Table of Contents

Introduction

What Is Fluency?

Fluency is the critical bridge between two key elements of reading—decoding and comprehension. In its 2000 report, the National Reading Panel defined it as "the ability to read text quickly, accurately, and with proper expression." Fluency has several dimensions. Successful readers must decode words accurately. But they must move beyond decoding and recognize words in connected text quickly and automatically. They must also read with expression in order to bring meaningful interpretation to the text. All three dimensions—accurate decoding, automaticity, and ability to read expressively—work together to create effective comprehension and overall success in reading.

In its 1994 study of reading, the National Assessment of Educational Progress (NAEP) established a clear connection between fluency and comprehension. NAEP defined fluency as the ease or "naturalness" of reading. It recognized certain key elements as contributing to fluency. These included the reader's grouping or phrasing of words as shown through intonation, stress, and pauses and the reader's adherence to the author's syntax. They also included expressiveness as reflected by the reader's interjection of a sense of feeling, anticipation, or characterization in oral reading. These elements are called *prosody*. When readers use appropriate volume, tone, emphasis, and phrasing, they give evidence of comprehension. They demonstrate that they are actively constructing meaning from the text.

Why Is Fluency Important?

Fluency is critical because it directly impacts the comprehension process. For years, teachers thought that if students could decode words accurately, they would become strong readers. Fluency, which has been referred to as a "neglected" aspect of reading, received little attention. Now it is recognized as one of the five critical components of reading.

Researchers have pointed out that people can successfully focus on only one thing at a time. They can, however, do more than one thing at a time if one of those things is so well learned that it can be done automatically. In its simplest form, reading can be seen as (1) word identification or decoding and (2) comprehension, or the active construction of meaning. Effective readers cannot focus on both of these processes at the same time. If a reader is focused almost entirely on decoding, that reader will have few resources left over for constructing meaning. Only when readers can read the words in connected text automatically are they free to focus their attention on making inferences, drawing conclusions, and applying other critical thinking skills associated with constructing meaning.

A fluent reader generally reads with speed and accuracy, but in addition usually displays these kinds of behaviors:

- Recognizes words automatically
- Applies graphophonic, semantic, and syntactic cues to recognize unfamiliar words
- Segments texts into meaningful chunks
- Emulates the sounds and rhythms of spoken language while reading aloud

A nonfluent reader, in contrast, may display these kinds of behaviors:

- Reads slowly and laboriously
- Processes text word-by-word in a choppy manner
- Frequently ignores punctuation
- Fails to use meaningful phrasing
- Shows little certainty when reading high-frequency words

Fluency does not mean only rapid reading. Occasionally, you will come across a nonfluent reader who is able to read text rapidly but fails to use appropriate phrasing. This reader often ignores meaning and punctuation. As a result, this reader struggles to answer questions about what has been read and fails to grasp the intent of the text.

Why Assess Fluency?

Students need to be fluent in order to be proficient readers. Their oral reading fluency can be improved through explicit training, but you need to assess their fluency level before you can determine what specific fluency-building activities and materials will be appropriate. In addition, students excel in reading when they are given opportunities to read as much connected text as possible at their independent level. Fluency assessment helps you determine what this level is.

The oral reading fluency assessments in this book answer this question: *How many words can a student read aloud per minute and how many of these words are read correctly*? This book also helps you observe reading performance beyond speed and accuracy by providing a rubric similar to the one developed by NAEP. This 4-level rubric takes into account additional aspects of fluency, such as prosody.

How and When to Assess

Kindergarten through Early First Grade

Until children can decode and automatically recognize many words by sight, they cannot be expected to read aloud effortlessly and expressively. That is why formally assessing their oral reading fluency at this early stage is not recommended. However, it is highly recommended that kindergarten children be involved in fluency-building activities, such as listening to books being read aloud and imitating auditory models of natural speech. Toward the end of kindergarten, children can be given opportunities to reread familiar, predictable, and decodable text to build fluency.

Some assessments for children at these grade levels are considered valuable. By assessing letter naming, phoneme segmentation, and sight word fluency during kindergarten and the early part of Grade 1, teachers can determine what type of fluency-building activities and materials to provide. Assessments for these skill areas appear on pages 8–13.

Mid-year of Grade 1 through Grade 6

Curriculum-based assessment of oral reading fluency is administered by asking a student to do a timed reading of a carefully selected on-level passage. As the student reads, you follow along in a copy of the same text and record errors such as omissions, substitutions, misreadings, insertions of words or parts of words, and hesitations of more than three seconds. Self-corrections and repetitions are not considered errors. To calculate the number of words read correctly in one minute, subtract the number of errors from the total number of words read. This process should be repeated periodically throughout the school year to monitor growth.

The Fluency Passages

The fluency passages serve two purposes. They can be administered three times a year as benchmark tests to determine if students are on track. They can also be used every unit so that you can monitor progress and determine if students are meeting instructional goals.

For Grade 1, there are 24 fiction and nonfiction fluency passages that you can use for informal assessment or to formally assess children who can decode phonologically and can automatically recognize many words by sight. It is recommended that oral reading fluency assessments begin mid-year. For Grades 2–6, there are 30 fiction and nonfiction passages per grade to help you assess fluency, using at least two selections every two to three weeks for most students. The page numbers on the chart below are a guide to help you decide which fluency passages to use each unit of the school year.

Unit	Grade 1	Grade 2	Grade 3	Grade 4	Grade 5	Grade 6
1	na	62–71	122–131	182–191	242–251	302–311
2	na	72–81	132–141	192–201	252–261	312–321
3	14–25	82–91	142–151	202–211	262–271	322–331
4	26–37	92–101	152–161	212–221	272–281	332–341
5	38–49	102–111	162–171	222–231	282–291	342–351
6	50–61	112–121	172–181	232–241	292–301	352–361

Curriculum-Based Oral Reading Fluency Norms

Use these norms to interpret your students' oral reading fluency abilities and to tailor instruction to their individual needs. Results are based on a one-minute timed sampling of students reading at least two passages aloud.

Grade	Percentile	Fall WCPM	Winter WCPM	Spring WCPM
1	90	NA	81	111
	75	NA	47	82
	50	NA	23	53
	25	NA	12	28
	10	NA	6	15
	SD	NA	32	39
2	90	106	125	142
	75	79	100	117
	50	51	72	89
	25	25	42	61
	10	11	18	31
	SD	37	41	42
3	90	128	146	162
	75	99	120	137
	50	71	92	107
	25	44	62	78
	10	21	36	48
	SD	40	43	44
4	90	145	166	180
	75	119	139	152
	50	194	112	123
	25	68	87	98
	10	45	61	72
	SD	40	41	43
5	90	166	182	194
	75	139	156	168
	50	110	127	139
	25	85	99	109
	10	61	74	83
	SD	45	44	45
6	90	177	195	204
	75	153	167	177
	50	127	140	150
	25	98	111	122
	10	68	82	93
	SD	42	45	44
7	90	180	192	202
	75	156	165	177
	50	128	138	150
	25	102	109	123
	10	79	88	98
	SD	40	43	41
8	90	185	193	199
	75	161	173	177
	50	133	146	151
	25	106	115	124
	10	77	84	97
	SD	43	45	41

A student's scores should fall within a range of ten WCPM above or below the score shown.

KEY
WCPM: Words correct per minute
SD: Average standard deviation of scores

SOURCE Hasbrouck, J. & Tindal, G. (2005) norms for oral reading fluency. Eugene, OR: Behavioral Research & Teaching, University of Oregon.

© Macmillan/McGraw-Hill

Administering Fluency Assessments and Using the Fluency Record

Directions

Give a student a reading passage he or she has not seen before. Fluency assessments are always done as "cold reads"; that is, they are done with material that is new to the person being tested. Explain that you would like the student to read the passage out loud and then answer two questions about it. Then say: *When you are ready, you may begin.* Start your stopwatch when the student reads the first word.

1. Follow along on your copy of the passage as the student reads. Place a line through each word that is read incorrectly or omitted.

2. Place a check above each word that is read correctly.

3. If the student substitutes or mispronounces a word, put a line through the word and write the word the student said above it.

4. If the student does not correctly say the word within 3 seconds, say the word for the student and circle the word to mark it as incorrect. Self-corrections and repetitions are not marked as errors.

5. At the end of one minute, stop your stopwatch and place a bracket (]) after the last word read by the student.

6. Have the student finish reading the passage.

7. Read the comprehension questions to the student. Have the student answer the comprehension questions orally.

How to Score

Record the information for each student on the fluency record sheet for that passage.

1. Look at the number in the left margin of the passage, on the same line as the bracket. (Note: In hyphenated words, individual words are counted as one word.) Add to this number all the words before the bracket to figure out how many words the student was able to read in one minute.

2. Count each word you circled or put a line through. The total is the number of errors made. Subtract this number from the number of words read in one minute to arrive at the Oral Reading Fluency Rate, or Words Correct Per Minute score.

3. Use this formula to score Oral Reading Accuracy:

$$\frac{\text{Total No. of Words Read} - \text{No. of Errors}}{\text{Total Number of Words Read}} \times 100$$

An Oral Reading Accuracy Scoring Chart is also provided on the inside of the back cover to help you calculate the percentage.

4. On the Prosody Rubric, circle 1, 2, 3, or 4 depending on your evaluation of the student's performance. A score of 4 is the highest possible score.

5. Write comments about oral reading performance on the sheet, including the student's ability to answer the comprehension questions.

Scoring Sample

The Oral Fluency Record Sheet is an assessment tool to help you record oral reading accuracy and important aspects of oral reading fluency. Information gathered from the fluency record sheet may be used to verify or clarify instructional decisions.

> Oral Reading Accuracy is a percentage score based on the total number of words read and the number of errors noted. The student should read 97% or more of the words correctly. A scoring chart for measuring Oral Reading Accuracy is provided on the inside back cover for your convenience.

> Oral Reading Fluency is a score that is equivalent to the total number of words read in one minute minus the number of errors made.

Oral Fluency Record Sheet

Name _____ Date _____

Oral Reading Accuracy: _____%   Circle: Fall Winter Spring

Oral Reading Fluency Score: _____ words correct per minute

Prosody Rubric: (Circle Score) 1 2 3 4 ◄──

> The Prosody Rubric is a rubric for evaluating oral reading performance. It groups observable behaviors into levels.

Comprehension Question Responses

#1 _____

#2 _____

Scoring Sample

    ✓ ✓ ✓ ✓ ✓ ✓ ✓ ✓ ✓ ✓ ✓
Jane and Dean were best pals. They rode their bikes to

    ✓   ✓ ✓ ✓ ✓ ✓ ✓ ✓ ✓
11   school (together.) At recess, they always played on the same

    ✓ ✓ ✓ ✓ ✓ ✓ ✓ ✓ ✓ ✓
21   team. Jane and Dean like to race home at school and do their

    ✓ ✓ ✓ ✓ ✓ ✓ ✓ ✓
34   homework together. Then Pepper came along. Pepper was Jane's

    ✓ ✓ ✓ ✓ ✓ ✓ ✓ ✓ ✓ ✓
43   new black puppy. Dean felt bad because Jane spent all her time with

    ✓ ✓ ✓ ✓ ✓ ✓ ✓ ✓ ✓ ✓ ✓
56   pepper now. Dean missed his best friend. One day, Dean sat on his

    ✓ ✓ ✓ ✓ ✓ ✓ ✓ ✓ ✓ ✓
69   (front) steps alone. He closed his eyes and thought about all the fun

    ✓ ✓ ✓ ✓ ✓ ✓ ✓
82   he and Jane used to have. Suddenly,] something licked his face and

94   Dean opened his eyes. Jane and Pepper had come to play. Now Dean

107   had two best pals. |||

> No. of words read corrrectly: 86/111

> No. of errors made: 3/111

Letter Naming Fluency Assessment

Instructions for Administering Letter Naming Fluency

1. Place the Letter Naming Fluency record sheet in front of the student.

2. Say these specific directions to the student:

   Here are some letters. Tell me the names of as many letters as you can. When I say, "Begin" start here (point to the first letter) *and go across the page. Point to each letter and tell me the name of that letter. If you come to a letter that you don't know, I'll tell it to you. Put your finger on the first letter. Ready, begin.*

3. Start your stopwatch. Follow along with the Letter Naming Fluency record sheet. Put a (/) through letters named incorrectly. Place a check above letters named correctly.

4. At the end of 1 minute, place a bracket (]) after the last letter named and say, *Stop.*

Directions for Scoring

1. If the student does not get any correct letter names within the first 10 letters (1 row), discontinue the task and record a score of zero.

2. If the student hesitates for 3 seconds on a letter, score the letter incorrect, and provide the correct letter to the student.

3. If the student provides the letter sound rather than the letter name, say: *Remember to tell me the letter name, not the sound it makes.* If the student continues providing letter sounds, mark each letter as incorrect, and make a note of this behavior at the bottom of the page.

4. Score a point for each correct letter the student names and record the total number of correct letters at the bottom of the sheet.

5. See the **Letter Naming Fluency Growth Table** on page 368 to obtain a letter naming fluency score.

Name _____ Date _____

Letter Naming Fluency	# correct
g a t X r F C j T z	__/10
K l q z b n y s I O	__/10
A e V u Q Y z M j a	__/10
f i W R g U d z S c	__/10
k M g D o J n p m h	__/10
C N E b u a g w V f	__/10
G Y i d e n S T t c	__/10
R F a m Z I w v C n	__/10
f s P o T W E j k Q	__/10
D U g e A b i y B d	__/10

Total ___/100

Phoneme Segmentation Fluency Assessment

Instructions for Administering Phoneme Segmentation

1. Make a copy of the Phoneme Segmentation Fluency record sheet. Use this sheet to record the student's oral responses.

2. Say these directions to the student:

I am going to say a word. Then, you tell me all the sounds you hear in the word. So if I say, "cat" you will say /c/ /a/ /t/. Let's try one. Tell me all the sounds in "hop."

3. If the student gives the correct response, /h/ /o/ /p/, then commend the student.

4. If the student gives an incorrect response, say: *The sounds in "hop" are /h/ /o/ /p/.* Ask the student to repeat the sounds: *Tell me all the sounds in "hop."*

5. Give the student the first word and start your stopwatch. Place a check above each correct sound segment produced. Put a slash (/) through incorrect sounds.

6. The maximum time for each sound segment is 3 seconds. If the student does not provide the next sound segment within 3 seconds, give the student the next word.

7. At the end of 1 minute, stop presenting words and scoring further responses. Add the number of sound segments produced correctly. Record the total number of sound segments produced correctly on the bottom of the scoring sheet.

Directions for Scoring

1. If the student has not given any sound segments correctly in the first five words, discontinue the task and put a score of zero. (0)

2. Place a check above the sound segments in the word that are correctly pronounced by the student. The student receives 1 point for each correct part of the word.

Both of the following examples are correct segmentations of words:

Word	Student Response	Scoring Procedure	Correct Segments
like	"l…i…k"	/l/ /i/ /k/	3/3
crack	"k..r..a..k"	/k/ /r/ /a/ /k/	4/4

3. Put a slash through segments pronounced incorrectly.

4. See the **Phoneme Segmentation Fluency Growth Table** on page 368 to obtain a phoneme segmentation fluency score.

Name _____ Date _____

Record Sheet

Phoneme Segmentation Fluency		# correct
man /m/ /a/ /n/	thing /th/ /i/ /ng/	___ /6
his /h/ /i/ /z/	kiss /k/ /i/ /s/	___ /6
brand /b/ /r/ /a/ /n/ /d/	match /m/ /a/ /t/ /ch/	___ /9
smile /s/ /m/ /ī/ /l/	froze /f/ /r/ /oa/ /z/	___ /8
press /p/ /r/ /e/ s/	cheat /ch/ /ea/ /t/	___ /7
slope /s/ /l/ /ō/ /p/	tide /t/ /ī/ /d/	___ /7
blend /b/ /l/ /e/ n/ /d/	gate /g/ /ā/ /t/	___ /8
lost /l/ /o/ /s/ /t/	shop /sh/ /o/ /p/	___ /7
jump /j/ /u/ /m/ /p/	drill /d/ /r/ /i/ /l/	___ /8
those /th/ /ō/ /s/	west /w/ /e/ /s/ /t/	___ /7
plug /p/ /l/ /u/ /g/	rush /r/ /u/ /sh/	___ /7
tape /t/ /ā/ /p/	inch /i/ /n/ /ch/	___ /6
plane /p/ /l/ /ā/ /n/	tube /t/ /ü/ b/	___ /7

Total ___ /93

Sight Word Fluency Assessment

Instructions for Administering the Assessment

Give student the assessment sheet, and have the student put his or her finger on the first word in the first row. Explain that you would like the student to read as many words as he or she can in one minute. Tell the student to point to each word and say the word. Then say: *When you are ready, you may begin.* Start your stopwatch, timing the student for one minute as he or she reads the words.

1. Follow along as the student reads. Place a check above each word that is said correctly.

2. Place a line through each word that is read incorrectly or omitted.

3. If the student substitutes or mispronounces a word, put a line through the word and write the word the student said above it.

4. If the student does not correctly say a word within 3 seconds, say the word for the student and mark the word as incorrect.

5. Say *Stop* at the end of one minute and place a bracket (]) after the last word read by the student.

Directions for Scoring

1. Count the total number of words read. This includes the words that are read correctly and incorrectly. Record that number on the table at the bottom of the sheet.

2. Count the number of errors for each line of words in the # of errors column. Record the total number of errors in the bottom table.

3. See the **Oral Reading Accuracy Scoring Chart** on the inside of the back cover to obtain a word accuracy rate.

Name _____ Date _____

Sight Word Fluency					# of errors
and	are	do	for	go	___ /5
has	have	he	here	is	___ /5
like	little	look	me	my	___ /5
play	said	see	she	to	___ /5
the	this	was	we	what	___ /5
where	with	you	jump	not	___ /5
up	too	yes	over	run	___ /5
come	good	on	that	very	___ /5
help	use	now	could	one	___ /5
two	they	her	does	who	___ /5
some	of	at	live	into	___ /5
many	out	want	under	show	___ /5

Total number of words read in one minute	
Number of errors	
Accuracy rate (see **Oral Reading Accuracy Scoring Chart**)	

My Dog Sam

Sam is my dog. He is a big dog.
I like Sam a lot. We have a lot of fun.
Sam runs with me. He is very quick.
Sam digs in the mud. Sam has mud on him.
Sam sits on me. I have mud on me.
I give Sam a bath. He likes it.
Sam gets wet. I get wet, too.
Sam likes me. I like Sam a lot.
We have a lot of fun.

1. Who is this story about?
2. How does Sam have fun?

Oral Fluency Record Sheet

Name _____ Date _____

Oral Reading Accuracy: _____%

Oral Reading Fluency Score: _____ words correct per minute

Prosody Rubric: (Circle Score) 1 2 3 4

Comprehension Question Responses

#1 _____

#2 _____

My Dog Sam

	Sam is my dog. He is a big dog.
9	I like Sam a lot. We have a lot of fun.
20	Sam runs with me. He is very quick.
28	Sam digs in the mud. Sam has mud on him.
38	Sam sits on me. I have mud on me.
47	I give Sam a bath. He likes it.
55	Sam gets wet. I get wet, too.
62	Sam likes me. I like Sam a lot.
70	We have a lot of fun. **76**

Number of words read: _____   Number of errors made: _____

Kit and Rex

Kit is a small cat. Rex is a big dog.
They have fun. Kit sits in a bag.
Rex tugs on the bag. Kit runs away.
Kit gets in a box. Rex gets in the box, too.
Kit runs out of the box. Rex looks for Kit.
He can not find Kit. Rex is very sad.
He sits down. Rex sees Kit in the box.
Rex runs to the box. He licks Kit.
Kit licks Rex back. Kit and Rex have fun.

1. Who is this story mostly about?

2. How are Kit and Rex different from other dogs and cats?

Oral Fluency Record Sheet

Name _____ Date _____

Oral Reading Accuracy: _____%

Oral Reading Fluency Score: _____ words correct per minute

Prosody Rubric: (Circle Score) 1 2 3 4

Comprehension Question Responses

#1 _____

#2 _____

Kit and Rex

	Kit is a small cat. Rex is a big dog.
10	They have fun. Kit sits in a bag.
18	Rex tugs on the bag. Kit runs away.
26	Kit gets in a box. Rex gets in the box, too.
37	Kit runs out of the box. Rex looks for Kit.
47	He can not find Kit. Rex is very sad.
56	He sits down. Rex sees Kit in the box.
65	Rex runs to the box. He licks Kit.
73	Kit licks Rex back. Kit and Rex have fun. **82**

Number of words read: _____   Number of errors made: _____

The Bug

I see a bug. It has six legs.
It is red. It is very small.
It is fun to look at it.
The bug is very busy.
I see it go up a hill.
I see it come down.
I see it dig. I see it stop.
The sun is out now. It is a hot sun.
It is time for a nap.
The bug naps in the sun.
I will nap in the sun, too.

1. What is this story mostly about?

2. Why does the bug take a nap?

Oral Fluency Record Sheet

Name _____ Date _____

Circle: Fall   Winter   Spring

Oral Reading Accuracy: _____%

Oral Reading Fluency Score: _____ words correct per minute

Prosody Rubric: (Circle Score) 1 2 3 4

Comprehension Question Responses

#1 _____

#2 _____

The Bug

	I see a bug. It has six legs.
8	It is red. It is very small.
15	It is fun to look at it.
22	The bug is very busy.
27	I see it go up a hill.
34	I see it come down.
39	I see it dig. I see it stop.
47	The sun is out now. It is a hot sun.
57	It is time for a nap.
63	The bug naps in the sun.
69	I will nap in the sun, too. **76**

Number of words read: _____   Number of errors made: _____

The Vet

Jan is a good vet.
She likes to help pets.
She can help cats and dogs.
She can help ducks and frogs.
She likes all pets.
Tim has a small dog. His dog is sick.
Jan looks at the dog.
She will help him get well.
Pam has a cat. Her cat has a bad leg.
Jan will help the cat. The cat will get well.
Soon the cat will run. Jan likes her job a lot.

1. Who is this story about?

2. Why is Jan a good vet?

Oral Fluency Record Sheet

Name _____ Date _____

Oral Reading Accuracy: _____%   Circle: Fall Winter Spring

Oral Reading Fluency Score: _____ words correct per minute

Prosody Rubric: (Circle Score) 1 2 3 4

Comprehension Question Responses

#1 _____

#2 _____

The Vet

	Jan is a good vet.
5	She likes to help pets.
10	She can help cats and dogs.
16	She can help ducks and frogs.
22	She likes all pets.
26	Tim has a small dog. His dog is sick.
35	Jan looks at the dog.
40	She will help him get well.
46	Pam has a cat. Her cat has a bad leg.
56	Jan will help the cat. The cat will get well.
66	Soon the cat will run. Jan likes her job a lot. 77

Number of words read: _____   Number of errors made: _____

Name _____ Date _____

Kim Gets to Eat

Meg and Kim are in bed. Meg gets up.
But Kim does not get up.
Meg gets a cup. She fills the cup with milk.
Kim is still not up. She is still in bed.
Meg runs to get Dad. Dad makes breakfast.
Kim gets up at last. She is glad to be up.
Kim likes breakfast with Meg and Dad.
Meg gets milk for Kim.
Now they will eat with Dad.
Breakfast is a lot of fun!

1. Who gets up first in the story?

2. When does this story take place?

Oral Fluency Record Sheet

Name _____ Date _____

Oral Reading Accuracy: _____%   Circle: Fall   Winter   Spring

Oral Reading Fluency Score: _____ words correct per minute

Prosody Rubric: (Circle Score) 1 2 3 4

Comprehension Question Responses

#1 _____

#2 _____

Kim Gets to Eat

	Meg and Kim are in bed. Meg gets up.
9	But Kim does not get up.
15	Meg gets a cup. She fills the cup with milk.
25	Kim is still not up. She is still in bed.
35	Meg runs to get Dad. Dad makes breakfast.
43	Kim gets up at last. She is glad to be up.
54	Kim likes breakfast with Meg and Dad.
61	Meg gets milk for Kim.
66	Now they will eat with Dad.
72	Breakfast is a lot of fun! **78**

Number of words read: _____   Number of errors made: _____

Fox and Frog

It is hot. Frog sits on a pad.
Frog sits still in the hot sun. He does not hop.
He does not jump. Frog is just too hot.
Fox is very sad. He wants to jump with Frog.
He wants to hop with Frog. But Frog just sits still.
Fox sits on a log. Fox comes up with a good plan.
Fox gets a very big fan for Frog.
Now Frog hops and jumps again.
Frog and Fox hop and jump together.
Fox is very glad.

1. Why does Frog sit still?

2. Why does Fox get the fan?

Oral Fluency Record Sheet

Name _____ Date _____

Oral Reading Accuracy: _____%   Circle: Fall   Winter   Spring

Oral Reading Fluency Score: _____ words correct per minute

Prosody Rubric: (Circle Score) 1 2 3 4

Comprehension Question Responses

#1 _____

#2 _____

Fox and Frog

	It is hot. Frog sits on a pad.
8	Frog sits still in the hot sun. He does not hop.
19	He does not jump. Frog is just too hot.
28	Fox is very sad. He wants to jump with Frog.
38	He wants to hop with Frog. But Frog just sits still.
49	Fox sits on a log. Fox comes up with a good plan.
61	Fox gets a very big fan for Frog.
69	Now Frog hops and jumps again.
75	Frog and Fox hop and jump together.
82	Fox is very glad. **86**

Number of words read: _____   Number of errors made: _____

Ducks

A duck is a kind of bird.

Ducks live in warm places. They live in cold places, too.

Ducks have short necks. Their wings are short, too.

Ducks like to swim. They spend lots of time in the water.

But ducks do not get wet.

Water rolls off a duck. How does this happen?

Ducks have oil on their tails.

They rub this oil on their feathers.

The oil stops the water. The feathers stay dry.

Ducks are fun to watch.

Do you like to watch ducks?

---

1. What is this story about?

2. Why do a duck's feathers stay dry?

Oral Fluency Record Sheet

Name _____ Date _____

Oral Reading Accuracy: _____%   Circle: Fall   Winter   Spring

Oral Reading Fluency Score: _____ words correct per minute

Prosody Rubric: (Circle Score) 1 2 3 4

Comprehension Question Responses

#1 _____

#2 _____

Ducks

	A duck is a kind of bird.
7	Ducks live in warm places. They live in cold places, too.
18	Ducks have short necks. Their wings are short, too.
27	Ducks like to swim. They spend lots of time in the water.
39	But ducks do not get wet.
45	Water rolls off a duck. How does this happen?
54	Ducks have oil on their tails.
60	They rub this oil on their feathers.
67	The oil stops the water. The feathers stay dry.
76	Ducks are fun to watch.
81	Do you like to watch ducks? **87**

Number of words read: _____   Number of errors made: _____

Seeds and Fruits

Most fruit trees grow from seeds.
People put seeds in the ground.
They water the seeds. A new tree grows.
Plants grow without people, too.
Animals take the seeds from place to place.
Wind and water can carry the seeds away, too.
Some fruits have many seeds.
Apples have lots and lots of seeds.
Some fruits have just one seed.
Think about a peach. The pit is the seed.
Seeds make new fruit trees all the time.
The trees grow and grow. Then we have good fruit to eat.

1. How do fruit trees grow?

2. What happens to the seeds that are carried by the wind?

Oral Fluency Record Sheet

Name _____ Date _____

Oral Reading Accuracy: _____%   Circle: Fall   Winter   Spring

Oral Reading Fluency Score: _____ words correct per minute

Prosody Rubric: (Circle Score) 1 2 3 4

Comprehension Question Responses

#1 _____

#2 _____

Seeds and Fruits

	Most fruit trees grow from seeds.
6	People put seeds in the ground.
12	They water the seeds. A new tree grows.
20	Plants grow without people, too.
25	Animals take the seeds from place to place.
33	Wind and water can carry the seeds away, too.
42	Some fruits have many seeds.
47	Apples have lots and lots of seeds.
54	Some fruits have just one seed.
60	Think about a peach. The pit is the seed.
69	Seeds make new fruit trees all the time.
77	The trees grow and grow. Then we have good fruit to eat. 89

Number of words read: _____   Number of errors made: _____

Name _____ Date _____

Kate and Jake

Kate is a snake. Jake is a turtle.
Jake wants to move fast like Kate.
Jake asks Fred the frog what to do.
Fred tells Jake that being slow is fine.
Jake still wants to be fast.
Jake is very sad.
He wants to be as fast as a snake.
Fred has an idea.
Fred tells Jake that a turtle has a shell.
The shell is Jake's home.
That is better than being fast.
Jake is glad now. He is not fast.
But he is always at home.

1. What is Jake's problem?

2. How does Fred help Jake solve his problem?

Oral Fluency Record Sheet

Name _____ Date _____

Oral Reading Accuracy: _____%   Circle: Fall Winter Spring

Oral Reading Fluency Score: _____ words correct per minute

Prosody Rubric: (Circle Score) 1 2 3 4

Comprehension Question Responses

#1 _____

#2 _____

Kate and Jake

	Kate is a snake. Jake is a turtle.
8	Jake wants to move fast like Kate.
15	Jake asks Fred the frog what to do.
23	Fred tells Jake that being slow is fine.
31	Jake still wants to be fast.
37	Jake is very sad.
41	He wants to be as fast as a snake.
50	Fred has an idea.
54	Fred tells Jake that a turtle has a shell.
63	The shell is Jake's home.
68	That is better than being fast.
74	Jake is glad now. He is not fast.
82	But he is always at home. **88**

Number of words read: _____   **Number of errors made:** _____

Name _____   Date _____

A Fun Lake

Dave's home is on a big lake.

Dave has a good time there. The lake is such fun.

Dave likes to jump in the lake. He likes to swim.

He likes to feed the ducks.

Dad sits under a tree.

He likes to be in the shade.

The sun makes him too hot.

Dad can eat his lunch and see Dave jump.

The lake is fun in the winter, too.

They dig a hole in the ice and fish.

They skate on the lake, too.

The lake is the best place to be.

1. How does Dave feel about the lake?

2. What does Dave like to do with his dad?

Oral Fluency Record Sheet

Name _____   Date _____

Oral Reading Accuracy: _____%   Circle: Fall   Winter   Spring
Oral Reading Fluency Score: _____ words correct per minute
Prosody Rubric: (Circle Score) 1 2 3 4
Comprehension Question Responses
#1 _____
#2 _____

A Fun Lake

	Dave's home is on a big lake.
7	Dave has a good time there. The lake is such fun.
18	Dave likes to jump in the lake. He likes to swim.
29	He likes to feed the ducks.
35	Dad sits under a tree.
40	He likes to be in the shade.
47	The sun makes him too hot.
53	Dad can eat his lunch and see Dave jump.
62	The lake is fun in the winter, too.
70	They dig a hole in the ice and fish.
79	They skate on the lake, too.
85	The lake is the best place to be. **93**

Number of words read: _____   Number of errors made: _____

Pets

A pet can add fun to your life.
Dogs and cats make good pets. So do fish.
Pigs and ducks can be pets, too.
You can have more than one pet.
But you must take care of them.
Some pets need a cage or bed.
You must make sure the pet eats and drinks.
You can brush its fur.
You should say nice things to your pet.
Pets like to play. If your pet runs, you can run.
If your pet swims, you can swim.
When your pet has fun, then so do you.

1. What things can you do for your pet?

2. What are two pets people can have?

Oral Fluency Record Sheet

Name _____ Date _____

Oral Reading Accuracy: _____%   Circle: Fall Winter Spring

Oral Reading Fluency Score: _____ words correct per minute

Prosody Rubric: (Circle Score) 1 2 3 4

Comprehension Question Responses

#1 _____

#2 _____

Pets

	A pet can add fun to your life.
8	Dogs and cats make good pets. So do fish.
17	Pigs and ducks can be pets, too.
24	You can have more than one pet.
31	But you must take care of them.
38	Some pets need a cage or bed.
45	You must make sure the pet eats and drinks.
54	You can brush its fur.
59	You should say nice things to your pet.
67	Pets like to play. If your pet runs, you can run.
78	If your pet swims, you can swim.
85	When your pet has fun, then so do you. 94

Number of words read: _____   **Number of errors made:** _____

Lifeguards

Lifeguards make it safe for us to swim.
But their job can be hard.
They must stay in the sun all day.
They must rush around to get things done.
They have to run fast and swim in the waves.
Every day they check the waves and the sand.
When waves are tall, they wave flags and ring a bell.
Clang! Clang! We stop and turn.
Lifeguards will now save a boy or girl.
Look at them run. See how fast they can swim.
They must be very brave.
Would you like to have this job?

1. What do lifeguards do?

2. What do you think is the hardest part about a
   lifeguard's job?

Oral Fluency Record Sheet

Name _____   Date _____

Oral Reading Accuracy: _____%   Circle: Fall Winter Spring
Oral Reading Fluency Score: _____ words correct per minute
Prosody Rubric: (Circle Score) 1 2 3 4
Comprehension Question Responses
#1 _____
#2 _____

Lifeguards

	Lifeguards make it safe for us to swim.
8	But their job can be hard.
14	They must stay in the sun all day.
22	They must rush around to get things done.
30	They have to run fast and swim in the waves.
40	Every day they check the waves and the sand.
49	When waves are tall, they wave flags and ring a bell.
60	Clang! Clang! We stop and turn.
66	Lifeguards will now save a boy or girl.
74	Look at them run. See how fast they can swim.
84	They must be very brave.
89	Would you like to have this job? **96**

Number of words read: _____   Number of errors made: _____

Ben's Birthday

Today is Ben's birthday.
I am helping Mom make a cake.
We mix eggs and milk.
Then Mom adds more good things.
The batter is thick and white.
Mom puts the batter into a pan.
She puts the pan into the oven.
"I think Ben will like his cake," I say.
Time passes. Then I think I smell smoke.
Is it the cake? Mom runs in. But the cake is fine.
Now we are ready for Ben's birthday.
Dad picks Ben up to see his cake.
Ben smiles and claps his hands.
"You are one year old today!" we all say.

1. What is the story about?

2. Why couldn't Ben bake the cake?

Oral Fluency Record Sheet

Name _____ Date _____

Oral Reading Accuracy: _____%   Circle: Fall Winter Spring
Oral Reading Fluency Score: _____ words correct per minute
Prosody Rubric: (Circle Score) 1 2 3 4
Comprehension Question Responses
#1 _____
#2 _____

Ben's Birthday

	Today is Ben's birthday.
4	I am helping Mom make a cake.
11	We mix eggs and milk.
16	Then Mom adds more good things.
22	The batter is thick and white.
28	Mom puts the batter into a pan.
35	She puts the pan into the oven.
42	"I think Ben will like his cake," I say.
51	Time passes. Then I think I smell smoke.
59	Is it the cake? Mom runs in. But the cake is fine.
71	Now we are ready for Ben's birthday.
78	Dad picks Ben up to see his cake.
86	Ben smiles and claps his hands.
92	"You are one year old today!" we all say. 101

Number of words read: _____   Number of errors made: _____

The Old Mirror

Joan is in a big room.
There are many boxes and an old trunk.
Then Joan sees an old mirror.
Joan looks in it.
She sees a girl in a long, white dress.
The dress is made of fine, old lace.
The girl has on a green hat.
But wait. The girl is Joan.
"I can see what I looked like long ago," thinks Joan.
"Mom!" Joan screams. "Please come quickly!"
Mom hears Joan call and runs to her room.
"It is fine, dear," she says. "It was just a dream."
Joan sits up in her bed and tells Mom about it.

1. What does Joan see in the mirror?

2. Why does Joan scream?

Oral Fluency Record Sheet

Name _____   Date _____

Oral Reading Accuracy: _____%   Circle: Fall Winter Spring
Oral Reading Fluency Score: _____ words correct per minute
Prosody Rubric: (Circle Score) 1 2 3 4
Comprehension Question Responses
#1 _____
#2 _____

The Old Mirror

	Joan is in a big room.
6	There are many boxes and an old trunk.
14	Then Joan sees an old mirror.
20	Joan looks in it.
24	She sees a girl in a long, white dress.
33	The dress is made of fine, old lace.
41	The girl has on a green hat.
48	But wait. The girl is Joan.
54	"I can see what I looked like long ago," thinks Joan.
65	"Mom!" Joan screams. "Please come quickly!"
71	Mom hears Joan call and runs to her room.
80	"It is fine, dear," she says. "It was just a dream."
91	Joan sits up in her bed and tells Mom about it. 102

Number of words read: _____   Number of errors made: _____

Name _____ Date _____

A New Turtle

Mom Turtle has an egg. It is a white egg.
It has a shape like a ball.
She makes a nest in the sand.
She slips her egg into the nest.
Will the egg hatch now? Yes, it will.
Look at the new turtle.
It will dig out of the nest.
But the sun is very hot. It makes the sand hot.
Hot sand can hurt the turtle.
So it will come out at night.
The sand will not be hot then.
The turtle will be safe.
Then it will rush to the lake.

1. What is this story mostly about?

2. Why does the turtle wait until night to go to the lake?

Oral Fluency Record Sheet

Name _____ Date _____

Oral Reading Accuracy: _____%   Circle: Fall Winter Spring
Oral Reading Fluency Score: _____ words correct per minute
Prosody Rubric: (Circle Score) 1 2 3 4
Comprehension Question Responses
#1 _____
#2 _____

A New Turtle

	Mom Turtle has an egg. It is a white egg.
10	It has a shape like a ball.
17	She makes a nest in the sand.
24	She slips her egg into the nest.
31	Will the egg hatch now? Yes, it will.
39	Look at the new turtle.
44	It will dig out of the nest.
51	But the sun is very hot. It makes the sand hot.
62	Hot sand can hurt the turtle.
68	So it will come out at night.
75	The sand will not be hot then.
82	The turtle will be safe.
87	Then it will rush to the lake. **94**

Number of words read: _____   Number of errors made: _____

Name _____ Date _____

Make a Mask

You can make a mask. A mask is fun to make.
The mask can look sad or glad or mad.
It can be a frog or a cat or a fox.
Pick a mask to make.
Then get some things.
Get a big bag. Then get some paint.
Cut the bag. Make eyes and a nose.
Take a brush and paint it.
What kind of mask did you make?
Did you make a frog or a cat? Did you make a fox?
Is it a sad mask? Is it a mad mask?
Put on your mask.
Will it make Mom and Dad jump?

1. What does this story tell you how to make?

2. What do you think is the hardest part about making the mask?

Oral Fluency Record Sheet

Name _____ Date _____

Oral Reading Accuracy: _____%   Circle: Fall Winter Spring
Oral Reading Fluency Score: _____ words correct per minute
Prosody Rubric: (Circle Score) 1 2 3 4
Comprehension Question Responses
#1 _____
#2 _____

Make a Mask

	You can make a mask. A mask is fun to make.
11	The mask can look sad or glad or mad.
20	It can be a frog or a cat or a fox.
31	Pick a mask to make.
36	Then get some things.
40	Get a big bag. Then get some paint.
48	Cut the bag. Make eyes and a nose.
56	Take a brush and paint it.
62	What kind of mask did you make?
69	Did you make a frog or a cat? Did you make a fox?
82	Is it a sad mask? Is it a mad mask?
92	Put on your mask.
96	Will it make Mom and Dad jump? 103

Number of words read: _____   Number of errors made: _____

Name _____   Date _____

The Nest

The wind was blowing. Bird was cold.
She turned around in her nest.
Then Bird saw the hole in her nest.
"Can I fix it?" Bird asked herself.
She asked Crow for help. Crow was eating.
She asked Jay for help. Jay just turned away.
"I can do it," said Bird. "I will show them."
Bird flew down to the ground.
She found six twigs. She picked up some fur.
Bird took them to her nest. It was time to work.
Bird put the twigs over the hole.
She put the fur over the twigs.
"I have fixed the hole," said Bird.
"Now I have a warm nest."

1. What does Bird use to fix her nest?

2. How does Bird feel at the end of the story?

Oral Fluency Record Sheet

Name _____ Date _____

Oral Reading Accuracy: _____%   Circle: Fall   Winter   Spring

Oral Reading Fluency Score: _____ words correct per minute

Prosody Rubric: (Circle Score) 1 2 3 4

Comprehension Question Responses

#1 _____

#2 _____

The Nest

	The wind was blowing. Bird was cold.
7	She turned around in her nest.
13	Then Bird saw the hole in her nest.
21	"Can I fix it?" Bird asked herself.
28	She asked Crow for help. Crow was eating.
36	She asked Jay for help. Jay just turned away.
45	"I can do it," said Bird. "I will show them."
55	Bird flew down to the ground.
61	She found six twigs. She picked up some fur.
70	Bird took them to her nest. It was time to work.
81	Bird put the twigs over the hole.
88	She put the fur over the twigs.
95	"I have fixed the hole," said Bird.
102	"Now I have a warm nest." **108**

Number of words read: _____ Number of errors made: _____

Kent Goes to Work

Kent works far away.
So he goes to work in a rocket.
His ride is loud and fast.
On one trip, Kent went to the moon.
His rocket landed in a dry sea.
Kent got out of the rocket. He walked on the moon.
Then Kent jumped in a moon car.
The car had big wheels. But the car moved slowly.
Kent drove the car around the moon.
He picked up rocks and dirt.
Then the moon car hit a bump. The car would not go.
So Kent left the moon car behind.
He loaded the rocket and took off for home.
I like the way Kent gets around. How about you?

1. What does Kent ride to get to work?

2. Is this story real or made up? How can you tell?

Oral Fluency Record Sheet

Name _____ Date _____

Oral Reading Accuracy: _____% Circle: Fall   Winter   Spring

Oral Reading Fluency Score: _____ words correct per minute

Prosody Rubric: (Circle Score) 1 2 3 4

Comprehension Question Responses

#1 _____

#2 _____

Kent Goes to Work

	Kent works far away.
4	So he goes to work in a rocket.
12	His ride is loud and fast.
18	On one trip, Kent went to the moon.
26	His rocket landed in a dry sea.
33	Kent got out of the rocket. He walked on the moon.
44	Then Kent jumped in a moon car.
51	The car had big wheels. But the car moved slowly.
61	Kent drove the car around the moon.
68	He picked up rocks and dirt.
74	Then the moon car hit a bump. The car would not go.
86	So Kent left the moon car behind.
93	He loaded the rocket and took off for home.
102	I like the way Kent gets around. How about you? 112

Number of words read: _____   Number of errors made: _____

Big and Small

Look up at the sky one night.
Do the stars look small?
In fact they are really quite big.
They are much bigger than Earth.
Do you know why they seem so small?
It is because they are so far away.
But we know a star that is not so far away.
It is the sun. The sun is made of hot gas.
It is hot gas that makes the sun glow.
Our bright sun may not seem that big.
But it is much bigger than Earth.
Other stars in the sky are even bigger than the sun.
Look up at the stars in the sky at night.
Now you know they are bigger than they look.

1. What is the main idea of this story?

2. Put the sun, Earth, and other stars in order from smallest to largest.

Oral Fluency Record Sheet

Name _____ Date _____

Oral Reading Accuracy: _____% Circle: Fall Winter Spring

Oral Reading Fluency Score: _____ words correct per minute

Prosody Rubric: (Circle Score) 1 2 3 4

Comprehension Question Responses

#1 _____

#2 _____

Big and Small

	Look up at the sky one night.
7	Do the stars look small?
12	In fact they are really quite big.
19	They are much bigger than Earth.
25	Do you know why they seem so small?
33	It is because they are so far away.
41	But we know a star that is not so far away.
52	It is the sun. The sun is made of hot gas.
63	It is hot gas that makes the sun glow.
72	Our bright sun may not seem that big.
80	But it is much bigger than Earth.
87	Other stars in the sky are even bigger than the sun.
98	Look up at the stars in the sky at night.
108	Now you know they are bigger than they look. 117

Number of words read: _____ Number of errors made: _____

A Home for Bats

Not all bats spend their days in caves.
Bats can live in many places.
Some bats hang from big trees.
Other bats live in old rock mines.
Bats can also live in old houses.
They may hide under low bridges.
Some bats can make tents with leaves.
They make their tents high up in a tree.
They rest under the tent.
Then they do not get wet.
Some bats hide in the homes of other animals.
Bats can find a home almost anywhere.
They will like it as long as it is dark.
Take a look around. Do you see any bats?

1. Name three places where bats live.

2. Why do bats only come out at night?

Oral Fluency Record Sheet

Name _____ Date _____

Oral Reading Accuracy: _____% Circle: Fall Winter Spring

Oral Reading Fluency Score: _____ words correct per minute

Prosody Rubric: (Circle Score) 1 2 3 4

Comprehension Question Responses

#1 _____

#2 _____

A Home for Bats

	Not all bats spend their days in caves.
8	Bats can live in many places.
14	Some bats hang from big trees.
20	Other bats live in old rock mines.
27	Bats can also live in old houses.
34	They may hide under low bridges.
40	Some bats can make tents with leaves.
47	They make their tents high up in a tree.
56	They rest under the tent.
61	Then they do not get wet.
67	Some bats hide in the homes of other animals.
76	Bats can find a home almost anywhere.
83	They will like it as long as it is dark.
93	Take a look around. Do you see any bats? 102

Number of words read: _____   Number of errors made: _____

Name _____ Date _____

Mike and the Bug

Mike dug a hole. He dropped a seed into the hole.
He put some dirt on top. Soon a stem came up.
Then ten beans popped out. Mike was excited.
A day went by. Mike looked at his plant again.
There were only eight beans.
He saw a fat bug on one bean.
"Did you eat my beans?" asked Mike.
"Yes, I did," said the bug. "I need food, too."
Mike picked up the bug. The bug was right.
"I will grow two plants every time," said Mike.
"One will be for me. The other will be for you."
"I will dig holes for the seeds," the bug said.
The bug winked at Mike. Mike winked back.

1. Who is this story about?

2. Why will Mike grow two plants every time?

Oral Fluency Record Sheet

Name _____ Date _____

Oral Reading Accuracy: _____%   Circle: Fall   Winter   Spring

Oral Reading Fluency Score: _____ words correct per minute

Prosody Rubric: (Circle Score) 1 2 3 4

Comprehension Question Responses

#1 _____

#2 _____

Mike and the Bug

	Mike dug a hole. He dropped a seed into the hole.
11	He put some dirt on top. Soon a stem came up.
22	Then ten beans popped out. Mike was excited.
30	A day went by. Mike looked at his plant again.
40	There were only eight beans.
45	He saw a fat bug on one bean.
53	"Did you eat my beans?" asked Mike.
60	"Yes, I did," said the bug. "I need food, too."
70	Mike picked up the bug. The bug was right.
79	"I will grow two plants every time," said Mike.
88	"One will be for me. The other will be for you."
99	"I will dig holes for the seeds," the bug said.
109	The bug winked at Mike. Mike winked back. 117

Number of words read: _____   Number of errors made: _____

Name _____ Date _____

The Dog Sled

Bill wanted one thing. He wanted to ride on a dog sled.

One day, Bill got what he wanted.

He met a man who ran sled dog trips.

The man showed Bill his dogs. Bill liked Lad the best.

Lad had thick fur. His eyes were big and bright.

Later the man took Bill to a sled.

Ten dogs were tied to the sled.

Lad was one of them.

Bill got into the sled. The dogs took off.

They pulled the sled over snow and ice.

The sled got back home at dark.

The man took off the ropes. Then he fed the dogs.

Bill had a great time.

He wants to ride on the sled again.

---

1. What did Bill want to do?

2. What time of year does this story take place?

Oral Fluency Record Sheet

Name _____ Date _____

Oral Reading Accuracy: _____%   Circle: Fall Winter Spring

Oral Reading Fluency Score: _____ words correct per minute

Prosody Rubric: (Circle Score) 1 2 3 4

Comprehension Question Responses

#1 _____

#2 _____

The Dog Sled

	Bill wanted one thing. He wanted to ride on a dog sled.
12	One day, Bill got what he wanted.
19	He met a man who ran sled dog trips.
28	The man showed Bill his dogs. Bill liked Lad the best.
39	Lad had thick fur. His eyes were big and bright.
49	Later the man took Bill to a sled.
57	Ten dogs were tied to the sled.
64	Lad was one of them.
69	Bill got into the sled. The dogs took off.
78	They pulled the sled over snow and ice.
86	The sled got back home at dark.
93	The man took off the ropes. Then he fed the dogs.
104	Bill had a great time.
109	He wants to ride on the sled again. 117

Number of words read: _____   Number of errors made: _____

You and Your Shadow

Do you like to play with your shadow?
You can use your hands to make pictures on a wall.
You can make animal heads and funny shapes.
Light makes the shadows.
Light might hit you on one side.
Your shadow would fall on the other side.
When you are outside, sunlight makes shadows.
The sun may make long shadows or short ones.
In the morning and evening, the sun is low.
Shadows are long.
At noon, the sun is high. Shadows are short.
Is your shadow in front of you?
Then the light is behind you.
Is your shadow behind you?
Then the light is in front of you.
You are never alone. You always have your shadow.

1. What makes shadows?
2. What would your shadow look like in the morning?

Oral Fluency Record Sheet

Name _____ Date _____

Oral Reading Accuracy: _____%   Circle: Fall Winter Spring

Oral Reading Fluency Score: _____ words correct per minute

Prosody Rubric: (Circle Score) 1 2 3 4

Comprehension Question Responses

#1 _____

#2 _____

You and Your Shadow

	Do you like to play with your shadow?
8	You can use your hands to make pictures on a wall.
19	You can make animal heads and funny shapes.
27	Light makes the shadows.
31	Light might hit you on one side.
38	Your shadow would fall on the other side.
46	When you are outside, sunlight makes shadows.
53	The sun may make long shadows or short ones.
62	In the morning and evening, the sun is low.
71	Shadows are long.
74	At noon, the sun is high. Shadows are short.
83	Is your shadow in front of you?
90	Then the light is behind you.
96	Is your shadow behind you?
101	Then the light is in front of you.
109	You are never alone. You always have your shadow. 118

Number of words read: _____   Number of errors made: _____

Our American Flag

Our flag is special to us.
It stands for our country. It is red, white, and blue.
The flag has 13 stripes. It has 50 stars.
There were 13 states when our country was born.
There are 50 states in our country now.
We call our flag the Stars and Stripes.
That is what we see when we look at the flag.
Here are some rules about the flag.
Fly the flag outside in good weather.
Take the flag down at night.
Take the flag inside when it rains.
Never let the flag touch the ground.
Follow these rules.
They show that you are proud of your flag.

1. What does each star stand for on the flag?

2. How can you care for your flag?

Oral Fluency Record Sheet

Name _____ Date _____

Oral Reading Accuracy: _____%   Circle: Fall Winter Spring

Oral Reading Fluency Score: _____ words correct per minute

Prosody Rubric: (Circle Score) 1 2 3 4

Comprehension Question Responses

#1 _____

#2 _____

Our American Flag

	Our flag is special to us.
6	It stands for our country. It is red, white, and blue.
17	The flag has 13 stripes. It has 50 stars.
26	There were 13 states when our country was born.
35	There are 50 states in our country now.
43	We call our flag the Stars and Stripes.
51	That is what we see when we look at the flag.
62	Here are some rules about the flag.
70	Fly the flag outside in good weather.
77	Take the flag down at night.
83	Take the flag inside when it rains.
90	Never let the flag touch the ground.
97	Follow these rules.
100	They show that you are proud of your flag. 109

Number of words read: _____   Number of errors made: _____

Soccer Camp

Kate and her big brother Ted like to play soccer. They are always bouncing or kicking a soccer ball. They play in the driveway and kick the ball into a net. Sometimes Kate and Ted play on the grass in their yard. On rainy days, they play in the basement. They go to soccer camp in the summer.

This summer, Ted goes to a different camp. Kate doesn't want to go to camp by herself. She frowns on her way to the field. But then she stops and smiles. She sees boys and girls running and kicking soccer balls. She will play soccer with many new friends!

1. What do Kate and Ted love to do?

2. Why doesn't Kate want to go to camp by herself?

Oral Fluency Record Sheet

Name _____   Date _____

Oral Reading Accuracy: _____%   Circle: Fall Winter Spring
Oral Reading Fluency Score: _____ words correct per minute
Prosody Rubric: (Circle Score) 1 2 3 4
Comprehension Question Responses
#1 _____
#2 _____

Soccer Camp

	Kate and her big brother Ted like to
8	play soccer. They are always bouncing or kicking
16	a soccer ball. They play in the driveway and kick the
27	ball into a net. Sometimes Kate and Ted play on
37	the grass in their yard. On rainy days, they play
47	in the basement. They go to soccer camp in
56	the summer.
58	This summer, Ted goes to a different camp.
66	Kate doesn't want to go to camp by herself. She
76	frowns on her way to the field. But then she stops
87	and smiles. She sees boys and girls running and
96	kicking soccer balls. She will play soccer with
104	many new friends! 107

Number of words read: _____   Number of errors made: _____

Name _____ Date _____

The New Friend

Jane and Dean were best pals. They rode their bikes to school together every day. They were both in Mrs. Green's class. At recess, they always played on the same baseball team. Jane and Dean liked to race home after school and do their homework together.

Then Pepper came along. Pepper was Jane's new black puppy. Dean felt sad because Jane spent all her time with Pepper now. Dean missed his best friend.

One day, Dean sat on his front steps alone. He closed his eyes and thought about all the fun he and Jane used to have.

Suddenly, something licked his face, and Dean opened his eyes. Jane and Pepper had come to play. Now Dean had two best pals.

1. Why was Dean sad?

2. Why do you think Jane and Pepper came to play?

Oral Fluency Record Sheet

Name _____ Date _____

Oral Reading Accuracy: _____%   Circle: Fall Winter Spring
Oral Reading Fluency Score: _____ words correct per minute
Prosody Rubric: (Circle Score) 1 2 3 4
Comprehension Question Responses
#1 _____
#2 _____

The New Friend

	Jane and Dean were best pals. They rode their
9	bikes to school together every day. They were both
18	in Mrs. Green's class. At recess, they always
26	played on the same baseball team. Jane and Dean
35	liked to race home after school and do their
44	homework together.
46	Then Pepper came along. Pepper was Jane's
53	new black puppy. Dean felt sad because Jane
61	spent all her time with Pepper now. Dean missed
70	his best friend.
73	One day, Dean sat on his front steps alone. He
83	closed his eyes and thought about all the fun he
93	and Jane used to have.
98	Suddenly, something licked his face, and Dean
105	opened his eyes. Jane and Pepper had come to
114	play. Now Dean had two best pals. 121

Number of words read: _____   Number of errors made: _____

© Macmillan/McGraw-Hill

How to Play Running Bases

Have you ever played a game called "running bases"? It is a lot of fun! You need two people to catch the ball and a group of people to run between the bases. You also need two bases and one ball. You can use many things as your bases. An old shirt or a paper plate will work fine.

To start the game, the catchers throw the ball to each other three times. Then the runners start running back and forth between the bases. The catchers try to tag them.

The runners have to be quick and smart, so they do not get tagged. After three tags, a runner can change places with a catcher. Then the game begins again.

1. What can you use as a base for "running bases"?

2. Why can't you play "running bases" with just three people?

Oral Fluency Record Sheet

Name _____ Date _____

Oral Reading Accuracy: _____%   Circle: Fall Winter Spring

Oral Reading Fluency Score: _____ words correct per minute

Prosody Rubric: (Circle Score) 1 2 3 4

Comprehension Question Responses

#1 _____

#2 _____

How to Play Running Bases

	Have you ever played a game called "running
8	bases"? It is a lot of fun! You need two people to
20	catch the ball and a group of people to run
30	between the bases. You also need two bases and
39	one ball. You can use many things as your bases.
49	An old shirt or a paper plate will work fine.
59	To start the game, the catchers throw the ball
68	to each other three times. Then the runners start
77	running back and forth between the bases. The
85	catchers try to tag them.
90	The runners have to be quick and smart, so
99	they do not get tagged. After three tags, a runner
109	can change places with a catcher. Then the game
118	begins again. 120

Number of words read: _____   Number of errors made: _____

Our Great Forests

Long ago, most of the eastern half of the United States was one big forest. The whole land was thickly covered with trees.

Today trees do not cover as big an area. As people spread out across the country, they cut down trees to create farms and cities. Now people are planting new forests to try to replace some of the ones that were cut down.

We have three kinds of forests in the United States. In one kind, the trees lose their leaves in the fall. In another kind, the trees stay green all year. The third kind is called a mixed forest. It has trees that lose their leaves along with trees that stay green.

If you ever visit a forest, look at the trees. See if you can tell what kind they are!

1. Describe three kinds of forests.

2. Why would someone cut down trees?

Oral Fluency Record Sheet

Name _____ Date _____

Oral Reading Accuracy: _____% Circle: Fall Winter Spring

Oral Reading Fluency Score: _____ words correct per minute

Prosody Rubric: (Circle Score) 1 2 3 4

Comprehension Question Responses

#1 _____

#2 _____

Our Great Forests

	Long ago, most of the eastern half of the
9	United States was one big forest. The whole land
18	was thickly covered with trees.
23	Today trees do not cover as big an area. As
33	people spread out across the country, they cut down
42	trees to create farms and cities. Now people are
51	planting new forests to try to replace some of the
61	ones that were cut down.
66	We have three kinds of forests in the
74	United States. In one kind, the trees lose their leaves
84	in the fall. In another kind, the trees stay green
94	all year. The third kind is called a mixed forest.
104	It has trees that lose their leaves along with trees
114	that stay green.
117	If you ever visit a forest, look at the trees.
127	See if you can tell what kind they are! 136

Number of words read: _____ Number of errors made: _____

Jake's Jar

Jake loves to read everything in sight! This is why he joined the school's reading club. Jake reads when he first wakes up in the morning. He reads a little at lunchtime. He reads right before he goes to sleep at night.

One day, Jake asked Mom how many books he had read so far. He and Mom forgot to count them. Mom found an old jar in the kitchen. Every time Jake finished a book, they put a dime into the jar. This would help them know how many books Jake had read.

When the jar was full, Jake wanted to buy a book to give to his reading club. Jake's mom cheered and said that was a wonderful idea!

1. What does Jake love to do?

2. How can the dimes in the jar help Jake tell how many books he has read?

Oral Fluency Record Sheet

Name _____ Date _____

Oral Reading Accuracy: _____% Circle: Fall Winter Spring

Oral Reading Fluency Score: _____ words correct per minute

Prosody Rubric: (Circle Score) 1 2 3 4

Comprehension Question Responses

#1 _____

#2 _____

Jake's Jar

	Jake loves to read everything in sight! This is
9	why he joined the school's reading club. Jake
17	reads when he first wakes up in the morning. He
27	reads a little at lunchtime. He reads right before he
37	goes to sleep at night.
42	One day, Jake asked Mom how many books he
51	had read so far. He and Mom forgot to count them.
62	Mom found an old jar in the kitchen. Every time
72	Jake finished a book, they put a dime into the jar.
83	This would help them know how many books Jake
92	had read.
94	When the jar was full, Jake wanted to buy a
104	book to give to his reading club. Jake's mom
113	cheered and said that was a wonderful idea! 121

Number of words read: _____ Number of errors made: _____

The Flower Sale

Mr. Bloom's class wanted to raise money for the school. They agreed to have a flower sale. Every child was given a job. Some children went from room to room to tell about the flowers. Others made posters to put up around the school. The children knew they needed to sell a lot of flowers.

On the day of the sale, Mr. Bloom went to the flower market and bought the flowers. Then the children got busy with new jobs. Some children counted the money, while others gave out the flowers.

At the end of the day, the children were tired but they felt great. Mr. Bloom asked the children what they wanted to purchase for the school. They wanted to buy more flowers.

1. What is the story mostly about?

2. Why did some children put up posters around the school?

© Macmillan/McGraw-Hill

Oral Fluency Record Sheet

Name _____   Date _____

Oral Reading Accuracy: _____%   Circle: Fall   Winter   Spring

Oral Reading Fluency Score: _____ words correct per minute

Prosody Rubric: (Circle Score) 1 2 3 4

Comprehension Question Responses

#1 _____

#2 _____

The Flower Sale

	Mr. Bloom's class wanted to raise money for
8	the school. They agreed to have a flower sale.
17	Every child was given a job. Some children went
26	from room to room to tell about the flowers. Others
36	made posters to put up around the school. The
45	children knew they needed to sell a lot of flowers.
55	On the day of the sale, Mr. Bloom went to the
66	flower market and bought the flowers. Then the
74	children got busy with new jobs. Some children
82	counted the money, while others gave out the flowers.
91	At the end of the day, the children were tired
101	but they felt great. Mr. Bloom asked the children what
111	they wanted to purchase for the school. They wanted
120	to buy more flowers. **124**

Number of words read: _____   Number of errors made: _____

Sharks

Sharks have lived on Earth for years and years. Today there are more than 350 different kinds. Sharks come in many sizes. The whale shark can be 36 feet in length. The smallest shark grows only to about 6 inches. Some sharks have big, sharp teeth. Others have very small teeth. But all sharks have one thing in common. They all must open their mouths to breathe. Sharks must keep their mouths open when they swim, or they will die.

Every year sharks are killed for many reasons. They get caught in fishing nets. Some are caught to be sold for shark meat or shark fin soup. Shark skin is sometimes used for belts. Other people hunt them because they think sharks are dangerous. Will sharks be around much longer?

1. How does a shark breathe?

2. Why are sharks in danger?

© Macmillan/McGraw-Hill

Oral Fluency Record Sheet

Name _____ Date _____

Oral Reading Accuracy: _____%   Circle: Fall Winter Spring
Oral Reading Fluency Score: _____ words correct per minute
Prosody Rubric: (Circle Score) 1 2 3 4
Comprehension Question Responses
#1 _____
#2 _____

Sharks

	Sharks have lived on Earth for years and years.
9	Today there are more than 350 different kinds. Sharks
18	come in many sizes. The whale shark can be 36
28	feet in length. The smallest shark grows only to about
38	6 inches. Some sharks have big, sharp teeth.
46	Others have very small teeth. But all sharks have one
56	thing in common. They all must open their mouths to
66	breathe. Sharks must keep their mouths open when
74	they swim, or they will die.
80	Every year sharks are killed for many
87	reasons. They get caught in fishing nets. Some
95	are caught to be sold for shark meat or shark fin
106	soup. Shark skin is sometimes used for belts.
114	Other people hunt them because they think
121	sharks are dangerous. Will sharks be around
128	much longer? 130

Number of words read: _____   Number of errors made: _____

Plants and Animals

Are there ways in which grass, birds, and people are all alike? Here are two. Grass, birds, and people are all living things. And all living things need to have food.

Plants and animals get food in different ways. Most plants cannot move around, so they need to make their own food. They use energy from the sun along with water, air, and parts of the soil to create food.

Animals cannot make their own food, but they can move around to find it. Animals chase after their food, fly across the sky to catch it, or figure out other ways to get their meals.

You are a kind of animal. How do you move around to get the different things you eat?

---

1. What is the passage mostly about?

2. How do people and plants get their food in different ways?

Oral Fluency Record Sheet

Name _____ Date _____

Oral Reading Accuracy: _____% Circle: Fall Winter Spring

Oral Reading Fluency Score: _____ words correct per minute

Prosody Rubric: (Circle Score) 1 2 3 4

Comprehension Question Responses

#1 _____

#2 _____

Plants and Animals

	Are there ways in which grass, birds, and
8	people are all alike? Here are two. Grass, birds, and
18	people are all living things. And all living things
27	need to have food.
31	Plants and animals get food in different ways.
39	Most plants cannot move around, so they need to
48	make their own food. They use energy from the sun
58	along with water, air, and parts of the soil to
68	create food.
70	Animals cannot make their own food, but they
78	can move around to find it. Animals chase after their
88	food, fly across the sky to catch it, or figure out
99	other ways to get their meals.
105	You are a kind of animal. How do you move
115	around to get the different things you eat? 123

Number of words read: _____ Number of errors made: _____

A Special Gift

Rachel wanted to give Michelle a special
birthday gift. But she had no money.

One afternoon Rachel noticed that Mrs. Will
next door was giving away old furniture. Old chairs
and tables were stacked on the sidewalk. Rachel
asked Mrs. Will if she could take one of the
wooden chairs.

"Sure," said Mrs. Will.

The chair was covered with cuts and marks,
but it looked strong. Rachel found cans of old paint
in her garage. There were lots of different colors.
Carefully she painted a bright sky and lots of
flowers on the chair.

Rachel took the chair to Michelle's birthday
party. She hid it behind a bush until it was time to
open presents.

"I love it!" screamed Michelle when she saw
the chair. What a special gift the chair made!

1. What did Rachel give Michelle for her birthday?

2. What made the gift special?

Oral Fluency Record Sheet

Name _____ Date _____

Oral Reading Accuracy: _____%   Circle: Fall   Winter   Spring

Oral Reading Fluency Score: _____ words correct per minute

Prosody Rubric: (Circle Score) 1 2 3 4

Comprehension Question Responses

#1 _____

#2 _____

A Special Gift

	Rachel wanted to give Michelle a special
7	birthday gift. But she had no money.
14	One afternoon Rachel noticed that Mrs. Will
21	next door was giving away old furniture. Old chairs
30	and tables were stacked on the sidewalk. Rachel
38	asked Mrs. Will if she could take one of the
48	wooden chairs.
50	"Sure," said Mrs. Will.
54	The chair was covered with cuts and marks,
62	but it looked strong. Rachel found cans of old paint
72	in her garage. There were lots of different colors.
81	Carefully she painted a bright sky and lots of
90	flowers on the chair.
94	Rachel took the chair to Michelle's birthday
101	party. She hid it behind a bush until it was time to
113	open presents.
115	"I love it!" screamed Michelle when she saw
123	the chair. What a special gift the chair made! 132

Number of words read: _____ Number of errors made: _____

Animal Watch

Jason and Pete decide to take a walk in
the forest. They know that the animals come to
the forest pond to drink. If the boys are very
quiet, they will be able to watch the animals.

The boys hide behind some tall bushes.
When they look over the bushes, they can see
the pond clearly.

Soon the boys hear a sound coming
closer and closer. It sounds like a deer or
perhaps a family of skunks.

Suddenly Pete gets a funny feeling in
his chest. "Hic," says Pete. "Hic, hic, hic.
I've got the hiccups!"

The boys hear the sound quickly
moving away.

"I'm sorry," says Pete. "I just can't be
quiet when I have the hiccups. Maybe we'll
have better luck next time."

1. Why do the boys go to the forest?

2. What makes the animals move away?

Oral Fluency Record Sheet

Name _____ Date _____

Oral Reading Accuracy: _____%   Circle: Fall   Winter   Spring

Oral Reading Fluency Score: _____ words correct per minute

Prosody Rubric: (Circle Score) 1 2 3 4

Comprehension Question Responses

#1 _____

#2 _____

Animal Watch

	Jason and Pete decide to take a walk in
9	the forest. They know that the animals come to
18	the forest pond to drink. If the boys are very
28	quiet, they will be able to watch the animals.
37	The boys hide behind some tall bushes.
44	When they look over the bushes, they can see
53	the pond clearly.
56	Soon the boys hear a sound coming
63	closer and closer. It sounds like a deer or
72	perhaps a family of skunks.
77	Suddenly Pete gets a funny feeling in
84	his chest. "Hic," says Pete. "Hic, hic, hic.
92	I've got the hiccups!"
96	The boys hear the sound quickly
102	moving away.
104	"I'm sorry," says Pete. "I just can't be
112	quiet when I have the hiccups. Maybe we'll
120	have better luck next time." **125**

Number of words read: _____   Number of errors made: _____

Working Dogs

Dogs make wonderful pets. They are fun to play with and can be very friendly. But did you know that dogs can have jobs, too? Many dogs work to help people in important ways.

Some dogs are trained to help blind people get around. They are called seeing-eye dogs. Other dogs are trained to assist deaf people. They can alert their owner to sounds like fire alarms and doorbells.

Most dogs have an excellent sense of smell. That is why police officers use them to find people who are lost or hurt. Dogs are also used for herding animals. They know just how to make the sheep and cows move along.

Dogs like to play, but they are hard workers, too!

1. What is this passage mostly about?

2. How could a trained dog help a deaf person during a fire?

Oral Fluency Record Sheet

Name _____ Date _____

Oral Reading Accuracy: _____%   Circle: Fall Winter Spring
Oral Reading Fluency Score: _____ words correct per minute
Prosody Rubric: (Circle Score) 1 2 3 4
Comprehension Question Responses
#1 _____
#2 _____

Working Dogs

	Dogs make wonderful pets. They are fun to
8	play with and can be very friendly. But did you
18	know that dogs can have jobs, too? Many dogs
27	work to help people in important ways.
34	Some dogs are trained to help blind people
42	get around. They are called seeing-eye dogs.
50	Other dogs are trained to assist deaf people.
58	They can alert their owner to sounds like fire
67	alarms and doorbells.
70	Most dogs have an excellent sense of smell.
78	That is why police officers use them to find
87	people who are lost or hurt. Dogs are also used
97	for herding animals. They know just how to make
106	the sheep and cows move along.
112	Dogs like to play, but they are hard
120	workers, too! **122**

Number of words read: _____   Number of errors made: _____

A Walk on the Ceiling

House flies can be real pests. They can also carry germs. But they can be very interesting to just watch.

Did you ever see a house fly walk on the ceiling? Did you wonder how house flies could do that? Like other insects, all flies have six legs. Each leg ends in a claw. The claw helps all kinds of flies hold on to walls and ceilings.

But a house fly has something else. Each of its claws has a little pad. When the house fly walks on something smooth, the pads become flat. The pads also give off a sticky liquid. This liquid acts like a glue. It holds the house fly to the ceiling.

Would you like to be like a house fly? Would you like to walk on the ceiling, too?

---

1. What helps house flies walk on ceilings?

2. Why should you never let flies walk on your food?

© Macmillan/McGraw-Hill

Oral Fluency Record Sheet

Name _____ Date _____

Oral Reading Accuracy: _____%   Circle: Fall   Winter   Spring

Oral Reading Fluency Score: _____ words correct per minute

Prosody Rubric: (Circle Score) 1 2 3 4

Comprehension Question Responses

#1 _____

#2 _____

A Walk on the Ceiling

	House flies can be real pests. They can also
9	carry germs. But they can be very interesting to
18	just watch.
20	Did you ever see a house fly walk on the
30	ceiling? Did you wonder how house flies could
38	do that? Like other insects, all flies have six legs.
48	Each leg ends in a claw. The claw helps all kinds
59	of flies hold on to walls and ceilings.
67	But a house fly has something else. Each
75	of its claws has a little pad. When the house fly
86	walks on something smooth, the pads become
93	flat. The pads also give off a sticky liquid.
102	This liquid acts like a glue. It holds the house
112	fly to the ceiling.
116	Would you like to be like a house fly?
125	Would you like to walk on the ceiling, too? 134

Number of words read: _____   Number of errors made: _____

Fun for Marge

Marge the cat did not feel like chasing mice today. She wanted some fun for a change. Marge strolled across the street and into a schoolyard. She wanted to watch what the children were doing there.

Marge slid through the door and hid in a cardboard box. Not long after that, someone picked up the box. Marge swayed as she was carried through a narrow hall. Then the swaying stopped.

In a flash, Marge was out of the box. She could not believe her eyes. All the children were running and chasing balls. Marge thought they were all pretending to be cats, and joined in the game.

Soon the children were chasing Marge, but she did not like this kind of fun. Marge ran down the hall and out the door. After that day, Marge thought chasing mice was just enough fun for a feline.

1. Why did Marge go to the schoolyard?

2. Why would Marge think the children were pretending to be cats?

Oral Fluency Record Sheet

Name _____ Date _____

Oral Reading Accuracy: _____%   Circle: Fall Winter Spring

Oral Reading Fluency Score: _____ words correct per minute

Prosody Rubric: (Circle Score) 1 2 3 4

Comprehension Question Responses

#1 _____

#2 _____

Fun for Marge

	Marge the cat did not feel like chasing mice
9	today. She wanted some fun for a change. Marge
18	strolled across the street and into a schoolyard.
26	She wanted to watch what the children were
34	doing there.
36	Marge slid through the door and hid in a
45	cardboard box. Not long after that, someone picked
53	up the box. Marge swayed as she was carried
62	through a narrow hall. Then the swaying stopped.
70	In a flash, Marge was out of the box. She could
81	not believe her eyes. All the children were running and
91	chasing balls. Marge thought they were all pretending
99	to be cats, and joined in the game.
107	Soon the children were chasing Marge,
113	but she did not like this kind of fun. Marge ran
124	down the hall and out the door. After that day,
134	Marge thought chasing mice was just enough
141	fun for a feline. 145

Number of words read: _____ Number of errors made: _____

The Art Museum

Mr. Lawn's class went to a new art museum.
This was not like any other museum they ever saw.
Everything in the museum was made from trash.

In the first hall, the children saw clothes.
Phil noticed that some coats were made from old
flags. The colors looked pretty. Jane spotted big rain
hats made from soda bottles. In the next hall, the
children played with toys. Sarah played with a
mouse made from boxes. Brooke and Tom raced tin
can cars. Kelly played with a ball that was made
from rubber bands.

In the last hall, the class saw a tiny town
with toothpick houses and red doors. The roads
were made from old wood. The stores were made
from milk jugs. When the children got back to class,
they made art from trash, too. The whole school
came to see their fine work.

1. What was different about the art museum in this story?

2. What did the children learn at the museum?

Oral Fluency Record Sheet

Name _____ Date _____

Oral Reading Accuracy: _____% Circle: Fall Winter Spring

Oral Reading Fluency Score: _____ words correct per minute

Prosody Rubric: (Circle Score) 1 2 3 4

Comprehension Question Responses

#1 _____

#2 _____

The Art Museum

	Mr. Lawn's class went to a new art museum.
9	This was not like any other museum they ever saw.
19	Everything in the museum was made from trash.
27	In the first hall, the children saw clothes.
35	Phil noticed that some coats were made from old
44	flags. The colors looked pretty. Jane spotted big rain
53	hats made from soda bottles. In the next hall, the
63	children played with toys. Sarah played with a
71	mouse made from boxes. Brooke and Tom raced tin
80	can cars. Kelly played with a ball that was made
90	from rubber bands.
93	In the last hall, the class saw a tiny town
103	with toothpick houses and red doors. The roads
111	were made from old wood. The stores were made
120	from milk jugs. When the children got back to class,
130	they made art from trash, too. The whole school
139	came to see their fine work. **145**

Number of words read: _____ Number of errors made: _____

The White House

The White House is the home of the President
of the United States. It is indeed a big, white house.
A painter would need 570 gallons of white paint to
cover all the outside walls!

The White House has six floors, 132 rooms,
and 32 bathrooms. Some rooms are for the
President's family and friends. Other rooms are
used as offices or for meetings. Parties and other
celebrations are held in some rooms. The biggest
room is the East Room. It is used for balls and
parties. The President has small dinners in the
Blue Room. Big dinners, on the other hand, take
place in the State Dining Room.

You would enjoy a visit to the White House.
The tour takes you to five of the rooms. You might
even meet the President!

1. What is this story about?

2. Tell what three of the rooms in the White House are
used for.

Oral Fluency Record Sheet

Name _____ Date _____

Oral Reading Accuracy: _____%   Circle: Fall Winter Spring
Oral Reading Fluency Score: _____ words correct per minute
Prosody Rubric: (Circle Score) 1 2 3 4
Comprehension Question Responses
#1 _____
#2 _____

The White House

	The White House is the home of the President
9	of the United States. It is indeed a big, white house.
20	A painter would need 570 gallons of white paint to
30	cover all the outside walls!
35	The White House has six floors, 132 rooms,
43	and 32 bathrooms. Some rooms are for the
51	President's family and friends. Other rooms are
58	used as offices or for meetings. Parties and other
67	celebrations are held in some rooms. The biggest
75	room is the East Room. It is used for balls and
86	parties. The President has small dinners in the
94	Blue Room. Big dinners, on the other hand, take
103	place in the State Dining Room.
109	You would enjoy a visit to the White House.
118	The tour takes you to five of the rooms. You might
129	even meet the President! 133

© Macmillan/McGraw-Hill

Number of words read: _____   Number of errors made: _____

Watch Out for Flying Foxes

Birds and insects can fly, but can foxes fly, too? The bat is the only flying mammal. Fruit bats, the largest of all bats, are sometimes called *flying foxes*.

There are almost 200 kinds of fruit bats. They are called fruit bats because they survive on fruits. Some fruit bats only drink the juice from fruit. Others eat whole fruits, seeds and all.

Most fruit bats have long noses, large eyes, pointy ears, and furry bodies. Some kinds have wings as long as six feet across. Fruit bats can be brown, gray, or black. They live in thick forests or swamps. Fruit bats are often found in trees in big groups called *camps*. Some camps have more than a thousand bats in them.

The next time you hear noise in the trees, look up. It might be a camp of fruit bats!

1. What is this article mostly about?

2. Why are fruit bats sometimes called *flying foxes*?

Oral Fluency Record Sheet

Name _____ Date _____

Oral Reading Accuracy: _____% Circle: Fall Winter Spring

Oral Reading Fluency Score: _____ words correct per minute

Prosody Rubric: (Circle Score) 1 2 3 4

Comprehension Question Responses

#1 _____

#2 _____

Watch Out for Flying Foxes

	Birds and insects can fly, but can foxes
8	fly, too? The bat is the only flying mammal.
17	Fruit bats, the largest of all bats, are sometimes
26	called *flying foxes*.
29	There are almost 200 kinds of fruit bats.
37	They are called fruit bats because they survive on
46	fruits. Some fruit bats only drink the juice from fruit.
56	Others eat whole fruits, seeds and all.
63	Most fruit bats have long noses, large eyes,
71	pointy ears, and furry bodies. Some kinds have
79	wings as long as six feet across. Fruit bats can be
90	brown, gray, or black. They live in thick forests or
100	swamps. Fruit bats are often found in trees in big
110	groups called *camps*. Some camps have more
117	than a thousand bats in them.
123	The next time you hear noise in the trees, look
133	up. It might be a camp of fruit bats! 142

Number of words read: _____ Number of errors made: _____

Grandma Nell

Grandma Nell moved in with us last month because she has been sick. It is still a little strange having Grandma in our home.

It is difficult to be around Grandma because she does not always answer when I ask her something. Talking seems to be hard for her. She hardly ever speaks. Mom says that is because she can't hear very well.

When I went home from school the other day, Grandma was in the kitchen. Something smelled really good, but I didn't want to go into the kitchen. After dinner, Grandma surprised us with a cherry pie. So that was what I had smelled! She put a huge slice on my plate. I smiled at Grandma and she smiled back at me.

Today, Grandma and I are baking an apple pie together. Grandma Nell is a good cook and teacher. We do not need to talk much when we are baking.

1. What makes it hard for Grandma Nell to talk to others?
2. Why didn't the granddaughter want to go into the kitchen?

© Macmillan/McGraw-Hill

Oral Fluency Record Sheet

Name _____ Date _____

Oral Reading Accuracy: _____%   Circle: Fall Winter Spring

Oral Reading Fluency Score: _____ words correct per minute

Prosody Rubric: (Circle Score) 1 2 3 4

Comprehension Question Responses

#1 _____

#2 _____

Grandma Nell

	Grandma Nell moved in with us last month
8	because she has been sick. It is still a little strange
19	having Grandma in our home.
24	It is difficult to be around Grandma because
32	she does not always answer when I ask her
41	something. Talking seems to be hard for her. She
50	hardly ever speaks. Mom says that is because she
59	can't hear very well.
63	When I went home from school the other day,
72	Grandma was in the kitchen. Something smelled
79	really good, but I didn't want to go into the kitchen.
90	After dinner, Grandma surprised us with a cherry pie.
99	So that was what I had smelled! She put a huge slice
111	on my plate. I smiled at Grandma and she smiled
121	back at me.
124	Today, Grandma and I are baking an apple
132	pie together. Grandma Nell is a good cook and
141	teacher. We do not need to talk much when we
151	are baking. 153

Number of words read: _____   Number of errors made: _____

A Job for Karla

Karla watched the actors on stage. They looked as if they were having so much fun. How could they do it while she could not? Whenever Karla got on stage, she felt awful. She would feel dizzy, then forget all her lines.

Still Karla did enjoy watching the play. Mitch was so good at saying his lines and Ann looked like a real queen. On the way home from school, Karla wondered how she could join her friends in the play. Surely there was a job for her, even if she was very shy.

The next day Karla saw a poster on the stage door. She read it. Karla just knew it was the perfect job for her.

That afternoon, Karla learned how to run a spotlight. Karla could watch the play and be part of the action. And she never had to step on stage!

---

1. What is the story mostly about?

2. What was written on the poster Karla read?

Oral Fluency Record Sheet

Name _____ Date _____

Oral Reading Accuracy: _____% Circle: Fall Winter Spring
Oral Reading Fluency Score: _____ words correct per minute
Prosody Rubric: (Circle Score) 1 2 3 4
Comprehension Question Responses
#1 _____
#2 _____

A Job for Karla

	Karla watched the actors on stage. They
7	looked as if they were having so much fun. How
17	could they do it while she could not? Whenever Karla
27	got on stage, she felt awful. She would feel dizzy,
37	then forget all her lines.
42	Still Karla did enjoy watching the play. Mitch
50	was so good at saying his lines and Ann looked
60	like a real queen. On the way home from school,
70	Karla wondered how she could join her friends in
79	the play. Surely there was a job for her, even if she
91	was very shy.
94	The next day Karla saw a poster on the stage
104	door. She read it. Karla just knew it was the perfect
115	job for her.
118	That afternoon, Karla learned how to run a
126	spotlight. Karla could watch the play and be
134	part of the action. And she never had to step
144	on stage! 146

Number of words read: _____   Number of errors made: _____

The Tiger Story

In the jungle a very large, striped cat sneaks up on a deer. Then it leaps. The deer gets away. The tiger does not chase its prey. It just looks for something else to eat.

Tigers are the world's biggest cats. One tiger can eat 9 to 15 pounds of meat a day. Tigers like living in thick forests or places with tall grass. They usually live alone.

Tigers do not live in groups like lions do. The only time you would see a group of tigers is when a mother tiger has cubs. Cubs stay with their mothers for about two years.

But getting a peek at a tiger with cubs in the wild is now a rare event. There are not too many tigers left. Today, twice as many tigers live in zoos as in the wild. Not enough wild places remain for them to live.

1. Tell two facts about tigers that you learned from the story.

2. Where do most tigers live today?

© Macmillan/McGraw-Hill

Oral Fluency Record Sheet

Name _____ Date _____

Oral Reading Accuracy: _____%   Circle: Fall Winter Spring

Oral Reading Fluency Score: _____ words correct per minute

Prosody Rubric: (Circle Score) 1 2 3 4

Comprehension Question Responses

#1 _____

#2 _____

The Tiger Story

	In the jungle a very large, striped cat sneaks
9	up on a deer. Then it leaps. The deer gets away. The
21	tiger does not chase its prey. It just looks for
31	something else to eat.
35	Tigers are the world's biggest cats. One tiger
43	can eat 9 to 15 pounds of meat a day. Tigers like
55	living in thick forests or places with tall grass. They
65	usually live alone.
68	Tigers do not live in groups like lions do. The
78	only time you would see a group of tigers is when
89	a mother tiger has cubs. Cubs stay with their
98	mothers for about two years.
103	But getting a peek at a tiger with cubs in
113	the wild is now a rare event. There are not too
124	many tigers left. Today, twice as many tigers live in
134	zoos as in the wild. Not enough wild places remain
144	for them to live. 148

Number of words read: _____   Number of errors made: _____

Common Cents

   If you have one hundred of these, you have a
dollar. What are we talking about? We are talking
about the penny. The penny is the most common coin
in the United States. The U.S. Mint produces more
than one thousand pennies every second. That adds up
to about 30 million pennies a day.

   The copper penny was the first coin made in
America. The first one was made in 1787. Since then,
there have been many different pictures on pennies.
Abraham Lincoln's picture went on the penny in
1909. The other side showed wheat. Today, Lincoln's
face is still on the penny.

   New pennies are now made of zinc. They have
only a tiny bit of copper in them. Over the years,
some things have changed with the penny, but one
thing remains the same. A penny is still worth
one cent.

---

1. Whose face is on the penny today?

2. Name two things that have changed about the penny
   over time.

© Macmillan/McGraw-Hill

Oral Fluency Record Sheet

Name _____ Date _____

Oral Reading Accuracy: _____%   Circle: Fall   Winter   Spring

Oral Reading Fluency Score: _____ words correct per minute

Prosody Rubric: (Circle Score) 1 2 3 4

Comprehension Question Responses

#1 _____

#2 _____

Common Cents

	If you have one hundred of these, you have a
10	dollar. What are we talking about? We are talking
19	about the penny. The penny is the most common coin
29	in the United States. The U.S. Mint produces more
38	than one thousand pennies every second. That adds up
47	to about 30 million pennies a day.
54	The copper penny was the first coin made in
63	America. The first one was made in 1787. Since then,
73	there have been many different pictures on pennies.
81	Abraham Lincoln's picture went on the penny in
89	1909. The other side showed wheat. Today, Lincoln's
97	face is still on the penny.
103	New pennies are now made of zinc. They have
112	only a tiny bit of copper in them. Over the years,
123	some things have changed with the penny, but one
132	thing remains the same. A penny is still worth
141	one cent. 143

© Macmillan/McGraw-Hill

Number of words read: _____   **Number of errors made:** _____

Name _____ Date _____

A Birthday Party

Molly turned eight on Sunday. She did not expect
a party because she knew her mom had millions of other
things to do. But that morning her mom told Molly that
they should take a walk in the park. When they got there,
Molly saw her closest friends. Five girls and three boys
all shouted, "Happy birthday!" Molly was really
surprised. Her mom had planned everything. There
were snacks. There were games to play. There was
even a cake with eight candles.

After eating yummy snacks, the friends
played games. Jack won a prize for making a funny
face. Kate won a balloon for blowing the biggest
bubble. Grace won marbles for hopping on one foot.
Everyone got stickers just because they took part
in a game.

Then the kids sang to Molly. She blew out the
candles and everyone ate cake. Molly was so
happy. She thanked all her friends for making her
birthday special. She hugged and kissed her
mom for giving her the best birthday ever.

1. Name two things that Molly did at her birthday party.

2. Why did Molly's mom suggest that they walk in the park?

Oral Fluency Record Sheet

Name _____ Date _____

Oral Reading Accuracy: _____%   Circle: Fall   Winter   Spring

Oral Reading Fluency Score: _____ words correct per minute

Prosody Rubric: (Circle Score) 1 2 3 4

Comprehension Question Responses

#1 _____

#2 _____

A Birthday Party

	Molly turned eight on Sunday. She did not expect
9	a party because she knew her mom had millions of other
20	things to do. But that morning her mom told Molly that
31	they should take a walk in the park. When they got there,
43	Molly saw her closest friends. Five girls and three boys
53	all shouted, "Happy birthday!" Molly was really
60	surprised. Her mom had planned everything. There
67	were snacks. There were games to play. There was
76	even a cake with eight candles.
82	After eating yummy snacks, the friends
88	played games. Jack won a prize for making a funny
98	face. Kate won a balloon for blowing the biggest
107	bubble. Grace won marbles for hopping on one foot.
116	Everyone got stickers just because they took part
124	in a game.
127	Then the kids sang to Molly. She blew out the
137	candles and everyone ate cake. Molly was so
145	happy. She thanked all her friends for making her
154	birthday special. She hugged and kissed her
161	mom for giving her the best birthday ever. 169

Number of words read: _____   Number of errors made: _____

The Marching Band

Mike played the flute at school, and Max played the drums. One day Mike and Max decided to form the school's first marching band.

"We need more members for our band," said Mike.

Max and Mike put up a sign asking anyone who played a musical instrument to join. They got several responses that day.

Chris really wanted to join the band, but he had one huge problem. He could not play any musical instrument. Beth also wanted to join the band, but she played the harp.

"How can you be in our band?" Mike asked Beth. "You play the harp sitting down. How can you march?"

All the band members wanted Beth to play in the band. But they also wanted to march. Then Max had an idea. He invited Beth and Chris to join the band.

Max said, "Chris will lead the band and pull a wagon with Beth and her harp on it."

The band members loved Max's idea and everyone else loved the marching band's great music.

---

1. What problem did Chris have in the story?

2. How did Max solve two problems with his idea?

Oral Fluency Record Sheet

Name _____ Date _____

Oral Reading Accuracy: _____%   Circle: Fall   Winter   Spring

Oral Reading Fluency Score: _____ words correct per minute

Prosody Rubric: (Circle Score) 1 2 3 4

Comprehension Question Responses

#1 _____

#2 _____

The Marching Band

	Mike played the flute at school, and Max played the
10	drums. One day Mike and Max decided to form the
20	school's first marching band.
24	"We need more members for our band," said Mike.
33	Max and Mike put up a sign asking anyone who
43	played a musical instrument to join. They got several
52	responses that day.
55	Chris really wanted to join the band, but he had
65	one huge problem. He could not play any musical
74	instrument. Beth also wanted to join the band, but she
84	played the harp.
87	"How can you be in our band?" Mike asked Beth.
97	"You play the harp sitting down. How can you march?"
107	All the band members wanted Beth to play in the
117	band. But they also wanted to march. Then Max had an
128	idea. He invited Beth and Chris to join the band.
138	Max said, "Chris will lead the band and pull a wagon
149	with Beth and her harp on it."
156	The band members loved Max's idea and everyone
164	else loved the marching band's great music. 171

Number of words read: _____   Number of errors made: _____

Name _____ Date _____

Being a Good Sport

How can you be a "good sport"? You should be a good winner and not a sore loser. Don't brag when you win or complain when you lose. Say kind words to the other team and to your own team, too. If someone on your team makes a mistake, do not make fun of the person or get mad. Do not blame anyone for losing the game. When someone plays well, say so. It will make both of you feel good. Show team spirit not just by yelling the loudest. Write a nice note to the players on your team, and given them special nicknames. Hang a banner at school on the day of a game.

Treat the other team the way you would want them to treat you. Make up a cheer to let them know you are good sports. If you win or lose, be sure to shake hands with the other team at the end of the game. Find something nice to say about the way they played. And do not forget to have fun.

1. What does being a "good sport" mean?

2. Which idea from the story about being a good sport are you most likely to use?

Oral Fluency Record Sheet

Name _____ Date _____

Oral Reading Accuracy: _____% Circle: Fall Winter Spring
Oral Reading Fluency Score: _____ words correct per minute
Prosody Rubric: (Circle Score) 1 2 3 4
Comprehension Question Responses
#1 _____
#2 _____

Being a Good Sport

	How can you be a "good sport"? You should be
10	a good winner and not a sore loser. Don't brag
20	when you win or complain when you lose. Say kind
30	words to the other team and to your own team, too.
41	If someone on your team makes a mistake, do
50	not make fun of the person or get mad. Do not
61	blame anyone for losing the game. When
68	someone plays well, say so. It will make both of
78	you feel good. Show team spirit not just by yelling
88	the loudest. Write a nice note to the players on
98	your team, and give them special nicknames.
105	Hang a banner at school on the day of a game.
116	Treat the other team the way you would want
125	them to treat you. Make up a cheer to let them
136	know you are good sports. If you win or lose, be
147	sure to shake hands with the other team at the
157	end of the game. Find something nice to say
166	about the way they played. And do not forget to
176	have fun. 178

Number of words read: _____ Number of errors made: _____

Fossils

Dinosaurs lived on Earth millions of years ago. Today we know a lot about them. How do we know so much? We learned about them from people who study the remains of dead plants and animals.

Fossils is the name we give to remains that have become hard and turned to stone. Not every plant or animal becomes a fossil when it dies. Some just dry up under the sun. Strong winds blow away others.

For a dead plant or animal to become a fossil, everything must be just right. Sand or mud has to cover the animal or plant quickly. That way, neither the wind nor the sun can destroy it. Then the sand or mud cover turns hard as a rock. Over time, the fossil takes shape.

To find fossils, we must dig for them. We might find a bone, a tooth, or part of a plant. We might even find a footprint! Every find is a clue that tells a little more about life many years ago.

1. How do people find fossils?

2. Why are the sun and the wind a problem when creating new fossils?

© Macmillan/McGraw-Hill

Oral Fluency Record Sheet

Name _____ Date _____

Oral Reading Accuracy: _____%   Circle: Fall   Winter   Spring

Oral Reading Fluency Score: _____ words correct per minute

Prosody Rubric: (Circle Score) 1 2 3 4

Comprehension Question Responses

#1 _____

#2 _____

Fossils

	Dinosaurs lived on Earth millions of years
7	ago. Today we know a lot about them. How do we
18	know so much? We learned about them from people
27	who study the remains of dead plants and animals.
36	Fossils is the name we give to remains that
45	have become hard and turned to stone. Not every
54	plant or animal becomes a fossil when it dies.
63	Some just dry up under the sun. Strong winds blow
73	away others.
75	For a dead plant or animal to become a fossil,
85	everything must be just right. Sand or mud has to
95	cover the animal or plant quickly. That way, neither
104	the wind nor the sun can destroy it. Then the sand or
116	mud cover turns hard as a rock. Over time, the fossil
127	takes shape.
129	To find fossils, we must dig for them. We might
139	find a bone, a tooth, or part of a plant. We might even
152	find a footprint! Every find is a clue that tells a little
164	more about life many years ago. 170

Number of words read: _____   Number of errors made: _____

Lily's First Movie

Nick lived on a ranch where several animals were trained to perform in shows and in movies. Nick's favorite was Lily, a baby elephant. Lily loved to play a trick on Nick. She would swing her trunk and if it hit him, she would put her head back as if she were laughing. Then Nick would laugh, too.

One day, moviemakers came to town. They needed a terrific animal performer for their movie. They watched Lily playing her trick on Nick and they were impressed by her actions. So the movie people took Lily away in a huge truck.

Lily was very sad because she missed Nick. She would not do her trick with the actors. The movie people tried to win her over, but she refused to budge. Then they talked with Nick's dad.

The next day, Nick appeared at the movie set. When Lily saw Nick, she hit him with her trunk, then put back her head and laughed. Then she hit him with her trunk again. The movie people laughed and clapped loudly. Now they had their star performer.

1. What was Lily's special trick?

2. Why wouldn't Lily do her trick with the actors?

Oral Fluency Record Sheet

Name _____ Date _____

Oral Reading Accuracy: _____% Circle: Fall Winter Spring

Oral Reading Fluency Score: _____ words correct per minute

Prosody Rubric: (Circle Score) 1 2 3 4

Comprehension Question Responses

#1 _____

#2 _____

Lily's First Movie

	Nick lived on a ranch where several animals were
9	trained to perform in shows and in movies. Nick's
18	favorite was Lily, a baby elephant. Lily loved to play
28	a trick on Nick. She would swing her trunk and if it
40	hit him, she would put her head back as if she
51	were laughing. Then Nick would laugh, too.
58	One day, moviemakers came to town. They needed
66	a terrific animal performer for their movie. They
74	watched Lily playing her trick on Nick and they were
84	impressed by her actions. So the movie people took Lily
94	away in a huge truck.
99	Lily was very sad because she missed Nick. She
108	would not do her trick with the actors. The movie people
119	tried to win her over, but she refused to budge. Then they
131	talked with Nick's dad.
135	The next day, Nick appeared at the movie set. When
145	Lily saw Nick, she hit him with her trunk, then put back
157	her head and laughed. Then she hit him with her trunk
168	again. The movie people laughed and clapped loudly.
176	Now they had their star performer. **182**

Number of words read: _____ Number of errors made: _____

One Last Thing

When Dad got a better job in the city, we had to move. Moving from a big house in the country to a city apartment was hard, especially for Mom. Dad said we should throw away anything we didn't need. He said our things would not all fit in the new apartment. If we must bring something, however, he said we could each take one last thing.

Mom had a hard time choosing what to throw away and what last thing to bring. Every day, she tried to get rid of something. But every item was a treasure to her. It was almost moving day, and Mom had not thrown anything away. Then my sister came up with an idea. She took pictures of all of Mom's treasures. We arranged the pictures in a big book, and then we named the book *One Last Thing*.

Mom was so happy with our present that she cried. She said they were happy tears. Moving would not be such a painful experience. She could take all her treasures. She would take *One Last Thing*.

---

1. Why couldn't Mom pack all of her treasures?

2. Why was *One Last Thing* a good title for the book?

© Macmillan/McGraw-Hill

Oral Fluency Record Sheet

Name _____ Date _____

Oral Reading Accuracy: _____%   Circle: Fall   Winter   Spring

Oral Reading Fluency Score: _____ words correct per minute

Prosody Rubric: (Circle Score) 1 2 3 4

Comprehension Question Responses

#1 _____

#2 _____

One Last Thing

	When Dad got a better job in the city, we had to
12	move. Moving from a big house in the country to a city
24	apartment was hard, especially for Mom. Dad said we
33	should throw away anything we didn't need. He said
42	our things would not all fit in the new apartment. If we
54	must bring something, however, he said we could each
63	take one last thing.
67	Mom had a hard time choosing what to throw
76	away and what last thing to bring. Every day, she tried
87	to get rid of something. But every item was a treasure to
99	her. It was almost moving day, and Mom had not thrown
110	anything away. Then my sister came up with an idea. She
121	took pictures of all of Mom's treasures. We arranged the
131	pictures in a big book, and then we named the book
142	*One Last Thing*.
145	Mom was so happy with our present that she
154	cried. She said they were happy tears. Moving would not
164	be such a painful experience. She could take all her
174	treasures. She would take *One Last Thing*. 181

Number of words read: _____   Number of errors made: _____

Name _____ Date _____

A Beautiful State

Maine is a beautiful state. You will find it along the northeast coast of the United States. It has a long coast with lots of little islands. The coast also has sandy beaches and quiet fishing villages.

Forests cover almost all of the state. Pine trees once made up most of the forests. That's why the state is called the Pine Tree State.

There are many interesting facts about Maine. Maine makes more wooden toothpicks than any other state. Maine is also the place where a group called the Camp Fire Girls started. The group is now called the Camp Fire Boys and Girls. It offers outdoor fun to children all over the country.

Here's another interesting fact. If you live in a cold place, you may wear earmuffs to keep your ears warm. A 15-year-old boy invented earmuffs in Maine in 1873. He later opened a factory to make earmuffs.

Will you take a trip to Maine? If you do, you will find yourself in a beautiful and interesting place: the Pine Tree State.

1. What covers most of the state of Maine?

2. Describe two interesting facts about Maine.

Oral Fluency Record Sheet

Name _____   Date _____

Oral Reading Accuracy: _____%   Circle: Fall Winter Spring
Oral Reading Fluency Score: _____ words correct per minute
Prosody Rubric: (Circle Score) 1 2 3 4
Comprehension Question Responses
#1 _____
#2 _____

A Beautiful State

	Maine is a beautiful state. You will find it
9	along the northeast coast of the United States. It has a
20	long coast with lots of little islands. The coast also
30	has sandy beaches and quiet fishing villages.
37	Forests cover almost all of the state. Pine trees
46	once made up most of the forests. That's why the state
57	is called the Pine Tree State.
63	There are many interesting facts about Maine.
70	Maine makes more wooden toothpicks than any other
78	state. Maine is also the place where a group called the
89	Camp Fire Girls started. The group is now called the
99	Camp Fire Boys and Girls. It offers outdoor fun
108	to children all over the country.
114	Here's another interesting fact. If you live in a
123	cold place, you may wear earmuffs to keep your ears
133	warm. A 15-year-old boy invented earmuffs in Maine
143	in 1873. He later opened a factory to make earmuffs.
153	Will you take a trip to Maine? If you do, you
164	will find yourself in a beautiful and interesting
172	place: the Pine Tree State. 177

Number of words read: _____   Number of errors made: _____

Horses of the Sea

Have you ever seen a seahorse? The seahorse got its name because its head looks like a horse. That is the only way they are the same.

A seahorse can be from six to twelve inches long. With a curved tail like a monkey's tail, it can attach itself to plants and reefs. Otherwise, strong ocean currents would sweep it away. Then it would be hard for the seahorse to eat and hide.

Its body is very tough. It has plates of armor that protect it from its enemies. The plates are heavy, so seahorses do not swim well. But they have a special fin on their backs. The fin flutters quickly. It moves the seahorse through the water.

Seahorses face several problems. Other sea creatures like to eat seahorses. But seahorses can protect themselves. They can change color like a chameleon. This helps them hide. Seahorses can see sideways. This helps them watch for enemies.

But the biggest problem seahorses face is water pollution. If we do not help clean the oceans where seahorses live, they might all die.

1. How does the seahorse protect itself from ocean currents?

2. How is the seahorse similar to a horse and a chameleon?

© Macmillan/McGraw-Hill

Oral Fluency Record Sheet

Name _____ Date _____

Oral Reading Accuracy: _____%   Circle: Fall   Winter   Spring

Oral Reading Fluency Score: _____ words correct per minute

Prosody Rubric: (Circle Score) 1 2 3 4

Comprehension Question Responses

#1 _____

#2 _____

Horses of the Sea

	Have you ever seen a seahorse? The seahorse got
9	its name because its head looks like a horse. That is the
21	only way they are the same.
27	A seahorse can be from six to twelve inches long.
37	With a curved tail like a monkey's tail, it can attach itself
49	to plants and reefs. Otherwise, strong ocean currents
57	would sweep it away. Then it would be hard for the
68	seahorse to eat and hide.
73	Its body is very tough. It has plates of armor that
84	protect it from its enemies. The plates are heavy, so
94	seahorses do not swim well. But they have a special fin
105	on their backs. The fin flutters quickly. It moves the
115	seahorse through the water.
119	Seahorses face several problems. Other sea
125	creatures like to eat seahorses. But seahorses can protect
134	themselves. They can change color like a chameleon.
142	This helps them hide. Seahorses can see sideways. This
151	helps them watch for enemies.
156	But the biggest problem seahorses face is water
164	pollution. If we do not help clean the oceans where
174	seahorses live, they might all die. **180**

© Macmillan/McGraw-Hill

Number of words read: _____   Number of errors made: _____

The Foolish Fox

Long ago a fox was out for a walk and
came to a fence. Behind the fence were some
plump, ripe grapes.

"Those grapes look so good," said the fox.
"They shall be my dinner." But the grapes were on the
other side of the fence. The fox was not thin enough
to crawl underneath it.

"I will go home and wait until I grow thin,"
thought the fox.

The fox ate nothing for three days. Then he
was thin enough to crawl under the fence, but he was
also very hungry. He went back to the fence, crawled
under, and gobbled up all the grapes that he wanted.
But he ate so many that he grew too fat to crawl under
the fence to go home.

"Now I must grow thin again," thought the
fox. "I must not eat anything."

The fox hid under the grape vines for three days.
He ate nothing, and after three days he could easily
squeeze back under the fence.

"Never again will I be so foolish," thought the
fox sadly as he made his way home.

1. Why couldn't the fox crawl under the fence the first time?

2. What lesson did the fox learn?

© Macmillan/McGraw-Hill

Oral Fluency Record Sheet

Name _____ Date _____

Oral Reading Accuracy: _____%   Circle: Fall Winter Spring
Oral Reading Fluency Score: _____ words correct per minute
Prosody Rubric: (Circle Score) 1 2 3 4
Comprehension Question Responses
#1 _____
#2 _____

The Foolish Fox

	Long ago a fox was out for a walk and
10	came to a fence. Behind the fence were some
19	plump, ripe grapes.
22	"Those grapes look so good," said the fox.
30	"They shall be my dinner." But the grapes were on the
41	other side of the fence. The fox was not thin enough
52	to crawl underneath it.
56	"I will go home and wait until I grow thin,"
66	thought the fox.
69	The fox ate nothing for three days. Then he
78	was thin enough to crawl under the fence, but he was
89	also very hungry. He went back to the fence, crawled
99	under, and gobbled up all the grapes that he wanted.
109	But he ate so many that he grew too fat to crawl under
122	the fence to go home.
127	"Now I must grow thin again," thought the
135	fox. "I must not eat anything."
141	The fox hid under the grape vines for three days.
151	He ate nothing, and after three days he could easily
161	squeeze back under the fence.
166	"Never again will I be so foolish," thought the
175	fox sadly as he made his way home. 183

Number of words read: _____ Number of errors made: _____

Name _____ Date _____

Sand Castle Friends

Liz was spending the summer vacation at the beach.
She didn't know any other kids, and she was starting to
feel lonely.

Liz walked down to the edge of the water and began
to build a sand castle. The castle had two floors and twelve
rooms before another girl came along.

"Hi, I'm Lucy. Can I add some flags to your
castle?" she asked.

"Flags sound great!" said Liz. Liz added more
rooms to the castle while Lucy made flags with twigs and
some tissue.

"To make this castle really great, let's cover the
walls with shells," said Lucy after the flags were done.

Lucy and Liz gathered shells along the shore. They
pressed the shells into the castle walls. The castle looked
beautiful. Soon the sky began to get dark. The ocean water
moved closer and closer to the castle. The girls watched as
the waves started to melt away their castle.

"Let's make a bigger castle tomorrow," said Lucy.
"Maybe we can even give it a tower."

"Wonderful!" said Liz. "See you then."

1. What did Lucy add first to the castle?

2. How did Liz feel at the end of the story?

Oral Fluency Record Sheet

Name _____ Date _____

Oral Reading Accuracy: _____%   Circle: Fall   Winter   Spring

Oral Reading Fluency Score: _____ words correct per minute

Prosody Rubric: (Circle Score) 1 2 3 4

Comprehension Question Responses

#1 _____

#2 _____

Sand Castle Friends

	Liz was spending the summer vacation at the beach.
9	She didn't know any other kids, and she was starting to
20	feel lonely.
22	Liz walked down to the edge of the water and began
33	to build a sand castle. The castle had two floors and twelve
45	rooms before another girl came along.
51	"Hi, I'm Lucy. Can I add some flags to your
61	castle?" she asked.
64	"Flags sound great!" said Liz. Liz added more
72	rooms to the castle while Lucy made flags with twigs and
83	some tissue.
85	"To make this castle really great, let's cover the
94	walls with shells," said Lucy after the flags were done.
104	Lucy and Liz gathered shells along the shore. They
113	pressed the shells into the castle walls. The castle looked
123	beautiful. Soon the sky began to get dark. The ocean water
134	moved closer and closer to the castle. The girls watched as
145	the waves started to melt away their castle.
153	"Let's make a bigger castle tomorrow," said Lucy.
161	"Maybe we can even give it a tower."
169	"Wonderful!" said Liz. "See you then." 175

Number of words read: _____   Number of errors made: _____

Saving Up

My class planned a trip to the aquarium. We decided to raise money for everyone's admission ticket. We earned the money by having a Good-to-Eat Sale at school.

Each morning for a week, everyone brought in something that was both delicious and healthy. I brought some enormous bran muffins. Miss Hansen brought in granola bar cookies. Other students brought raisins, carrot sticks, and banana bread.

We had a wide assortment of treats to sell. We set up our table where the school buses and cars dropped off their passengers. Each morning, we arranged the goods on the table.

As students were dropped off, they saw the delicious foods. Everyone was surprised to see what was for sale. No one could pass our table without stopping.

The sale was a huge success. We earned enough money for everyone to attend the class trip. The class cannot wait to see all of the sharks and the rare fish at the aquarium.

1. How did the class earn money for their trip?
2. What did the class mean by foods that were "good to eat"?

Oral Fluency Record Sheet

Name _____ Date _____

Oral Reading Accuracy: _____% Circle: Fall Winter Spring

Oral Reading Fluency Score: _____ words correct per minute

Prosody Rubric: (Circle Score) 1 2 3 4

Comprehension Question Responses

#1 _____

#2 _____

Saving Up

	My class planned a trip to the aquarium. We decided
10	to raise money for everyone's admission ticket. We earned
19	the money by having a Good-to-Eat Sale at school.
30	Each morning for a week, everyone brought in
38	something that was both delicious and healthy. I brought
47	some enormous bran muffins. Miss Hansen brought in
55	granola bar cookies. Other students brought raisins, carrot
63	sticks, and banana bread.
67	We had a wide assortment of treats to sell. We set
78	up our table where the school buses and cars dropped off
89	their passengers. Each morning, we arranged the goods on
98	the table.
100	As students were dropped off, they saw the delicious
109	foods. Everyone was surprised to see what was for sale.
119	No one could pass our table without stopping.
127	The sale was a huge success. We earned enough
136	money for everyone to attend the class trip. The class
146	cannot wait to see all of the sharks and the rare fish
158	at the aquarium. 161

Number of words read: _____ **Number of errors made:** _____

Bumpy Travels

Last evening, Dad and I spent a couple of hours reading a book about America's early pioneers. The book described families traveling in covered wagons pulled by horses, oxen, or mules. All of a family's possessions were inside each wagon. The family had to carry food for their journey, too.

I thought it would be fun to travel that way, but Dad explained that back then, travel was difficult. He asked how I would feel if I had to ride long distances in a wagon that bumped all day long. If someone didn't want to stay inside the wagon, the only other choice was to walk beside it.

I told Dad I would have to think about that one. Dad and I talked about our drive through Kansas last summer. Even by car, the drive took a long time. We did not, however, have to worry about feeding oxen along the way.

Traveling is easier and more convenient now, but I still think a journey in a covered wagon would be a great adventure.

1. What is this passage mostly about?

2. What is one difference between riding in a covered wagon and riding in a car?

Oral Fluency Record Sheet

Name _____ Date _____

Oral Reading Accuracy: _____%   Circle: Fall Winter Spring
Oral Reading Fluency Score: _____ words correct per minute
Prosody Rubric: (Circle Score) 1 2 3 4
Comprehension Question Responses
#1 _____
#2 _____

Bumpy Travels

	Last evening, Dad and I spent a couple of hours
10	reading a book about America's early pioneers. The book
19	described families traveling in covered wagons pulled by
27	horses, oxen, or mules. All of a family's possessions were
37	inside each wagon. The family had to carry food for their
48	journey, too.
50	I thought it would be fun to travel that way, but
61	Dad explained that back then, travel was difficult. He asked
71	how I would feel if I had to ride long distances in a wagon
85	that bumped all day long. If someone didn't want to stay
96	inside the wagon, the only other choice was to walk
106	beside it.
108	I told Dad I would have to think about that one.
119	Dad and I talked about our drive through Kansas last summer.
130	Even by car, the drive took a long time. We did not,
142	however, have to worry about feeding oxen along the way.
152	Traveling is easier and more convenient now, but I
161	still think a journey in a covered wagon would be a
172	great adventure. 174

© Macmillan/McGraw-Hill

Number of words read: _____   Number of errors made: _____

Basketball on Wheels

Basketball is a challenging sport to play. Players need strength to move up and down the court and bounce the ball while they are on the move. They also need to be alert for the opportunity to pass. Basketball players cannot relax or let their attention stray for a second. People who play basketball work as a team and depend on each other for support. The same is true for people who play basketball from wheelchairs.

The United States has many basketball teams for children in wheelchairs. The children on these teams bounce the ball, pass, and shoot from their wheelchairs. They learn to move quickly in their chairs and keep track of the ball. They must also be good at passing and shooting. They need a lot of balance, energy, and upper-body strength. Just think how high the basketball hoop looks when you are sitting down.

Wheelchair basketball is an excellent way for children in wheelchairs to be on a team. These players show us we can all be strong if we make the effort.

1. Name three things that are needed by all kinds of basketball players.

2. Why is it important for children in wheelchairs to get the chance to play basketball?

© Macmillan/McGraw-Hill

Oral Fluency Record Sheet

Name _____ Date _____

Oral Reading Accuracy: _____%   Circle: Fall   Winter   Spring

Oral Reading Fluency Score: _____ words correct per minute

Prosody Rubric: (Circle Score) 1 2 3 4

Comprehension Question Responses

#1 _____

#2 _____

Basketball on Wheels

	Basketball is a challenging sport to play. Players need
9	strength to move up and down the court and bounce the ball while
22	they are on the move. They also need to be alert for the opportunity
36	to pass. Basketball players cannot relax or let their attention stray
47	for a second. People who play basketball work as a team and
59	depend on each other for support. The same is true for people who
72	play basketball from wheelchairs.
76	The United States has many basketball teams for
84	children in wheelchairs. The children on these teams bounce
93	the ball, pass, and shoot from their wheelchairs. They learn to
104	move quickly in their chairs and keep track of the ball. They
116	must also be good at passing and shooting. They need a lot of
129	balance, energy, and upper-body strength. Just think how
138	high the basketball hoop looks when you are sitting down.
148	Wheelchair basketball is an excellent way for children
156	in wheelchairs to be on a team. These players show us we can
169	all be strong if we make the effort. 177

Number of words read: _____   Number of errors made: _____

Name _____ Date _____

Snakes of Many Colors

You might think snakes do not need protection, but they do. Certain kinds of mammals, such as pigs and mongooses, prey on snakes. Large birds, such as the serpent eagle, think they make fine meals. Even other snakes, such as the King Cobra, will hunt certain snakes.

Snakes often use colors to protect themselves from predators. The bright colors of some snakes, like the Mangrove snake, warn enemies that the snake is poisonous. Other snakes only pretend to be poisonous. The bright red, black, and white scales of the Pueblan milk snake, which are arranged in bands, make animals think the snake is poisonous even though it is not.

Snakes also use their colors to hide themselves from predators. For example, the bright green cat snake lives high in a tree in the rainforest. The snake stays coiled around a branch during the day. It looks just like a vine, fooling animals that might want to make it their dinner.

These snakes need their colorful scales to stay safe. After all, it is a dangerous world, even for a snake.

1. How do snakes use color to protect themselves?

2. Why is the world dangerous for snakes?

Oral Fluency Record Sheet

Name _____ Date _____

Oral Reading Accuracy: _____% Circle: Fall Winter Spring

Oral Reading Fluency Score: _____ words correct per minute

Prosody Rubric: (Circle Score) 1 2 3 4

Comprehension Question Responses

#1 _____

#2 _____

Snakes of Many Colors

	You might think snakes do not need protection,
8	but they do. Certain kinds of mammals, such as pigs and
19	mongooses, prey on snakes. Large birds, such as the
28	serpent eagle, think they make fine meals. Even other
37	snakes, such as the King Cobra, will hunt certain snakes.
47	Snakes often use colors to protect themselves from
55	predators. The bright colors of some snakes, like the
64	Mangrove snake, warn enemies that the snake is poisonous.
73	Other snakes only pretend to be poisonous. The bright red,
83	black, and white scales of the Pueblan milk snake, which
93	are arranged in bands, make animals think the snake is
103	poisonous even though it is not.
109	Snakes also use their colors to hide themselves
117	from predators. For example, the bright green cat snake
126	lives high in a tree in the rainforest. The snake stays coiled
138	around a branch during the day. It looks just like a vine,
150	fooling animals that might want to make it their dinner.
160	These snakes need their colorful scales to stay safe.
169	After all, it is a dangerous world, even for a snake. **180**

Number of words read: _____ Number of errors made: _____

Name _____ Date _____

The Kitchen

Mama never wanted to be in the kitchen. She said
she had spent so much time helping her mama in the
kitchen that she never wanted to see a pot or pan or a cutting
board again. Still she managed to prepare good meals for
our family.

I didn't share my mother's feelings about cooking. I
especially loved baking. I loved the look of Grandma's old
mixing bowls and the smell and feel of finely sifted flour,
creamy butter, and cold eggs fresh from the refrigerator.

On the day before Mama's birthday, she decided
to treat herself to a new haircut. After she left, I went into
the kitchen and found Grandma's recipe book. In a jiffy, I
had flour, eggs, sugar, butter, and spices in a bowl. I mixed
them together, put the batter into a pan, and put the pan into
the oven. When Mama got home, I made her close her eyes.

"Happy birthday," I said, holding the biggest, best
birthday cake ever.

"My little baker," Mama said proudly.

---

1. What is the main idea of this story?

2. How did Mama feel when she saw her birthday cake?

Oral Fluency Record Sheet

Name _____ Date _____

Oral Reading Accuracy: _____% Circle: Fall Winter Spring

Oral Reading Fluency Score: _____ words correct per minute

Prosody Rubric: (Circle Score) 1 2 3 4

Comprehension Question Responses

#1 _____

#2 _____

The Kitchen

	Mama never wanted to be in the kitchen. She said
10	she had spent so much time helping her mama in the
21	kitchen that she never wanted to see a pot or pan or a cutting
35	board again. Still she managed to prepare good meals for
45	our family.
47	I didn't share my mother's feelings about cooking. I
56	especially loved baking. I loved the look of Grandma's old
66	mixing bowls and the smell and feel of finely sifted flour,
77	creamy butter, and cold eggs fresh from the refrigerator.
86	On the day before Mama's birthday, she decided
94	to treat herself to a new haircut. After she left, I went into
107	the kitchen and found Grandma's recipe book. In a jiffy, I
118	had flour, eggs, sugar, butter, and spices in a bowl. I mixed
130	them together, put the batter into a pan, and put the pan into
143	the oven. When Mama got home, I made her close her eyes.
155	"Happy birthday," I said, holding the biggest, best
163	birthday cake ever.
166	"My little baker," Mama said proudly. **172**

Number of words read: _____ Number of errors made: _____

A Good Friend

Misha stumbled into her room and sank down miserably onto her bed. She wished she could take back her angry and thoughtless words. She had told her best friend that she did not like her. She hadn't really meant it, but the angry words had just poured out.

Misha knew that she was jealous of Anna's talent for drawing. Anna could draw so beautifully, and Misha so wanted to be an artist. Misha felt her tears dripping onto her pillow, and then she felt something chilly and damp touch her arm. She looked down and saw her playful cat, Oliver.

Oliver meowed and rubbed against Misha's shoulder. The tearful girl began to stroke the affectionate cat. She petted him tenderly until her tears stopped. Oliver purred and rolled playfully onto his back. He patted Misha's hand, and Misha chuckled loudly.

Oliver knew how to make her forget her troubles. He was a good friend. Misha wanted to be a good friend, too. She decided to draw Anna a portrait of Oliver.

1. Why was Misha upset?

2. What did Oliver's actions persuade Misha to do?

Oral Fluency Record Sheet

Name _____   Date _____

Oral Reading Accuracy: _____%   Circle: Fall   Winter   Spring

Oral Reading Fluency Score: _____ words correct per minute

Prosody Rubric: (Circle Score) 1 2 3 4

Comprehension Question Responses

#1 _____

#2 _____

A Good Friend

	Misha stumbled into her room and sank down
8	miserably onto her bed. She wished she could take back her
19	angry and thoughtless words. She had told her best friend
29	that she did not like her. She hadn't really meant it, but the
42	angry words had just poured out.
48	Misha knew that she was jealous of Anna's talent
57	for drawing. Anna could draw so beautifully, and Misha
66	so wanted to be an artist. Misha felt her tears dripping
77	onto her pillow, and then she felt something chilly and
87	damp touch her arm. She looked down and saw her playful
98	cat, Oliver.
100	Oliver meowed and rubbed against Misha's shoulder.
107	The tearful girl began to stroke the affectionate cat. She petted
118	him tenderly until her tears stopped. Oliver purred and rolled
128	playfully onto his back. He patted Misha's hand, and Misha
138	chuckled loudly.
140	Oliver knew how to make her forget her troubles. He
150	was a good friend. Misha wanted to be a good friend, too. She
163	decided to draw Anna a portrait of Oliver. 171

Number of words read: _____   Number of errors made: _____

Thunderhead Clouds

Forces that form a thunderhead cloud can build over
a long period of time. We do not recognize that these forces
are operating until a large dark cloud forms overhead. The
forces that create thunderhead clouds are hot and cold air.

Warm air rises into the clouds. The air keeps moving
up, spilling over the top of clouds. Water vapor, or
little drops of water, are in this warm air.

As the warm air rises, it causes the water vapor to
cool and form bigger drops of water and even small ice
crystals. The clouds rise up as more air travels upward.

Inside the cloud is a roller coaster of air. The air
goes up rapidly, then it gets very cold and falls down
rapidly. Heavy rain, lightning, thunder, and hail may come
from the thunderhead cloud. The forces of hot and cold air
have combined to create one of nature's most amazing
shows, a thunderstorm.

1. What is the passage mostly about?

2. Why does the writer compare what is happening inside the cloud to
   a roller coaster?

Oral Fluency Record Sheet

Name _____ Date _____

Oral Reading Accuracy: _____%   Circle: Fall Winter Spring
Oral Reading Fluency Score: _____ words correct per minute
Prosody Rubric: (Circle Score) 1 2 3 4
Comprehension Question Responses
#1 _____
#2 _____

Thunderhead Clouds

	Forces that form a thunderhead cloud can build over
9	a long period of time. We do not recognize that these forces
21	are operating until a large dark cloud forms overhead. The
31	forces that create thunderhead clouds are hot and cold air.
41	Warm air rises into the clouds. The air keeps moving
51	up, spilling over the top of clouds. Water vapor, or
61	little drops of water, are in this warm air.
70	As the warm air rises, it causes the water vapor to
81	cool and form bigger drops of water and even small ice
92	crystals. The clouds rise up as more air travels upward.
102	Inside the cloud is a roller coaster of air. The air
113	goes up rapidly, then it gets very cold and falls down
124	rapidly. Heavy rain, lightning, thunder, and hail may come
133	from the thunderhead cloud. The forces of hot and cold air
144	have combined to create one of nature's most amazing
153	shows, a thunderstorm. 156

Number of words read: _____   Number of errors made: _____

The Polar Regions

There are two polar regions in the world: the South Pole and the North Pole.

Antarctica lies in the South Pole. It consists of tall mountains, icy glaciers, and miles and miles of frozen land. Most of the land is covered by a thick layer of ice. Because of the ice and the cold, very few forms of life can survive in Antarctica.

The North Pole, however, can support some life. In the summer, areas of the North Pole become warm enough for berries and vegetables to grow. In other parts of the North Pole, the ice melts, but the water cannot drain into the frozen soil. Instead, the water remains on the surface. Flowering plants, such as the Arctic poppy, can take root and grow there. These pretty flowers bring color to this white land.

The Arctic Ocean is also in the North Pole region. It has thousands of islands and much of it is covered by ice all year long. But even on the ice, many plants and animals can live.

1. Why are there very few forms of life in Antarctica?

2. What forms of life exist in the North Pole?

© Macmillan/McGraw-Hill

Oral Fluency Record Sheet

Name _____ Date _____

Oral Reading Accuracy: _____%   Circle: Fall Winter Spring
Oral Reading Fluency Score: _____ words correct per minute
Prosody Rubric: (Circle Score) 1 2 3 4
Comprehension Question Responses
#1 _____
#2 _____

The Polar Regions

	There are two polar regions in the world: the South
10	Pole and the North Pole.
15	Antarctica lies in the South Pole. It consists of tall
25	mountains, icy glaciers, and miles and miles of frozen land.
35	Most of the land is covered by a thick layer of ice. Because
48	of the ice and the cold, very few forms of life can survive in
62	Antarctica.
63	The North Pole, however, can support some life. In
72	the summer, areas of the North Pole become warm enough
82	for berries and vegetables to grow. In other parts of the
93	North Pole, the ice melts, but the water cannot drain into
104	the frozen soil. Instead, the water remains on the surface.
114	Flowering plants, such as the Arctic poppy, can take root
124	and grow there. These pretty flowers bring color to this
134	white land.
136	The Arctic Ocean is also in the North Pole region. It
147	has thousands of islands and much of it is covered by ice all
160	year long. But even on the ice, many plants and animals
171	can live. **173**

Number of words read: _____   Number of errors made: _____

Name _____ Date _____

The Pet Rock

Emma still has the pet rock she received for her birthday five years ago. It is still one of her favorite possessions. It is gray with fuzzy orange feet and a lavender tail. Its eyes are outlined in blue and white crayon, and its mouth is drawn in red crayon.

Rob brought the pet rock to Emma's birthday party when she turned six. It was wrapped in a huge yellow box with an enormous bright red bow. When Emma opened the box, she found another box inside wrapped in sparkly green paper. Inside that box was another box wrapped in pink tissue paper. Finally, inside that box was her pet rock.

It was the best gift Emma got that year and the only one she still has from her sixth birthday. It was special and different because Rob had made it himself.

Emma keeps it on a shelf in her room next to the trophy she won at last year's swim competition. When Emma looks at the rock, she remembers Rob, her party that year, and what friendship really means. It is still one of her best memories.

1. Why was Rob's gift so special and different ?
2. What was unusual about the way the pet rock was wrapped?

Oral Fluency Record Sheet

Name _____ Date _____

Oral Reading Accuracy: _____%   Circle: Fall Winter Spring

Oral Reading Fluency Score: _____ words correct per minute

Prosody Rubric: (Circle Score) 1 2 3 4

Comprehension Question Responses

#1 _____

#2 _____

The Pet Rock

	Emma still has the pet rock she received for her
10	birthday five years ago. It is still one of her favorite
21	possessions. It is gray with fuzzy orange feet and a
31	lavender tail. Its eyes are outlined in blue and white crayon,
42	and its mouth is drawn in red crayon.
50	Rob brought the pet rock to Emma's birthday party
59	when she turned six. It was wrapped in a huge yellow box
71	with an enormous bright red bow. When Emma opened the
81	box, she found another box inside wrapped in sparkly green
91	paper. Inside that box was another box wrapped in pink
101	tissue paper. Finally, inside that box was her pet rock.
111	It was the best gift Emma got that year and the only
123	one she still has from her sixth birthday. It was special and
135	different because Rob had made it himself.
142	Emma keeps it on a shelf in her room next to the
154	trophy she won at last year's swim competition. When
163	Emma looks at the rock, she remembers Rob, her party that
174	year, and what friendship really means. It is still one of
185	her best memories. **188**

Number of words read: _____ Number of errors made: _____

A Messy Job

The weekend had arrived, and more than anything, Dad wanted to relax in his favorite chair on the front porch. But he still had to wax and polish the car and paint the garage door. Unless he found someone to assist him, Dad realized it would be hours before he could relax.

Dad had an idea. He would walk to the hardware store and pick up some paint supplies, and while he was gone, Kyle, my brother, could wax the car.

Just as Dad left for the store, he told Kyle to use some "elbow grease." Kyle was probably not paying close attention to Dad. He was probably thinking about something else he considered more important.

After Dad left, Kyle went down to the basement and found a container labeled "Grease." When Dad returned, there was Kyle with grease covering his elbows. Dad's mouth dropped open in surprise. He laughed at the sight of Kyle running his greasy elbows over the car.

Now when Dad gives Kyle something to do, he chooses his words more carefully.

1. What did Dad really mean when he told Kyle to use "elbow grease"?

2. What lesson did Dad learn in this story?

Oral Fluency Record Sheet

Name _____ Date _____

Oral Reading Accuracy: _____%   Circle: Fall   Winter   Spring

Oral Reading Fluency Score: _____ words correct per minute

Prosody Rubric: (Circle Score) 1 2 3 4

Comprehension Question Responses

#1 _____

#2 _____

A Messy Job

	The weekend had arrived, and more than anything,
8	Dad wanted to relax in his favorite chair on the front porch.
20	But he still had to wax and polish the car and paint the
33	garage door. Unless he found someone to assist him, Dad
43	realized it would be hours before he could relax.
52	Dad had an idea. He would walk to the hardware
62	store and pick up some paint supplies, and while he was
73	gone, Kyle, my brother, could wax the car.
81	Just as Dad left for the store, he told Kyle to use
93	some "elbow grease." Kyle was probably not paying close
102	attention to Dad. He was probably thinking about
110	something else he considered more important.
116	After Dad left, Kyle went down to the basement
125	and found a container labeled "Grease." When Dad returned,
134	there was Kyle with grease covering his elbows. Dad's
143	mouth dropped open in surprise. He laughed at the sight of
154	Kyle running his greasy elbows over the car.
162	Now when Dad gives Kyle something to do, he
171	chooses his words more carefully. 176

© Macmillan/McGraw-Hill

Number of words read: _____   Number of errors made: _____

Name _____ Date _____

Polar Bears

Polar bears live in the icy North, in regions bordering the Arctic Ocean. In spite of their large size, polar bears are excellent swimmers. They can swim long distances through icy cold waters to hunt for fish, seals, walruses, and other animals that live in the sea. They also love to play in the water.

Polar bears have pads of fur on the soles of their feet and five long, curved claws on each of their paws. The fur keeps their feet warm while they walk on the ice, and the claws help them grip the slippery ice.

A polar bear's fur is thick and heavy. This fur along with a layer of fat helps to protect the polar bear's body from the Arctic cold. The color of the fur is creamy white, which helps the polar bear look like the snow and ice that surrounds it. Thanks to the white fur, a polar bear can creep up on a seal without being noticed.

Polar bears and their babies are happy in their Arctic home.

1. What protects the body of a polar bear from the cold?

2. Why would you think a polar bear wouldn't swim very well?

© Macmillan/McGraw-Hill

Oral Fluency Record Sheet

Name _____ Date _____

Oral Reading Accuracy: _____% Circle: Fall Winter Spring

Oral Reading Fluency Score: _____ words correct per minute

Prosody Rubric: (Circle Score) 1 2 3 4

Comprehension Question Responses

#1 _____

#2 _____

Polar Bears

	Polar bears live in the icy North, in regions
9	bordering the Arctic Ocean. In spite of their large size,
19	polar bears are excellent swimmers. They can swim long
28	distances through icy cold waters to hunt for fish, seals,
38	walruses, and other animals that live in the sea. They also
49	love to play in the water.
55	Polar bears have pads of fur on the soles of their
66	feet and five long, curved claws on each of their paws. The
78	fur keeps their feet warm while they walk on the ice, and
90	the claws help them grip the slippery ice.
98	A polar bear's fur is thick and heavy. This fur along
109	with a layer of fat helps to protect the polar bear's body
121	from the Arctic cold. The color of the fur is creamy white,
133	which helps the polar bear look like the snow and ice that
145	surrounds it. Thanks to the white fur, a polar bear can
156	creep up on a seal without being noticed.
164	Polar bears and their babies are happy in their
173	Arctic home. **175**

Number of words read: _____ Number of errors made: _____

Name _____ Date _____

Sun Facts

The sun is important to everything on Earth. Light and heat from the sun give warmth and energy to all life on the planet.

But the sun is really just a star. It looks larger because it is much closer to us than other stars. Compared with other stars, the sun is just medium-size. But compared with Earth, it is very large indeed. If the sun were a hollow ball, it would take one million Earth-size balls to fill it up.

The temperature of any place on Earth depends on the position of the sun. Places near the equator are hot because the sun shines almost directly overhead at noon. On the other hand, places near the North Pole and the South Pole are cold. This is because the sun almost never rises above the horizon there.

Scientists know a good deal about the sun, but they still have much to learn. As they learn, they hope to find better ways to use the sun's power on Earth.

1. Why is the sun important to everything on Earth?
2. Which sun fact did you find most interesting? Why?

Oral Fluency Record Sheet

Name _____ Date _____

Oral Reading Accuracy: _____%   Circle: Fall Winter Spring

Oral Reading Fluency Score: _____ words correct per minute

Prosody Rubric: (Circle Score) 1 2 3 4

Comprehension Question Responses

#1 _____

#2 _____

Sun Facts

	The sun is important to everything on Earth. Light
9	and heat from the sun give warmth and energy to all life
21	on the planet.
24	But the sun is really just a star. It looks larger
35	because it is much closer to us than other stars. Compared
46	with other stars, the sun is just medium-size. But
56	compared with Earth, it is very large indeed. If the sun
67	were a hollow ball, it would take one million Earth-size
78	balls to fill it up.
83	The temperature of any place on Earth depends on
92	the position of the sun. Places near the equator are hot
103	because the sun shines almost directly overhead at noon.
112	On the other hand, places near the North Pole and the South
124	Pole are cold. This is because the sun almost never rises
135	above the horizon there.
139	Scientists know a good deal about the sun, but they
149	still have much to learn. As they learn, they hope to find
161	better ways to use the sun's power on Earth. 170

Number of words read: _____   Number of errors made: _____

The Wink

The day of the big winter concert had arrived. Rosa
played the violin in the school orchestra, and tonight she
would be giving a solo performance in front of an audience
for the first time.

Rosa was nervous all day, and she was even more
uncomfortable and scared when she left for the concert.
Rosa went backstage to wait for her turn. One after another,
members of the orchestra played their instruments. Kelly
played the trumpet, Jack played the drums, and Max played
the French horn. When it was time for her friend Sam to
play the piano, Rosa peeked out from behind the curtain
to watch. Sam looked confident, and his playing was
smooth and clear. Then Rosa saw her parents in the third
row. Her father caught her eye and winked.

Suddenly, Rosa felt very confident. She stepped onto
the stage, adjusted the music stand, and set her music in
place. Then she began to play. When the song was over, the
audience clapped loudly. Rosa grinned, winked at her parents,
and ran offstage. Rosa's stage fright was over.

1. What is the story mostly about?
2. Why is "The Wink" a good title for this story?

Oral Fluency Record Sheet

Name _____ Date _____

Oral Reading Accuracy: _____% Circle: Fall Winter Spring

Oral Reading Fluency Score: _____ words correct per minute

Prosody Rubric: (Circle Score) 1 2 3 4

Comprehension Question Responses

#1 _____

#2 _____

The Wink

	The day of the big winter concert had arrived. Rosa
10	played the violin in the school orchestra, and tonight she
20	would be giving a solo performance in front of an audience
31	for the first time.
35	Rosa was nervous all day, and she was even more
45	uncomfortable and scared when she left for the concert.
54	Rosa went backstage to wait for her turn. One after another,
65	members of the orchestra played their instruments. Kelly
73	played the trumpet, Jack played the drums, and Max played
83	the French horn. When it was time for her friend Sam to
95	play the piano, Rosa peeked out from behind the curtain
105	to watch. Sam looked confident, and his playing was
114	smooth and clear. Then Rosa saw her parents in the third
125	row. Her father caught her eye and winked.
133	Suddenly, Rosa felt very confident. She stepped onto
141	the stage, adjusted the music stand, and set her music in
152	place. Then she began to play. When the song was over, the
164	audience clapped loudly. Rosa grinned, winked at her parents,
173	and ran offstage. Rosa's stage fright was over. 181

Number of words read: _____ Number of errors made: _____

Name _____ Date _____

The Gift of Friendship

I never went anywhere without my favorite lucky marble. It was very old, and it sparkled with incredibly pretty swirls of silver, lavender, and green inside. Likewise, my friend Hillary never went anywhere without one of the lucky key chain animals she collects. Her favorites were the camel and the octopus. Good friends know this kind of thing about each other.

Hillary's birthday was approaching. I wanted to buy her a new key chain animal, but I had already spent my entire allowance. My friend Pam collects them, too, so I traded my lucky marble for one of Pam's key chain animals. It was a shiny little butterfly.

Hillary had been upset when I told her about my marble, but just seeing the look on her face today at her birthday party would make it worthwhile.

When Hillary saw what I gave her, she almost cried. Then she told me that she had traded one of her key chain animals for a marble just like the one I used to have.

Being good friends, Hillary and I had a good laugh about our gifts.

1. What is "The Gift of Friendship" mostly about?
2. How did the writer get Hillary's gift?

Oral Fluency Record Sheet

Name _____ Date _____

Oral Reading Accuracy: _____%   Circle: Fall Winter Spring
Oral Reading Fluency Score: _____ words correct per minute
Prosody Rubric: (Circle Score) 1 2 3 4
Comprehension Question Responses
#1 _____
#2 _____

The Gift of Friendship

	I never went anywhere without my favorite lucky
8	marble. It was very old, and it sparkled with incredibly
18	pretty swirls of silver, lavender, and green inside. Likewise,
27	my friend Hillary never went anywhere without one of the
37	lucky key chain animals she collects. Her favorites were the
47	camel and the octopus. Good friends know this kind of
57	thing about each other.
61	Hillary's birthday was approaching. I wanted to buy
69	her a new key chain animal, but I had already spent my
81	entire allowance. My friend Pam collects them, too, so I
91	traded my lucky marble for one of Pam's key chain
101	animals. It was a shiny little butterfly.
108	Hillary had been upset when I told her about my
118	marble, but just seeing the look on her face today at her
130	birthday party would make it worthwhile.
136	When Hillary saw what I gave her, she almost cried.
146	Then she told me that she had traded one of her key chain
159	animals for a marble just like the one I used to have.
171	Being good friends, Hillary and I had a good laugh
181	about our gifts. 184

Number of words read: _____   Number of errors made: _____

Name _____ Date _____

The Giant Panda

The giant panda is an animal with a chubby, black-and-white body and black legs. Its head is large and round, and its white face has black patches around each eye.

Panda cubs are extremely tiny when they are born, weighing only about five ounces. As adults, however, giant pandas can weigh as much as 350 pounds.

Giant pandas live only in places where there are bamboo forests with plenty of bamboo shoots for them to eat. Because of this, they are found only on high mountain slopes in western and southwestern China. Giant pandas can spend 16 hours a day eating. In one year, a panda can eat more than 10,000 pounds of bamboo. Although the giant panda eats chiefly bamboo shoots, it sometimes eats other plants, fish, and small animals, too.

As a special gift to the people of the United States, China gave two giant pandas to the National Zoo in Washington, D.C., in 1972. The pandas lived there for many years, eating bamboo shoots and making all of the zoo visitors laugh.

1. Where do giant pandas live?
2. Why were the giant pandas from China a good gift?

Oral Fluency Record Sheet

Name _____   Date _____

Oral Reading Accuracy: _____%   Circle: Fall Winter Spring
Oral Reading Fluency Score: _____ words correct per minute
Prosody Rubric: (Circle Score) 1 2 3 4
Comprehension Question Responses
#1 _____
#2 _____

The Giant Panda

	The giant panda is an animal with a chubby, black-
10	and-white body and black legs. Its head is large and round,
22	and its white face has black patches around each eye.
32	Panda cubs are extremely tiny when they are born,
41	weighing only about five ounces. As adults, however, giant
50	pandas can weigh as much as 350 pounds.
58	Giant pandas live only in places where there are
67	bamboo forests with plenty of bamboo shoots for them to eat.
78	Because of this, they are found only on high mountain
88	slopes in western and southwestern China. Giant pandas
96	can spend 16 hours a day eating. In one year, a panda can
109	eat more than 10,000 pounds of bamboo. Although the
118	giant panda eats chiefly bamboo shoots, it sometimes eats
127	other plants, fish, and small animals, too.
134	As a special gift to the people of the United States,
145	China gave two giant pandas to the National Zoo in
155	Washington, D.C., in 1972. The pandas lived there for many
165	years, eating bamboo shoots and making all of the zoo
175	visitors laugh. 177

Number of words read: _____   Number of errors made: _____

Name _____ Date _____

Fads

Suppose one day a girl comes to school wearing a fake braid made out of yarn. The next day three girls come to school with fake braids. Soon all the girls in school are wearing the braids.

That is how a fad starts. A few people start doing something different, and then all of a sudden everybody starts to copy them.

In the 1950s, one popular fad for teenage girls was wearing their father's big, white shirts. Another fad for girls at the same time was wearing felt skirts with cutouts of poodles on them. During the 1970s, people wore blue jeans with fancy stitching on them as a fad. In recent years boys have worn baggy pants and baseball caps turned around backward.

Not all fads are about clothes. Some fads involve sports. In the 1990s, students on college campuses kicked around a small, colorful, leather ball. They called this game hacky sack. Hacky sack players kept the ball off the ground by using their knees and feet. Students loved playing this game during their free time.

When people look back at certain fads they may wonder why they were so popular. But when "everyone is doing it," fads are just a way for people to have some fun.

1. How does a fad start?
2. Name three fads from the past.

© Macmillan/McGraw-Hill

Oral Fluency Record Sheet

Name _____ Date _____

Oral Reading Accuracy: _____%   Circle: Fall   Winter   Spring

Oral Reading Fluency Score: _____ words correct per minute

Prosody Rubric: (Circle Score) 1 2 3 4

Comprehension Question Responses

#1 _____

#2 _____

Fads

	Suppose one day a girl comes to school wearing a
10	fake braid made out of yarn. The next day three girls
21	come to school with fake braids. Soon all the girls in
32	school are wearing the braids.
37	That is how a fad starts. A few people start doing
48	something different, and then all of a sudden everybody
57	starts to copy them.
61	In the 1950s, one popular fad for teenage girls was
71	wearing their father's big, white shirts. Another fad for
80	girls at the same time was wearing felt skirts with cutouts
91	of poodles on them. During the 1970s, people wore blue
101	jeans with fancy stitching on them as a fad. In recent
112	years boys have worn baggy pants and baseball caps
121	turned around backward.
124	Not all fads are about clothes. Some fads involve
133	sports. In the 1990s, students on college campuses kicked
142	around a small, colorful, leather ball. They called this game
152	hacky sack. Hacky sack players kept the ball off the ground
163	by using their knees and feet. Students loved playing this game
174	during their free time.
178	When people look back at certain fads they may wonder
188	why they were so popular. But when "everyone is doing it,"
199	fads are just a way for people to have some fun. **210**

Number of words read: _____ Number of errors made: _____

One Birthday for All

Every family has traditions. Traditions are things people do year after year. Beth King's family has many traditions they celebrate, but Beth's favorite tradition is about birthdays.

Because Beth has so many aunts, uncles, and cousins, it is impossible to celebrate each birthday. So once a year, on the third Saturday in July, Beth's relatives have one big birthday celebration for everyone. The adults stay at Beth's grandparents' house. The children sleep in tents on the lawn.

Everyone brings food and every meal is a feast. The cousins play soccer. Grandpa and the uncles sit on the wide porch and drink homemade lemonade. The aunts have a softball game. Everyone roots for their favorite team.

Afterward, everyone eats hamburgers and fresh corn. At the end, Grandma brings out a big frosted cake.

Every year, after the family birthday celebration, Beth goes to bed and starts thinking about next year's birthday party.

1. What is Beth's favorite family tradition?

2. Why does the family have their birthday celebration in the summer?

© Macmillan/McGraw-Hill

Oral Fluency Record Sheet

Name _____ Date _____

Oral Reading Accuracy: _____%   Circle: Fall Winter Spring
Oral Reading Fluency Score: _____ words correct per minute
Prosody Rubric: (Circle Score) 1 2 3 4
Comprehension Question Responses
#1 _____
#2 _____

One Birthday for All

	Every family has traditions. Traditions are things
7	people do year after year. Beth King's family has many
17	traditions they celebrate, but Beth's favorite tradition is
25	about birthdays.
27	Because Beth has so many aunts, uncles, and
35	cousins, it is impossible to celebrate each birthday.
43	So once a year, on the third Saturday in July, Beth's
54	relatives have one big birthday celebration for everyone.
62	The adults stay at Beth's grandparents' house. The
70	children sleep in tents on the lawn.
77	Everyone brings food and every meal is a feast.
86	The cousins play soccer. Grandpa and the uncles sit
95	on the wide porch and drink homemade lemonade.
103	The aunts have a softball game. Everyone roots for their
113	favorite team.
115	Afterward, everyone eats hamburgers and fresh
121	corn. At the end, Grandma brings out a big frosted cake.
132	Every year, after the family birthday celebration,
139	Beth goes to bed and starts thinking about next year's
149	birthday party. 151

Number of words read: _____   Number of errors made: _____

Fruit Fun

Ellen's favorite pastime was making things, so she was delighted when her aunt sent her a box of modeling clay. The clay was soft and gooey, and Ellen could press and mold it into all kinds of shapes.

Ellen started by creating different kinds of fruits—apples, bananas, oranges, pears, plums, grapefruit, peaches, and lemons. She arranged her best pieces of fruit in a fancy china bowl, and when her mother saw the bowl, she was amazed at how real the fruit looked. That gave Ellen and her mother an idea, and together they set the pretty bowl in the center of the dining room table.

That evening when Dad came home, he immediately noticed the fruit bowl.

"Those peaches look so ripe and delicious!" Dad exclaimed.

Ellen started laughing and she couldn't stop.

"What are you laughing at?" Dad demanded.

Dad reached out and chose the prettiest peach. Right away he realized why Ellen was laughing.

"You completely fooled me," he said. "This peach certainly looks good enough to eat."

1. What did Ellen make with the modeling clay?

2. Why did Ellen laugh when her father said the peaches look delicious?

Oral Fluency Record Sheet

Name _____ Date _____

Oral Reading Accuracy: _____% Circle: Fall Winter Spring

Oral Reading Fluency Score: _____ words correct per minute

Prosody Rubric: (Circle Score) 1 2 3 4

Comprehension Question Responses

#1 _____

#2 _____

Fruit Fun

	Ellen's favorite pastime was making things, so
7	she was delighted when her aunt sent her a box of
18	modeling clay. The clay was soft and gooey, and Ellen
28	could press and mold it into all kinds of shapes.
38	Ellen started by creating different kinds of
45	fruits—apples, bananas, oranges, pears, plums,
51	grapefruit, peaches, and lemons. She arranged her
58	best pieces of fruit in a fancy china bowl, and when
69	her mother saw the bowl, she was amazed at how real
80	the fruit looked. That gave Ellen and her mother an
90	idea, and together they set the pretty bowl in the
100	center of the dining room table.
106	That evening when Dad came home, he
113	immediately noticed the fruit bowl.
118	"Those peaches look so ripe and delicious!"
125	Dad exclaimed.
127	Ellen started laughing and she couldn't stop.
134	"What are you laughing at?" Dad demanded.
141	Dad reached out and chose the prettiest peach.
149	Right away he realized why Ellen was laughing.
157	"You completely fooled me," he said. "This
164	peach certainly looks good enough to eat." 171

Number of words read: _____ **Number of errors made:** _____

Babe

Babe Ruth might be the most famous baseball player who ever lived. His batting ability along with his colorful personality brought huge crowds to his games. But his road to fame was challenging and difficult.

Babe was born on February 6, 1895, as George Herman Ruth, Jr., to a poor family in Baltimore. When Babe was seven, his parents sent him to live at a school for boys. Although he visited home several times over the next few years, the school was his real home until he turned nineteen years old.

The school was strict, and baseball was the only game the boys were allowed to play. Luckily for Babe, there was a teacher at the school who took a special liking to Babe.

That teacher was also a wonderful baseball player. He could hit a ball hard and far. The teacher worked with Babe hour after hour, teaching him to hit and pitch and catch.

When Babe left the school, he was ready to make his way in the world. And Babe's way was baseball. He became a national hero.

1. Where was Babe's real home when he was growing up?
2. Who helped Babe the most in choosing his career?

Oral Fluency Record Sheet

Name _____ Date _____

Oral Reading Accuracy: _____% Circle: Fall Winter Spring

Oral Reading Fluency Score: _____ words correct per minute

Prosody Rubric: (Circle Score) 1 2 3 4

Comprehension Question Responses

#1 _____

#2 _____

Babe

	Babe Ruth might be the most famous baseball
8	player who ever lived. His batting ability along with his
18	colorful personality brought huge crowds to his games.
26	But his road to fame was challenging and difficult.
35	Babe was born on February 6, 1895, as George Herman
45	Ruth, Jr., to a poor family in Baltimore. When Babe was
56	seven, his parents sent him to live at a school for boys.
68	Although he visited home several times over the next few
78	years, the school was his real home until he turned
88	nineteen years old.
91	The school was strict, and baseball was the only
100	game the boys were allowed to play. Luckily for Babe,
110	there was a teacher at the school who took a special liking
122	to Babe.
124	That teacher was also a wonderful baseball player.
132	He could hit a ball hard and far. The teacher worked with
144	Babe hour after hour, teaching him to hit and pitch and catch.
156	When Babe left the school, he was ready to make his
167	way in the world. And Babe's way was baseball. He became a
179	national hero. 181

Number of words read: _____ Number of errors made: _____

Power from the Wind

Every day we experience what the wind does. A gentle wind may mess up our hair while a strong wind may knock down trees.

Long ago, people experienced what the wind did, too, and they learned how to put the wind to work. Persians developed windmills about 1,500 years ago. They used wind power to pump water for their crops and to grind grain for bread. Before using wind power, people pumped water and ground grain by hand or by animal power.

In time, the use of wind power spread to other parts of the world. Windmills became very popular in Holland, where people used them to drain water from the land and to grind grain. These windmills had four long arms.

People all over the world still use windmills to pump water and to grind grain, but now windmills are also used to produce electricity. As other types of power become more expensive, wind power becomes more attractive and valuable.

People are finding new ways to use this source of power that will continue as long as we have the wind.

1. What are three uses for windmills?
2. Why will we always be able to use wind power?

Oral Fluency Record Sheet

Name _____ Date _____

Oral Reading Accuracy: _____%   Circle: Fall Winter Spring

Oral Reading Fluency Score: _____ words correct per minute

Prosody Rubric: (Circle Score) 1 2 3 4

Comprehension Question Responses

#1 _____

#2 _____

Power from the Wind

	Every day we experience what the wind does. A
9	gentle wind may mess up our hair while a strong wind may
21	knock down trees.
24	Long ago, people experienced what the wind did,
32	too, and they learned how to put the wind to work.
43	Persians developed windmills about 1,500 years ago. They
51	used wind power to pump water for their crops and to grind
63	grain for bread. Before using wind power, people pumped
72	water and ground grain by hand or by animal power.
82	In time, the use of wind power spread to other parts
93	of the world. Windmills became very popular in Holland,
102	where people used them to drain water from the land and to
114	grind grain. These windmills had four long arms.
122	People all over the world still use windmills to
131	pump water and to grind grain, but now windmills are also
142	used to produce electricity. As other types of power
151	become more expensive, wind power becomes more
158	attractive and valuable.
161	People are finding new ways to use this source of
171	power that will continue as long as we have the wind. 182

Number of words read: _____ Number of errors made: _____

The Turtle Experiment

Joyce hopes to work as a scientist studying animals all over the world. For now she practices by observing her pet turtle, Marvin. Joyce keeps a record of Marvin's activities, including charts to show which foods he prefers.

Joyce's mom suggests that Joyce do some more research by talking to the owner of the local pet store. Joyce thinks this is an excellent idea. When she speaks to the pet store owner, he mentions that some turtles are unhappy in glass cages. This information gives Joyce an idea for an experiment.

Joyce decides to build a new home for Marvin. Her mother helps her put up a fence around a clear space in the backyard, and then they bring out stones and water. They take Marvin from his glass cage and place him inside his new home. Joyce studies Marvin to see if he prefers his new home.

After a week of close observation, Joyce reviews her records and sees that Marvin has been eating and playing more than ever before! Mom and Joyce decide that Marvin prefers the backyard to the glass cage.

"Great experiment," says Mom.

1. What was Joyce's turtle experiment?
2. What did Joyce do each day during the experiment?

Oral Fluency Record Sheet

Name _____ Date _____

Oral Reading Accuracy: _____%

Circle: Fall Winter Spring

Oral Reading Fluency Score: _____ words correct per minute

Prosody Rubric: (Circle Score) 1 2 3 4

Comprehension Question Responses

#1 _____

#2 _____

The Turtle Experiment

	Joyce hopes to work as a scientist studying animals
9	all over the world. For now she practices by observing her
20	pet turtle, Marvin. Joyce keeps a record of Marvin's
29	activities, including charts to show which foods he prefers.
38	Joyce's mom suggests that Joyce do some more
46	research by talking to the owner of the local pet store.
57	Joyce thinks this is an excellent idea. When she speaks to
68	the pet store owner, he mentions that some turtles are
78	unhappy in glass cages. This information gives Joyce an
87	idea for an experiment.
91	Joyce decides to build a new home for Marvin. Her
101	mother helps her put up a fence around a clear space in the
114	backyard, and then they bring out stones and water. They
124	take Marvin from his glass cage and place him inside his
135	new home. Joyce studies Marvin to see if he prefers his
146	new home.
148	After a week of close observation, Joyce reviews
156	her records and sees that Marvin has been eating and
166	playing more than ever before! Mom and Joyce decide that
176	Marvin prefers the backyard to the glass cage.
184	"Great experiment," says Mom. 188

© Macmillan/McGraw-Hill

Number of words read: _____ Number of errors made: _____

Ruiz's Toy Chest

Ruiz is almost nine, and he has decided that he has outgrown his old toys. He goes to his toy chest and empties out all his old playthings. His wooden helicopter, some coloring books, his stuffed giraffe, his parrot puppet, and all his other old toys are spread around him on the floor.

"I'll bet the little kid next door would really enjoy playing with some of this stuff," Ruiz thinks to himself as he looks at all of his old toys.

Ruiz picks up his stuffed giraffe with its black nose, orange stripes, long neck, and funny feet. He remembers how he used to pretend he was on the grassy plains of Africa riding on his giraffe.

"Maybe I'll keep my giraffe after all," thinks Ruiz, and he puts the giraffe back into the toy chest.

Ruiz peers into the toy chest. "My giraffe looks really lonely in there," he thinks. "I'd better put the other toys back in so that he'll have some more company."

Ruiz collects all the other toys and puts them back into the toy chest. "I think I'll keep all these old friends a little bit longer," he says to himself.

1. Why does Ruiz plan to give away his old toys?
2. Why does Ruiz decide to keep his old giraffe?

Oral Fluency Record Sheet

Name _____ Date _____

Oral Reading Accuracy: _____%   Circle: Fall Winter Spring

Oral Reading Fluency Score: _____ words correct per minute

Prosody Rubric: (Circle Score) 1 2 3 4

Comprehension Question Responses

#1 _____

#2 _____

Ruiz's Toy Chest

	Ruiz is almost nine, and he has decided that he
10	has outgrown his old toys. He goes to his toy chest
21	and empties out all his old playthings. His wooden
30	helicopter, some coloring books, his stuffed giraffe,
37	his parrot puppet, and all his other old toys are spread
48	around him on the floor.
53	"I'll bet the little kid next door would really
62	enjoy playing with some of this stuff," Ruiz thinks to
72	himself as he looks at all of his old toys.
82	Ruiz picks up his stuffed giraffe with its black
91	nose, orange stripes, long neck, and funny feet. He
100	remembers how he used to pretend he was on the
110	grassy plains of Africa riding on his giraffe.
118	"Maybe I'll keep my giraffe after all," thinks
126	Ruiz, and he puts the giraffe back into the toy chest.
137	Ruiz peers into the toy chest. "My giraffe
145	looks really lonely in there," he thinks. "I'd better put
155	the other toys back in so that he'll have some
165	more company."
167	Ruiz collects all the other toys and puts them
176	back into the toy chest. "I think I'll keep all these old
188	friends a little bit longer," he says to himself. **197**

Number of words read: _____ Number of errors made: _____

The Largest Plants

Trees are the largest of all plants. They provide
homes for birds and other animals, and they protect us from
the sun and the wind. But trees are important in other
ways, too.

Wood from trees helps us build our homes and furniture.
Wood gives us pulp for paper which goes into making plastic.
Some trees produce the milky material that is used to create
rubber. Other trees provide substances used in medicines.

Trees give us many foods, too, such as grapefruits,
olives, chocolate, coconuts, and walnuts. In many states,
vast orchards make large quantities of cherries, peaches,
figs, plums, and apples.

Trees have three parts. The roots hold the tree in the
ground. They soak up water and vitamins needed to help
the tree grow. The trunk and branches carry sap and hold
the leaves in the sunlight. The leaves make the tree's food.
Leaves use the light from the sun to take a gas called
carbon dioxide from the air. The leaves mix this gas with
oxygen and water to make the food the tree needs
to grow.

1. Name three foods we get from trees.
2. Name one thing in this room that comes from trees.

Oral Fluency Record Sheet

Name _____   Date _____

Oral Reading Accuracy: _____%   Circle: Fall   Winter   Spring
Oral Reading Fluency Score: _____ words correct per minute
Prosody Rubric: (Circle Score) 1 2 3 4
Comprehension Question Responses
#1 _____
#2 _____

The Largest Plants

	Trees are the largest of all plants. They provide
9	homes for birds and other animals, and they protect us from
20	the sun and the wind. But trees are important in other
31	ways, too.
33	Wood from trees helps us build our homes and furniture.
43	Wood gives us pulp for paper which goes into making plastic.
54	Some trees produce the milky material that is used to create
65	rubber. Other trees provide substances used in medicines.
73	Trees give us many foods, too, such as grapefruits,
82	olives, chocolate, coconuts, and walnuts. In many states,
90	vast orchards make large quantities of cherries, peaches,
98	figs, plums, and apples.
102	Trees have three parts. The roots hold the tree in the
113	ground. They soak up water and vitamins needed to help
123	the tree grow. The trunk and branches carry sap and hold
134	the leaves in the sunlight. The leaves make the tree's food.
145	Leaves use the light from the sun to take a gas called
157	carbon dioxide from the air. The leaves mix this gas with
168	oxygen and water to make the food the tree needs
178	to grow. 180

Number of words read: _____   Number of errors made: _____

Chimps That Talk

Have you ever been to the zoo and watched the chimpanzees? Chimpanzees are among the most playful, curious, and interesting animals at the zoo. They often entertain visitors by dancing around, waving their arms, and making hooting noises. Often they come right up to visitors as if they want to have a chat.

For many years, scientists have watched chimpanzees use grunts, hoots, and howls to tell each other about things like food and danger. Scientists wondered if chimpanzees could talk with humans and decided to try to teach them sign language. In sign language, hand and finger movements are used to mean different things.

At first, the chimpanzees would copy the signs the scientists made. For example, the scientist would make the signs for "I want to eat" as the chimpanzees ate a meal and the chimps would copy them. Later, the chimpanzees would make the sign "I want to eat" all by themselves. After a while, chimpanzees learned to make their own signs to show what they wanted.

Would you like to have a conversation with a chimpanzee? Maybe someday you will.

1. What is "Chimps That Talk" mostly about?
2. How do chimpanzees communicate?

Oral Fluency Record Sheet

Name _____ Date _____

Oral Reading Accuracy: _____%   Circle: Fall Winter Spring
Oral Reading Fluency Score: _____ words correct per minute
Prosody Rubric: (Circle Score) 1 2 3 4
Comprehension Question Responses
#1 _____
#2 _____

Chimps That Talk

	Have you ever been to the zoo and watched the
10	chimpanzees? Chimpanzees are among the most playful,
17	curious, and interesting animals at the zoo. They often
26	entertain visitors by dancing around, waving their arms,
34	and making hooting noises. Often they come right up to
44	visitors as if they want to have a chat.
53	For many years, scientists have watched chimpanzees
60	use grunts, hoots, and howls to tell each other about things like
72	food and danger. Scientists wondered if chimpanzees could
80	talk with humans and decided to try to teach them sign
91	language. In sign language, hand and finger movements are
100	used to mean different things.
105	At first, the chimpanzees would copy the signs the
114	scientists made. For example, the scientist would make the
123	signs for "I want to eat" as the chimpanzees ate a meal and the
137	chimps would copy them. Later, the chimpanzees would make
146	the sign "I want to eat" all by themselves. After a while,
158	chimpanzees learned to make their own signs to show what
168	they wanted.
170	Would you like to have a conversation with a chimpanzee?
180	Maybe someday you will. 184

Number of words read: _____   Number of errors made: _____

Wolf Watchers

Benjamin was thrilled to be on vacation in Montana. His parents wanted to observe timber wolves in their natural environment.

The first day, his family woke up early and hiked several miles with a guide to a wooded area. During the night, they had heard a wolf's howl, so they were certain there were wolves nearby. They knew that wolves were becoming rare, that they avoided people, and that the best time to spot a wolf was at sunrise. For a long time, they saw deer and elk, but no wolves.

Suddenly they heard leaves crunching softly. Nobody made a sound. Sure enough, it was a wolf! Benjamin's family watched the large, gray wolf for ten minutes before it vanished into the woods. They made plaster casts out of the wolf's tracks. But Benjamin wanted to do something to help the wolves survive.

"You can write a letter to show your support of timber wolves," the guide said.

Benjamin wrote a letter after he finished breakfast. He would remember the trip, and the wolf, for a long time.

1. What did Benjamin's family do in Montana?

2. What would the wolf have done if it had known there were people nearby?

© Macmillan/McGraw-Hill

Oral Fluency Record Sheet

Name _____   Date _____

Oral Reading Accuracy: _____%   Circle: Fall   Winter   Spring
Oral Reading Fluency Score: _____ words correct per minute
Prosody Rubric: (Circle Score) 1 2 3 4
Comprehension Question Responses
#1 _____
#2 _____

Wolf Watchers

	Benjamin was thrilled to be on vacation in Montana.
9	His parents wanted to observe timber wolves in their
18	natural environment.
20	The first day, his family woke up early and hiked
30	several miles with a guide to a wooded area. During the
41	night, they had heard a wolf's howl, so they were certain
52	there were wolves nearby. They knew that wolves were
61	becoming rare, that they avoided people, and that the best
71	time to spot a wolf was at sunrise. For a long time, they
84	saw deer and elk, but no wolves.
91	Suddenly they heard leaves crunching softly.
97	Nobody made a sound. Sure enough, it was a wolf!
107	Benjamin's family watched the large, gray wolf for ten
116	minutes before it vanished into the woods. They made
125	plaster casts out of the wolf's tracks. But Benjamin
134	wanted to do something to help the wolves survive.
143	"You can write a letter to show your support of
153	timber wolves," the guide said.
158	Benjamin wrote a letter after he finished breakfast.
166	He would remember the trip, and the wolf, for a
176	long time. 178

Number of words read: _____   Number of errors made: _____

Fire in the Locker Room

Jason was in the showers near the locker room when he thought he smelled something burning. He dashed into the locker room and saw flames shooting out of several lockers.

Jason was unsure what to do. Other kids had gotten into trouble for pulling the fire alarm, and Jason didn't want any trouble. He ran outside and began shouting "Fire, fire!" He was able to get the attention of a teacher, but at first the teacher didn't believe him. There had been a couple of false alarms lately. But the teacher went into the locker room and saw the fire spreading.

Jason, the teacher, and the track coach grabbed the school fire hoses and managed to put out most of the flames. But flames continued to pop up here and there, and the fire department had to come to make sure the fire was completely out.

No one knew how the fire had started, but the principal thanked Jason for his quick action. Jason had stopped more damage from happening to his school.

1. What is this story mostly about?
2. How did Jason's actions help the school?

Oral Fluency Record Sheet

Name _____ Date _____

Oral Reading Accuracy: _____% Circle: Fall Winter Spring
Oral Reading Fluency Score: _____ words correct per minute
Prosody Rubric: (Circle Score) 1 2 3 4
Comprehension Question Responses
#1 _____
#2 _____

Fire in the Locker Room

	Jason was in the showers near the locker room
9	when he thought he smelled something burning. He
17	dashed into the locker room and saw flames shooting
26	out of several lockers.
30	Jason was unsure what to do. Other kids had
39	gotten into trouble for pulling the fire alarm, and
48	Jason didn't want any trouble. He ran outside and
57	began shouting "Fire, fire!" He was able to get the
67	attention of a teacher, but at first the teacher didn't
77	believe him. There had been a couple of false alarms
87	lately. But the teacher went into the locker room
96	and saw the fire spreading.
101	Jason, the teacher, and the track coach grabbed
109	the school fire hoses and managed to put out most of the
121	flames. But flames continued to pop up here and there,
131	and the fire department had to come to make sure the fire
143	was completely out.
146	No one knew how the fire had started, but the
156	principal thanked Jason for his quick action. Jason
164	had stopped more damage from happening to his school. 173

Number of words read: _____ Number of errors made: _____

Bill Peet, Writer and Artist

Bill Peet is a popular children's writer and artist. Many of his books have animal characters because he loved to draw animals. The animals act like people and were often like people Bill Peet knew.

Before he began writing children's books, Bill Peet wrote and drew illustrations for the movies. He worked on famous films like *Peter Pan* and *Sleeping Beauty.*

Many of Bill Peet's books are very funny, but at the same time they talk about serious problems. In his book *Farewell to Shady Glade,* a group of animals has to leave its home because people want to put up buildings where they live. The animals lose their home, and the reader doesn't know if they will find a new one.

Other books give lessons about life. The book *Kermit the Hermit* is about a selfish crab. After a boy rescues him, Kermit learns that it is important to share.

Through Bill Peet's books, both children and adults get to see the world through new eyes. They get to laugh, but at the same time they get to learn important lessons about life.

1. Who is Bill Peet?
2. Why is Bill Peet an important writer?

Oral Fluency Record Sheet

Name _____ Date _____

Oral Reading Accuracy: _____%   Circle: Fall Winter Spring

Oral Reading Fluency Score: _____ words correct per minute

Prosody Rubric: (Circle Score) 1 2 3 4

Comprehension Question Responses

#1 _____

#2 _____

Bill Peet, Writer and Artist

8	Bill Peet is a popular children's writer and artist. Many of his books have animal characters
16	
26	because he loved to draw animals. The animals act like people and were often like people Bill Peet knew.
35	Before he began writing children's books, Bill Peet
43	wrote and drew illustrations for the movies. He worked
52	on famous films like *Peter Pan* and *Sleeping Beauty*.
61	Many of Bill Peet's books are very funny, but at
71	the same time they talk about serious problems. In his
81	book *Farewell to Shady Glade,* a group of animals has to
92	leave its home because people want to put up buildings
102	where they live. The animals lose their home, and the
112	reader doesn't know if they will find a new one.
122	Other books give lessons about life. The book
130	*Kermit the Hermit* is about a selfish crab. After a boy
141	rescues him, Kermit learns that it is important
149	to share.
151	Through Bill Peet's books, both children and
158	adults get to see the world through new eyes. They get to
170	laugh, but at the same time they get to learn important
181	lessons about life. **184**

Number of words read: _____   Number of errors made: _____

Plants in Danger

Did you know that some plants are endangered? One in eight plants on Earth is dying out, and we may never see them again.

Scientists call a plant endangered if they expect it to die off completely in the next 20 years. They hope that special efforts will be made to protect the plant so that it can continue to survive.

There are several reasons why some plants are endangered. People damage the homes of many kinds of plants when they build new homes or farms. When they cut down trees to clear the land, they destroy the places that have been the plants' homes. In some places, too many sheep or other animals graze on the land and eat all the plants that grew there. Sometimes areas along the coast are filled in for homes and businesses. The plants that grew there are destroyed.

A group called Green Kids has gotten together to teach about endangered plants and to show that kids can make a difference. Each spring, Green Kids visit schools across Canada to perform funny skits about the environment. The skits teach kids how to help save our natural world.

1. What does it mean when a plant is endangered?
2. What are two reasons why plants are endangered?

Oral Fluency Record Sheet

Name _____ Date _____

Oral Reading Accuracy: _____%   Circle: Fall   Winter   Spring
Oral Reading Fluency Score: _____ words correct per minute
Prosody Rubric: (Circle Score) 1 2 3 4
Comprehension Question Responses
#1 _____
#2 _____

Plants in Danger

	Did you know that some plants are endangered?
8	One in eight plants on Earth is dying out, and we may
20	never see them again.
24	Scientists call a plant endangered if they expect it
33	to die off completely in the next 20 years. They hope that
45	special efforts will be made to protect the plant so that it
57	can continue to survive.
61	There are several reasons why some plants are
69	endangered. People damage the homes of many kinds
77	of plants when they build new homes or farms. When
87	they cut down trees to clear the land, they destroy the
98	places that have been the plants' homes. In some
107	places, too many sheep or other animals graze on the
117	land and eat all the plants that grew there. Sometimes
127	areas along the coast are filled in for homes and
137	businesses. The plants that grew there are destroyed.
145	A group called Green Kids has gotten together
153	to teach about endangered plants and to show that
162	kids can make a difference. Each spring, Green Kids
171	visit schools across Canada to perform funny skits
179	about the environment. The skits teach kids how to
188	help save our natural world. **193**

Number of words read: _____   **Number of errors made:** _____

Name _____ Date _____

Tree Trouble

Scott overheard his mother and a neighbor outside
his apartment door. They were discussing the grove of oak
trees next to the apartment building. The city government
was planning to remove the trees to create space for new
apartments.

Scott was shocked. Surely they were not talking
about his favorite place! Scott loved the grove. It was shady
and cool in the summer, and it was the perfect spot for
building forts in the winter. And Scott could always go
there when he wanted to be alone.

Scott's neighbors were upset about losing the
grove, too, but no one knew what action to take. Scott
decided to hold a meeting for everyone in his apartment.
Almost everyone was interested and almost everyone came.
They discussed many ideas and finally decided to write
letters to the local newspaper.

After the newspaper printed the letters, more people
in the community became aware of the city's plans. Some
protested and wrote letters of their own.

Soon the city chose a new place for the apartments.
The grove was saved!

1. Why did Scott love the grove so much?

2. How did letter-writing save the grove of oak trees?

Oral Fluency Record Sheet

Name _____   Date _____

Oral Reading Accuracy: _____%   Circle: Fall Winter Spring
Oral Reading Fluency Score: _____ words correct per minute
Prosody Rubric: (Circle Score) 1 2 3 4
Comprehension Question Responses
#1 _____
#2 _____

Tree Trouble

	Scott overheard his mother and a neighbor outside
8	his apartment door. They were discussing the grove of oak
18	trees next to the apartment building. The city government
27	was planning to remove the trees to create space for new
38	apartments.
39	Scott was shocked. Surely they were not talking
47	about his favorite place! Scott loved the grove. It was shady
58	and cool in the summer, and it was the perfect spot for
70	building forts in the winter. And Scott could always go
80	there when he wanted to be alone.
87	Scott's neighbors were upset about losing the
94	grove, too, but no one knew what action to take. Scott
105	decided to hold a meeting for everyone in his apartment.
115	Almost everyone was interested and almost everyone came.
123	They discussed many ideas and finally decided to write
132	letters to the local newspaper.
137	After the newspaper printed the letters, more people
145	in the community became aware of the city's plans. Some
155	protested and wrote letters of their own.
162	Soon the city chose a new place for the apartments.
172	The grove was saved! **176**

Number of words read: _____   Number of errors made: _____

Farmer Paul's New Scarecrow

Every summer Farmer Paul knew he would
have trouble with crows. The last time Farmer Paul
had put up a scarecrow, the crows had seemed to
realize that if it were real it would move. After a
while they had swooped down and pecked at the
straw under its shirt and pulled at the straw in
its hat.

One day, Farmer Paul noticed a man-like
figure made of lightweight plastic on the roof of a
store. The figure was filled with air, and every time
the wind blew, it waved its head, arms, and legs. The
plastic man looked very much alive.

Farmer Paul bought one of the plastic figures,
and after he planted his corn, he attached the figure to
a tall stick. He gave it overalls and a shirt just like the
kind he wore, and he covered its head with a dark
wig. Whenever the wind blew even a little, the plastic
man moved.

The plastic man worked, and the big, black
crows were fooled. Farmer Paul's crops grew tall and
healthy, and the crows did not bother his fields
ever again.

1. What was Farmer Paul's new scarecrow made of?
2. What was the difference between the old scarecrow and the new one?

© Macmillan/McGraw-Hill

Oral Fluency Record Sheet

Name _____ Date _____

Oral Reading Accuracy: _____%   Circle: Fall Winter Spring

Oral Reading Fluency Score: _____ words correct per minute

Prosody Rubric: (Circle Score) 1 2 3 4

Comprehension Question Responses

#1 _____

#2 _____

Farmer Paul's New Scarecrow

	Every summer Farmer Paul knew he would
7	have trouble with crows. The last time Farmer Paul
16	had put up a scarecrow, the crows had seemed to
26	realize that if it were real it would move. After a
37	while they had swooped down and pecked at the
46	straw under its shirt and pulled at the straw in
56	its hat.
58	One day, Farmer Paul noticed a man-like
66	figure made of lightweight plastic on the roof of a
76	store. The figure was filled with air, and every time
86	the wind blew, it waved its head, arms, and legs. The
97	plastic man looked very much alive.
103	Farmer Paul bought one of the plastic figures,
111	and after he planted his corn, he attached the figure to
122	a tall stick. He gave it overalls and a shirt just like the
135	kind he wore, and he covered its head with a dark
146	wig. Whenever the wind blew even a little, the plastic
156	man moved.
158	The plastic man worked, and the big, black
166	crows were fooled. Farmer Paul's crops grew tall and
175	healthy, and the crows did not bother his fields
184	ever again. 186

Number of words read: _____ **Number of errors made:** _____

Name _____ Date _____

The Saturday Morning Project

One Friday night, Julie slept over at Grandma's house. She was excited. She did not know what to expect. Grandma always surprised her.

The next morning, Grandma said they were making pancakes. First, they sifted flour, salt, and baking powder into a bowl. Next, Julie beat eggs in another bowl. Grandma melted butter in a pot. She added the melted butter and milk to the eggs. After that Julie added the dry ingredients. Then she stirred everything together.

The best part came next. Grandma made the pancakes. But they were not just any old pancakes. They were in the shape of letters. She melted butter in a pan. Then she drew a J with some batter in the hot butter. Next, Grandma drew a U, then an L, then an I, and then an E. Grandma made one pancake for each letter in Julie's name.

Grandma put the five pancakes on a plate. They spelled J U L I E. Julie got to eat her own name for breakfast. She ate her name with jam! It was a great breakfast!

1. What was special about Grandma's pancakes?
2. How did Julie feel about staying at Grandma's house?

Oral Fluency Record Sheet

Name _____   Date _____

Oral Reading Accuracy: _____%   Circle: Fall Winter Spring

Oral Reading Fluency Score: _____ words correct per minute

Prosody Rubric: (Circle Score) 1 2 3 4

Comprehension Question Responses

#1 _____

#2 _____

The Saturday Morning Project

	One Friday night, Julie slept over at Grandma's house. She
10	was excited. She did not know what to expect. Grandma always
21	surprised her.
23	The next morning, Grandma said they were making
31	pancakes. First, they sifted flour, salt, and baking powder into a
42	bowl. Next, Julie beat eggs in another bowl. Grandma melted
52	butter in a pot. She added the melted butter and milk to
64	the eggs. After that Julie added the dry ingredients. Then she
75	stirred everything together.
78	The best part came next. Grandma made the pancakes. But
88	they were not just any old pancakes. They were in the shape of
101	letters. She melted butter in a pan. Then she drew a J with some
115	batter in the hot butter. Next, Grandma drew a U, then an L, then an
130	I, and then an E. Grandma made one pancake for each letter in
143	Julie's name.
145	Grandma put the five pancakes on a plate. They spelled
155	J U L I E. Julie got to eat her own name for breakfast. She ate her
168	name with jam! It was a great breakfast! **176**

© Macmillan/McGraw-Hill

Number of words read: _____   Number of errors made: _____

Summer Camping

Last summer, Tony and his brother went camping with their mom. They drove around the park for a long time. Finally, they found the perfect campsite. They decided to set up camp on a quiet spot surrounded by tall trees.

Their tent was shaped like an igloo. It was big enough for the three of them. It was made of thin red nylon cloth. It had a door that zipped and unzipped as they went in and out. It also had three windows covered with netting. There were lots of bugs in the woods. The windows stopped the bugs from coming in.

For cooking, they had a little stove. Mom set the stove at the end of a picnic table. Finally, they were ready for their first picnic under the trees. They had a tasty meal of barbecued chicken and boiled corn. Then the boys helped clean up.

When it got dark, they made a fire. They toasted some marshmallows, told stories, and sang songs. It was nice to be together under the stars.

1. What is the story mostly about?
2. What did Tony and his family do when it got dark?

Oral Fluency Record Sheet

Name _____ Date _____

Oral Reading Accuracy: _____%   Circle: Fall   Winter   Spring

Oral Reading Fluency Score: _____ words correct per minute

Prosody Rubric: (Circle Score) 1 2 3 4

Comprehension Question Responses

#1 _____

#2 _____

Summer Camping

	Last summer, Tony and his brother went camping with
9	their mom. They drove around the park for a long time. Finally,
21	they found the perfect campsite. They decided to set up camp on a
34	quiet spot surrounded by tall trees.
40	Their tent was shaped like an igloo. It was big enough for
52	the three of them. It was made of thin red nylon cloth. It had a door
68	that zipped and unzipped as they went in and out. It also had three
82	windows covered with netting. There were lots of bugs in the
93	woods. The windows stopped the bugs from coming in.
102	For cooking, they had a little stove. Mom set the stove at
114	the end of a picnic table. Finally, they were ready for their first
127	picnic under the trees. They had a tasty meal of barbecued chicken
139	and boiled corn. Then the boys helped clean up.
148	When it got dark, they made a fire. They toasted some
159	marshmallows, told stories, and sang songs. It was nice to be
170	together under the stars. 174

Number of words read: _____ Number of errors made: _____

Name _____ Date _____

Deep Sleep

Making it through the winter is hard for many animals. Some animals and insects, like birds and butterflies, are able to migrate to warmer places. Other animals, such as bears, cannot make such a far move.

To survive the icy weather, many bears go to sleep. This sleep is called hibernation. Preparing for this deep sleep keeps bears busy throughout late summer and fall. During this time, they must eat a lot of berries and fish. The food helps them gain at least 40 pounds a week. They must store enough body fat because they have to live off this fat while asleep.

For its long sleep, a bear finds a cave or hollow log. Its heart rate may drop from 40 to 10 beats a minute. Most bears start hibernating in early October. When they wake up around April or May, they are very hungry. Be very careful if you know there are bears near where you are living. You would not want to be in the path of a hungry bear.

1. Why do bears sleep during the winter?
2. Why are bears especially dangerous in the spring?

Oral Fluency Record Sheet

Name _____   Date _____

Oral Reading Accuracy: _____%   Circle: Fall   Winter   Spring
Oral Reading Fluency Score: _____ words correct per minute
Prosody Rubric: (Circle Score) 1 2 3 4
Comprehension Question Responses
#1 _____
#2 _____

Deep Sleep

	Making it through the winter is hard for many animals. Some
11	animals and insects, like birds and butterflies, are able to migrate to
23	warmer places. Other animals, such as bears, cannot make such a
34	far move.
36	To survive the icy weather, many bears go to sleep. This sleep
48	is called hibernation. Preparing for this deep sleep keeps bears busy
59	throughout late summer and fall. During this time, they must eat a lot
72	of berries and fish. The food helps them gain at least 40 pounds a
86	week. They must store enough body fat because they have to live off
99	this fat while asleep.
103	For its long sleep, a bear finds a cave or hollow log. Its heart
117	rate may drop from 40 to 10 beats a minute. Most bears start
130	hibernating in early October. When they wake up around April or
141	May, they are very hungry. Be very careful if you know there are bears
155	near where you are living. You would not want to be in the path
169	of a hungry bear. 173

Number of words read: _____   Number of errors made: _____

Name _____   Date _____

Sunflowers

Which flower looks very cheerful? Many people would
answer the sunflower. Most sunflowers bloom between July and
October. There are more than 60 different kinds. Some grow as tall
as 10 feet. A big sunflower may be as wide as a foot. It may have
more than 1,000 seeds.

The first sunflowers grew wild in North America. The
Spanish explorers first saw them in New Mexico. They took seeds
back to Spain. Soon people all over Europe grew sunflowers.

Sunflowers have many uses. The seeds give us a kind of
oil. This oil is good for cooking. It is also used to make margarine.
We also eat their seeds. Sunflowers also provide food for birds,
butterflies, and insects.

Not all sunflowers are yellow. Some are red. Some are
white. But the most popular sunflowers are yellow ones.

Sunflowers are easy to grow. They grow in many different
soils. They can live in different climates. Many kinds do not need a
lot of water. But they all need a lot of sun. You will always find
sunflowers facing the sun.

1. What are sunflower seeds used for?

2. Why are sunflowers easy to grow?

Oral Fluency Record Sheet

Name _____ Date _____

Oral Reading Accuracy: _____% Circle: Fall Winter Spring

Oral Reading Fluency Score: _____ words correct per minute

Prosody Rubric: (Circle Score) 1 2 3 4

Comprehension Question Responses

#1 _____

#2 _____

Sunflowers

	Which flower looks very cheerful? Many people would
8	answer the sunflower. Most sunflowers bloom between July and
17	October. There are more than 60 different kinds. Some grow as tall
29	as 10 feet. A big sunflower may be as wide as a foot. It may have
45	more than 1,000 seeds.
49	The first sunflowers grew wild in North America. The
58	Spanish explorers first saw them in New Mexico. They took seeds
69	back to Spain. Soon people all over Europe grew sunflowers.
79	Sunflowers have many uses. The seeds give us a kind of
90	oil. This oil is good for cooking. It is also used to make margarine.
104	We also eat their seeds. Sunflowers also provide food for birds,
115	butterflies, and insects.
118	Not all sunflowers are yellow. Some are red. Some are
128	white. But the most popular sunflowers are yellow ones.
137	Sunflowers are easy to grow. They grow in many different
147	soils. They can live in different climates. Many kinds do not need a
160	lot of water. But they all need a lot of sun. You will always find
175	sunflowers facing the sun. **179**

Number of words read: _____ Number of errors made: _____

Name _____   Date _____

The Beach Wagon

In the summer, David lived near the beach. He went to the
beach every day. He took his beach ball, pail, towel, and umbrella
down to the beach in an old red wagon.

One day David looked at the beat-up wagon. "That wagon
could look a lot better," he thought. "I could turn it into my super
beach wagon."

David thought and thought. What should a beach wagon
look like? At last, he had an idea. He bought a big can of glue. He
got a brush to spread the glue. Then he rolled the wagon down to
the beach.

David opened the glue. He spread glue on the sides of the
wagon. He covered the sides with glue. Then he filled his pail with
sand. He tossed sand onto the wet glue. Lots of sand stuck. Soon
the wagon was not red anymore. It was coated with sand.

"I think the wagon still needs something," thought David.
He looked for pretty rocks. He found some shells. He put more
glue on the wagon. He stuck on the rocks and shells.

"Yes!" smiled David. "Now I have a real beach wagon."

1. What is the story mainly about?
2. How did David turn his old wagon into a beach wagon?

Oral Fluency Record Sheet

Name _____ Date _____

Oral Reading Accuracy: _____%   Circle: Fall   Winter   Spring

Oral Reading Fluency Score: _____ words correct per minute

Prosody Rubric: (Circle Score) 1 2 3 4

Comprehension Question Responses

#1 _____

#2 _____

The Beach Wagon

	In the summer, David lived near the beach. He went to the
12	beach every day. He took his beach ball, pail, towel, and umbrella
24	down to the beach in an old red wagon.
33	One day David looked at the beat-up wagon. "That wagon
44	could look a lot better," he thought. "I could turn it into my super
58	beach wagon."
60	David thought and thought. What should a beach wagon
69	look like? At last, he had an idea. He bought a big can of glue. He
85	got a brush to spread the glue. Then he rolled the wagon down to
99	the beach.
101	David opened the glue. He spread glue on the sides of the
113	wagon. He covered the sides with glue. Then he filled his pail with
126	sand. He tossed sand onto the wet glue. Lots of sand stuck. Soon
139	the wagon was not red anymore. It was coated with sand.
150	"I think the wagon still needs something," thought David.
159	He looked for pretty rocks. He found some shells. He put more
171	glue on the wagon. He stuck on the rocks and shells.
182	"Yes!" smiled David. "Now I have a real beach wagon." **192**

Number of words read: _____   Number of errors made: _____

How Skunk Got His Stripes

Skunk did not always have white stripes. Long ago, he was all black. He was black from the tip of his nose to the end of his tail. At night, this was a big problem for the other animals. They could not see Skunk coming.

"We have to solve this problem!" said Bobcat. Skunk had sprayed him just the night before with his scent.

"It is not my fault," said Skunk. "You animals come crashing through my home in the middle of the night. You scare me half to death. What do you expect me to do?"

"I have an idea," said Fawn shyly. Everyone turned to the youngster in surprise. "Perhaps we should give Skunk white spots like mine. Then we could see him in the dark."

Even Skunk thought this was a fine solution. So Bobcat borrowed a bucket of white paint from a farmer's barn. Squirrel said he would paint spots on Skunk.

Squirrel started painting Skunk's back. But then he came to Skunk's tail. He saw that his tail was too bushy for polka dots. The animals decided that stripes would work just as well. And to this day, all skunks have striped tails.

1. What problem were the animals trying to solve?
2. What was Squirrel's solution?

Oral Fluency Record Sheet

Name _____ Date _____

Oral Reading Accuracy: _____%   Circle: Fall Winter Spring

Oral Reading Fluency Score: _____ words correct per minute

Prosody Rubric: (Circle Score) 1 2 3 4

Comprehension Question Responses

#1 _____

#2 _____

How Skunk Got His Stripes

	Skunk did not always have white stripes. Long ago, he
10	was all black. He was black from the tip of his nose to the end
25	of his tail. At night, this was a big problem for the other
38	animals. They could not see Skunk coming.
45	"We have to solve this problem!" said Bobcat. Skunk
54	had sprayed him just the night before with his scent.
64	"It is not my fault," said Skunk. "You animals come
74	crashing through my home in the middle of the night. You
85	scare me half to death. What do you expect me to do?"
97	"I have an idea," said Fawn shyly. Everyone turned to
107	the youngster in surprise. "Perhaps we should give Skunk
116	white spots like mine. Then we could see him in the dark."
128	Even Skunk thought this was a fine solution. So Bobcat
138	borrowed a bucket of white paint from a farmer's barn.
148	Squirrel said he would paint spots on Skunk.
156	Squirrel started painting Skunk's back. But then he
164	came to Skunk's tail. He saw that his tail was too bushy for
177	polka dots. The animals decided that stripes would work just as
188	well. And to this day, all skunks have striped tails. 198

Number of words read: _____   Number of errors made: _____

An Old Way of Life

The Eskimos are a people who live near the Arctic. It is very cold there. For thousands of years, the Eskimos found ways to live in the cold. Most of them lived near the sea. The sea gave them food. They hunted seals and whales. They caught fish. On land, they hunted a kind of deer called the caribou.

The Eskimos made clothing from the skins of animals they hunted. In summer most Eskimos made tents of animal skins. They sailed in boats made of animal skins. In winter, most Eskimos lived in houses made of snow or sod. In the coldest places, some Eskimos lived in houses made of snow all year long.

Eskimo life began to change in the 1800s. People from Europe started hunting for whales where the Eskimos lived. Fur traders arrived. The Eskimos worked with the whalers and fur traders. Soon many of the animals that the Eskimos needed were almost gone.

Today most Eskimos live in towns. They live in modern houses. They buy food at stores. But they always remember the old ways.

1. How did Eskimos use animal skins?
2. Why did life change for the Eskimos in the 1800s?

© Macmillan/McGraw-Hill

Oral Fluency Record Sheet

Name _____ Date _____

Oral Reading Accuracy: _____%   Circle: Fall   Winter   Spring

Oral Reading Fluency Score: _____ words correct per minute

Prosody Rubric: (Circle Score) 1 2 3 4

Comprehension Question Responses

#1 _____

#2 _____

An Old Way of Life

	The Eskimos are a people who live near the Arctic. It is
12	very cold there. For thousands of years, the Eskimos found ways to
24	live in the cold. Most of them lived near the sea. The sea gave
38	them food. They hunted seals and whales. They caught fish. On
49	land, they hunted a kind of deer called the caribou.
59	The Eskimos made clothing from the skins of animals they
69	hunted. In summer most Eskimos made tents of animal skins. They
80	sailed in boats made of animal skins. In winter, most Eskimos
91	lived in houses made of snow or sod. In the coldest places, some
104	Eskimos lived in houses made of snow all year long.
114	Eskimo life began to change in the 1800s. People from
124	Europe started hunting for whales where the Eskimos lived. Fur
134	traders arrived. The Eskimos worked with the whalers and fur
144	traders. Soon many of the animals that the Eskimos needed were
155	almost gone.
157	Today most Eskimos live in towns. They live in modern
167	houses. They buy food at stores. But they always remember
177	the old ways. **180**

Number of words read: _____ Number of errors made: _____

Name _____ Date _____

A Special Honor

Sometimes, many people admire a person. They want to honor that person. One way to honor a person is to put his or her picture on a stamp.

The United States printed its first postage stamp in 1847. The first five-cent stamp showed Benjamin Franklin. The first ten-cent stamp showed George Washington.

Stamps honor all kinds of people. They honor artists and writers. They honor soldiers and teachers. Do you have sports heroes? How about people in music? They may be on stamps.

Anyone can ask the Post Office to honor someone with a stamp. Is there someone you would like to honor? Write a letter. Send the letter to the Postmaster General. Give the person's full name. Tell when the person was born. Also, tell when the person died. The person cannot be alive. Tell why you admire the person.

A group of citizens reads the letters. They may have to read thousands of them. The group talks about the people. They tell the Postmaster what they think. He or she picks the person.

Who knows? It will take at least three years. But perhaps your person will be chosen for a stamp.

1. What is the passage mainly about?
2. How are people chosen for the special stamps?

© Macmillan/McGraw-Hill

Oral Fluency Record Sheet

Name _____ Date _____

Oral Reading Accuracy: _____%   Circle: Fall Winter Spring

Oral Reading Fluency Score: _____ words correct per minute

Prosody Rubric: (Circle Score) 1 2 3 4

Comprehension Question Responses

#1 _____

#2 _____

A Special Honor

	Sometimes, many people admire a person. They want to
9	honor that person. One way to honor a person is to put his or her
24	picture on a stamp.
28	The United States printed its first postage stamp in 1847.
38	The first five-cent stamp showed Benjamin Franklin. The first
48	ten-cent stamp showed George Washington.
54	Stamps honor all kinds of people. They honor artists and
64	writers. They honor soldiers and teachers. Do you have sports
74	heroes? How about people in music? They may be on stamps.
85	Anyone can ask the Post Office to honor someone with a
96	stamp. Is there someone you would like to honor? Write a letter.
108	Send the letter to the Postmaster General. Give the person's full
119	name. Tell when the person was born. Also, tell when the person
131	died. The person cannot be alive. Tell why you admire the person.
143	A group of citizens reads the letters. They may have to read
155	thousands of them. The group talks about the people. They tell the
167	Postmaster what they think. He or she picks the person.
177	Who knows? It will take at least three years. But perhaps
188	your person will be chosen for a stamp. 196

Number of words read: _____   Number of errors made: _____

An Amusing Story

In fourth grade, Rob wrote a story called "What If Ants Wore Pants." He even drew pictures to go with the story.

"What a great picture book idea, Rob!" said his teacher, Mr. Yetto. Mr. Yetto gave Rob some large sheets of paper to make the book. Rob began to work right away. Rob drew big pictures for his story. Then, he printed his words at the bottom of each page. Mr. Yetto made holes at the top of each sheet and put rings through the holes. He then hung the rings on a frame. This way, Rob could flip each page easily.

The book turned out really well. Mr. Yetto asked Rob to read his story to the kindergarten class. The next day, Rob and Mr. Yetto shared the big book with the kindergarten children. Rob flipped each page and read the story aloud. The children laughed at every page. They loved the funny pictures of llamas in pajamas. Their favorite, though, were the buffaloes in ski clothes.

Rob never felt as proud as he did that day. Perhaps Rob will grow up to be a writer or artist—or both.

1. Where were the words written in Rob's book?
2. What happened when Rob read his book to the young children?

Oral Fluency Record Sheet

Name _____ Date _____

Oral Reading Accuracy: _____%

Circle: **Fall   Winter   Spring**

Oral Reading Fluency Score: _____ words correct per minute

Prosody Rubric: (Circle Score) 1 2 3 4

Comprehension Question Responses

#1 _____

#2 _____

An Amusing Story

	In fourth grade, Rob wrote a story called "What If Ants
11	Wore Pants." He even drew pictures to go with the story.
22	"What a great picture book idea, Rob!" said his teacher,
32	Mr. Yetto. Mr. Yetto gave Rob some large sheets of paper to make
45	the book. Rob began to work right away. Rob drew big pictures
57	for his story. Then, he printed his words at the bottom of each page.
71	Mr. Yetto made holes at the top of each sheet and put rings through
85	the holes. He then hung the rings on a frame. This way, Rob could
99	flip each page easily.
103	The book turned out really well. Mr. Yetto asked Rob to
114	read his story to the kindergarten class. The next day, Rob and Mr.
127	Yetto shared the big book with the kindergarten children. Rob
137	flipped each page and read the story aloud. The children laughed at
149	every page. They loved the funny pictures of llamas in pajamas.
160	Their favorite, though, were the buffaloes in ski clothes.
169	Rob never felt as proud as he did that day. Perhaps Rob will
182	grow up to be a writer or artist—or both. **192**

Number of words read: _____   **Number of errors made:** _____

Name _____   Date _____

A Castle Visit

Lola had seen castles in fairy tales. Castles looked
wonderful in the stories. Now Lola was with her family in
France. She was visiting real castles.

The day was cold. The wind was blowing. The family was
at a big stone castle. It stood on top of a tall hill. High walls went
all around it.

Dad said that castles were homes for kings and nobles.
These people used them for protection. Family members, servants,
and soldiers also lived there.

The family walked across a bridge. They went through a
main gate. Lola saw how thick the walls were. Mom said that the
walls were 33 feet thick!

They climbed up to the top of the walls. Lola thought about
being a guard on these walls. You could see all around. You could
watch for enemies.

The family walked back down. They went into a big hall.
They visited bedrooms. They saw the kitchen. All the rooms were
cold and damp. The wind seemed to come right in.

"This castle is different from the ones in books," Lola
thought. "I wouldn't want to live here. I like our own house. It's nice
and cozy."

1. Why did people build castles?

2. What did Lola think about the castle?

Oral Fluency Record Sheet

Name _____   Date _____

Oral Reading Accuracy: _____%   Circle: Fall Winter Spring
Oral Reading Fluency Score: _____ words correct per minute
Prosody Rubric: (Circle Score) 1 2 3 4
Comprehension Question Responses
#1 _____
#2 _____

A Castle Visit

	Lola had seen castles in fairy tales. Castles looked
9	wonderful in the stories. Now Lola was with her family in
20	France. She was visiting real castles.
26	The day was cold. The wind was blowing. The family was
37	at a big stone castle. It stood on top of a tall hill. High walls went
53	all around it.
56	Dad said that castles were homes for kings and nobles.
66	These people used them for protection. Family members, servants,
75	and soldiers also lived there.
80	The family walked across a bridge. They went through a
90	main gate. Lola saw how thick the walls were. Mom said that the
103	walls were 33 feet thick!
108	They climbed up to the top of the walls. Lola thought about
120	being a guard on these walls. You could see all around. You could
133	watch for enemies.
136	The family walked back down. They went into a big hall.
147	They visited bedrooms. They saw the kitchen. All the rooms were
158	cold and damp. The wind seemed to come right in.
168	"This castle is different from the ones in books," Lola
178	thought. "I wouldn't want to live here. I like our own house. It's nice
192	and cozy." 194

© Macmillan/McGraw-Hill

Number of words read: _____   Number of errors made: _____

New Products for People

People create ideas for new products all the time.
Some new products are made just for fun. Others improve
people's quality of life.

A big company now makes swim goggles without straps.
You stick the goggles on your face. There are two separate lenses.
You stick each one over an eye. They stay in place even when you
dive. Speed swimmers use them to swim even faster.

Another company makes a new kind of toothbrush box. It
has a special kind of light. The light kills germs. Just leave your
toothbrush inside. You can be sure it will be really clean.

Do you think watermelons are too heavy? Plant scientists
have now come up with a smaller watermelon. It weighs only 4 to
6 pounds. It tastes sweeter than big watermelons. Now you won't
have to carry heavy watermelons to picnics anymore. You can take
small, light ones instead.

Do your shoelaces keep coming loose? Now you can get
rubbery tubes to keep them tied. They are easy to put on the laces.
They also last until your shoes wear out.

Do you have an idea that will develop a new product for people?
What is your idea?

---

1. What is this passage mainly about?
2. Why do people develop new products?

© Macmillan/McGraw-Hill

Oral Fluency Record Sheet

Name _____   Date _____

Oral Reading Accuracy: _____%   Circle: Fall Winter Spring
Oral Reading Fluency Score: _____ words correct per minute
Prosody Rubric: (Circle Score) 1 2 3 4
Comprehension Question Responses
#1 _____
#2 _____

New Products for People

	People create ideas for new products all the time.
9	Some new products are made just for fun. Others improve
19	people's quality of life.
23	A big company now makes swim goggles without straps.
32	You stick the goggles on your face. There are two separate lenses.
44	You stick each one over an eye. They stay in place even when you
58	dive. Speed swimmers use them to swim even faster.
67	Another company makes a new kind of toothbrush box. It
77	has a special kind of light. The light kills germs. Just leave your
90	toothbrush inside. You can be sure it will be really clean.
101	Do you think watermelons are too heavy? Plant scientists
110	have now come up with a smaller watermelon. It weighs only 4 to
123	6 pounds. It tastes sweeter than big watermelons. Now you won't
134	have to carry heavy watermelons to picnics anymore. You can take
145	small, light ones instead.
149	Do your shoelaces keep coming loose? Now you can get
159	rubbery tubes to keep them tied. They are easy to put on the laces.
173	They also last until your shoes wear out.
181	Do you have an idea that will develop a new product for people?
194	What is your idea? **198**

Number of words read: _____   Number of errors made: _____

Let's Go Skating

You can have fun and get lots of exercise with in-line roller skates. In-line skates have all their wheels lined up in one row. Many people think that in-line skates are easier to move around on than skates with four wheels. Balance is the most important thing. The hardest part is learning how to stop.

Before you try in-line skating, get equipment to protect yourself. Wear elbow pads and knee pads. You should wear wrist guards, safety gloves, and a helmet as well.

Find a smooth, flat surface to begin learning. Be sure you are away from traffic and away from people on foot. Learn how to stop before you begin rolling. Put your arms out in front of you for balance. Then, slide one foot forward and press hard on the brake pad under that heel.

Now you're ready to try in-line skating. Start off in a slight crouch position. Then, put your weight on one foot and push off with the other foot. You should push off to the side. Go slowly and get into the rhythm. Soon you'll be having so much fun you won't want to stop.

1. According to the passage, what is the hardest thing to learn with in-line skating?

2. What is the author's opinion of in-line skating?

Oral Fluency Record Sheet

Name _____ Date _____

Oral Reading Accuracy: _____%   Circle: Fall Winter Spring
Oral Reading Fluency Score: _____ words correct per minute
Prosody Rubric: (Circle Score) 1 2 3 4
Comprehension Question Responses
#1 _____
#2 _____

Let's Go Skating

	You can have fun and get lots of exercise with in-line roller
13	skates. In-line skates have all their wheels lined up in one row.
26	Many people think that in-line skates are easier to move around on
39	than skates with four wheels. Balance is the most important thing.
50	The hardest part is learning how to stop.
58	Before you try in-line skating, get equipment to protect
68	yourself. Wear elbow pads and knee pads. You should wear wrist
79	guards, safety gloves, and a helmet as well.
87	Find a smooth, flat surface to begin learning. Be sure you
98	are away from traffic and away from people on foot. Learn how to
111	stop before you begin rolling. Put your arms out in front of you for
125	balance. Then, slide one foot forward and press hard on the brake
137	pad under that heel.
141	Now you're ready to try in-line skating. Start off in a slight
154	crouch position. Then, put your weight on one foot and push off
166	with the other foot. You should push off to the side. Go slowly
179	and get into the rhythm. Soon you'll be having so much fun you
192	won't want to stop. **196**

© Macmillan/McGraw-Hill

Number of words read: _____   Number of errors made: _____

Saving the Sea Otters

I grew up in Alaska. I was 16 in 1989. That year, a big oil ship had an accident. It ran into a reef near where I lived. A big hole opened up in the bottom of the ship. The ship had millions of gallons of oil on board. Oil began to spill into the water. It spilled out for 12 hours.

Many sea otters lived in the water. I loved to watch the otters play. They spend most of their time on the surface of the water. This is where the oil stayed. The oil got into the otters' fur. It made their fur stick together. This let cold water reach their skin. Many of the animals froze to death. Others licked their fur. They swallowed the oil. It poisoned them.

I wanted to help rescue the sea otters. I got together with lots of other people. We worked around the clock. We cleaned the animals. We fed them. Animal doctors came to check them. At last, many of the animals were ready to go back into the water. We took them to places where there was no oil.

I was glad to help save the otters. These animals are like our neighbors.

1. What is this story mainly about?
2. How did the oil spill affect the sea otters?

Oral Fluency Record Sheet

Name _____   Date _____

Oral Reading Accuracy: _____%   Circle: Fall   Winter   Spring

Oral Reading Fluency Score: _____ words correct per minute

Prosody Rubric: (Circle Score) 1 2 3 4

Comprehension Question Responses

#1 _____

#2 _____

Saving the Sea Otters

	I grew up in Alaska. I was 16 in 1989. That year, a big oil
15	ship had an accident. It ran into a reef near where I lived. A big
30	hole opened up in the bottom of the ship. The ship had millions of
44	gallons of oil on board. Oil began to spill into the water. It spilled
58	out for 12 hours.
62	Many sea otters lived in the water. I loved to watch the
74	otters play. They spend most of their time on the surface of the
87	water. This is where the oil stayed. The oil got into the otters' fur.
101	It made their fur stick together. This let cold water reach their skin.
114	Many of the animals froze to death. Others licked their fur. They
126	swallowed the oil. It poisoned them.
132	I wanted to help rescue the sea otters. I got together with
144	lots of other people. We worked around the clock. We cleaned the
156	animals. We fed them. Animal doctors came to check them. At
167	last, many of the animals were ready to go back into the water. We
181	took them to places where there was no oil.
190	I was glad to help save the otters. These animals are like
202	our neighbors. **204**

Number of words read: _____   Number of errors made: _____

A Special Dessert

It was Mother's Day. Claire wanted to make a special cake.

"Mom loves walnut cake," she thought. "She loves apple pie. She loves pumpkin bread, too. I will mix them together. The new dessert will be three times as delicious."

Claire mixed everything in a large bowl. Then, she looked at the clock. Mom would be home soon. The cake needed to bake for 30 minutes. The pie and the bread each needed to bake for 45 minutes.

"I will add it all together," Claire thought. She poured the batter into a big baking pan. She put the pan into the oven. Then she set the timer for two hours.

Mom came home at six o'clock. "Happy Mother's Day," Claire sang. "Come see your surprise."

Mom saw the big cake on the kitchen table. Claire cut slices for Mom and herself. They both took bites. Mom looked like she was in pain. Claire could only say, "Ugh!"

The cake was hard on the outside. It was sticky on the inside. And it did not taste good.

Claire explained what she had done. Mom just laughed. "Things may only be good alone," she said. "They may not be better when you put them together. But thanks. It's the thought that counts. And this thought was very nice indeed."

---

1. What is this story mostly about?

2. Why did Claire put together the ingredients from all three desserts?

© Macmillan/McGraw-Hill

Oral Fluency Record Sheet

Name _____   Date _____

Oral Reading Accuracy: _____%   Circle: Fall   Winter   Spring
Oral Reading Fluency Score: _____ words correct per minute
Prosody Rubric: (Circle Score) 1 2 3 4
Comprehension Question Responses
#1 _____
#2 _____

A Special Dessert

	It was Mother's Day. Claire wanted to make a special cake.
11	"Mom loves walnut cake," she thought. "She loves apple
20	pie. She loves pumpkin bread, too. I will mix them together. The
32	new dessert will be three times as delicious."
40	Claire mixed everything in a large bowl. Then, she looked
50	at the clock. Mom would be home soon. The cake needed to bake
63	for 30 minutes. The pie and the bread each needed to bake for
76	45 minutes.
78	"I will add it all together," Claire thought. She poured the
84	batter into a big baking pan. She put the pan into the oven. Then
103	she set the timer for two hours.
110	Mom came home at six o'clock. "Happy Mother's Day,"
119	Claire sang. "Come see your surprise."
125	Mom saw the big cake on the kitchen table. Claire cut
136	slices for Mom and herself. They both took bites. Mom looked like
148	she was in pain. Claire could only say, "Ugh!"
157	The cake was hard on the outside. It was sticky on the
169	inside. And it did not taste good.
176	Claire explained what she had done. Mom just laughed.
185	"Things may only be good alone," she said. "They may not be
197	better when you put them together. But thanks. It's the thought that
209	counts. And this thought was very nice indeed." **217**

Number of words read: _____   Number of errors made: _____

Play Ball

What do baseball players need? To start with, they need a bat and a ball. A baseball bat is long and round. Most bats are made of ash wood. The bat cannot be longer than 46 inches. It cannot be thicker than 2 ¾ inches at any point. A baseball is small, hard, and round. It weighs about 5 ounces. It has a tiny cork ball at the center. Layers of rubber and yarn are tightly wrapped around this ball. The cover of the ball is made of two pieces of white cowhide. These are sewn together with thick red thread.

Next, players need a special padded leather glove. They also need shoes with spikes on the soles. The spikes help them stop and start quickly.

At bat, players wear a batting helmet. This is a special hard cap. The helmet protects batters in case they are hit in the head with the ball.

In baseball, a pitcher pitches the ball to a catcher. Catchers have special equipment to protect them. They wear a metal mask over their faces. They also wear padded cloth covers over their chests. To protect their legs, they wear hard shin guards.

Baseball can be safe and fun. Are you ready to play ball?

1. What is a baseball made of?
2. Why do baseball players wear special clothing?

Oral Fluency Record Sheet

Name _____ Date _____

Oral Reading Accuracy: _____%   Circle: Fall Winter Spring
Oral Reading Fluency Score: _____ words correct per minute
Prosody Rubric: (Circle Score) 1 2 3 4
Comprehension Question Responses
#1 _____
#2 _____

Play Ball

	What do baseball players need? To start with, they need a
11	bat and a ball. A baseball bat is long and round. Most bats are
25	made of ash wood. The bat cannot be longer than 46 inches. It
38	cannot be thicker than 2 ¾ inches at any point. A baseball is
50	small, hard, and round. It weighs about 5 ounces. It has a tiny cork
64	ball at the center. Layers of rubber and yarn are tightly wrapped
76	around this ball. The cover of the ball is made of two pieces of
90	white cowhide. These are sewn together with thick red thread.
100	Next, players need a special padded leather glove. They also
110	need shoes with spikes on the soles. The spikes help them stop and
123	start quickly.
125	At bat, players wear a batting helmet. This is a special hard
137	cap. The helmet protects batters in case they are hit in the head
150	with the ball.
153	In baseball, a pitcher pitches the ball to a catcher. Catchers
164	have special equipment to protect them. They wear a metal mask
175	over their faces. They also wear padded cloth covers over their
186	chests. To protect their legs, they wear hard shin guards.
196	Baseball can be safe and fun. Are you ready to play ball? **208**

Number of words read: _____   Number of errors made: _____

Plant Art

Topiary is a garden art. The artists do not use paintbrushes. They use clippers. To make a topiary sculpture, the artist cuts away leaves and twigs. After a lot of clipping and trimming, a shape will form.

The shape might be a ball. It might be a cone. It might be an animal. It might look like a bear or lion. It might be shaped like a seal.

Some animal shapes are made with wire frames. First, the artist puts a plant into dirt at the foot of the frame. Then, the plant grows up over the wire. After a long time, the plant covers the wire. The artist now trims it to look like an animal.

Topiary artists use many different kinds of plants. They use ivy and box hedges. Some even use daisy bushes. The kinds of plants that work best are thick with leaves. The leaves hide the branches. That way the shape is leafy green.

You can practice this old art. Many garden shops sell wire frames. You can choose from a variety of shapes.

Today, you may see big green sheep at a shopping center. You may see a green horse at a hotel. Think about how much time an artist has spent making these animals.

1. What is this article mostly about?
2. What kinds of shapes do topiary artists create?

© Macmillan/McGraw-Hill

Oral Fluency Record Sheet

Name _____ Date _____

Oral Reading Accuracy: _____% Circle: Fall Winter Spring
Oral Reading Fluency Score: _____ words correct per minute
Prosody Rubric: (Circle Score) 1 2 3 4
Comprehension Question Responses
#1 _____
#2 _____

Plant Art

	Topiary is a garden art. The artists do not use paintbrushes.
11	They use clippers. To make a topiary sculpture, the artist cuts away
23	leaves and twigs. After a lot of clipping and trimming, a shape
35	will form.
37	The shape might be a ball. It might be a cone. It might be
51	an animal. It might look like a bear or lion. It might be shaped like
66	a seal.
68	Some animal shapes are made with wire frames. First, the
78	artist puts a plant into dirt at the foot of the frame. Then, the plant
93	grows up over the wire. After a long time, the plant covers the
106	wire. The artist now trims it to look like an animal.
117	Topiary artists use many different kinds of plants. They use
127	ivy and box hedges. Some even use daisy bushes. The kinds of
139	plants that work best are thick with leaves. The leaves hide the
151	branches. That way the shape is leafy green.
159	You can practice this old art. Many garden shops sell wire
170	frames. You can choose from a variety of shapes.
179	Today, you may see big green sheep at a shopping center.
190	You may see a green horse at a hotel. Think about how much time
204	an artist has spent making these animals. 211

Number of words read: _____ Number of errors made: _____

Climbing the Walls

Jill's dad loved rock climbing. He took many trips to the mountains. He wanted Jill to come with him. But first Jill had to learn about climbing.

Jill was excited. She and her dad found a climbing wall in town. Jill put on a helmet and climbing shoes. Then she put on ropes and other gear. Jill's ropes were fastened to the floor. From there, they went around her dad's waist. Then, they went up to the top of the wall.

"I will hold the rope tight," her dad said. "You will be safe. Just go slowly."

Jill looked up at the wall. She saw places for her hands and feet. The top looked far away.

Jill started up. She went from spot to spot. She reached out with her hands. She pushed hard with her feet. At last, she was near the top.

"I can't climb this last bit," she called down.

"Just try," her dad called back. "I'm holding you."

Jill took hold of something small with her hand. She bent down. Then she jumped. Her hand felt the top of the wall. She pulled herself up. She had made it.

"Will you ever do that again?" asked her dad after Jill got back down.

"Oh, yes!" said Jill. "That was great!"

1. What is this story mostly about?
2. Do you think Jill felt safe the whole time she was climbing? Why?

© Macmillan/McGraw-Hill

Oral Fluency Record Sheet

Name _____ Date _____

Oral Reading Accuracy: _____%   Circle: Fall Winter Spring
Oral Reading Fluency Score: _____ words correct per minute
Prosody Rubric: (Circle Score) 1 2 3 4
Comprehension Question Responses
#1 _____
#2 _____

Climbing the Walls

	Jill's dad loved rock climbing. He took many trips to the
11	mountains. He wanted Jill to come with him. But first Jill had to
24	learn about climbing.
27	Jill was excited. She and her dad found a climbing wall in
39	town. Jill put on a helmet and climbing shoes. Then she put on
52	ropes and other gear. Jill's ropes were fastened to the floor. From
64	there, they went around her dad's waist. Then, they went up to the
77	top of the wall.
81	"I will hold the rope tight," her dad said. "You will be safe.
94	Just go slowly."
97	Jill looked up at the wall. She saw places for her hands and
110	feet. The top looked far away.
116	Jill started up. She went from spot to spot. She reached out
128	with her hands. She pushed hard with her feet. At last, she was
141	near the top.
144	"I can't climb this last bit," she called down.
153	"Just try," her dad called back. "I'm holding you."
162	Jill took hold of something small with her hand. She bent
173	down. Then she jumped. Her hand felt the top of the wall. She
186	pulled herself up. She had made it.
193	"Will you ever do that again?" asked her dad after Jill got
205	back down.
207	"Oh, yes!" said Jill. "That was great!" **214**

Number of words read: _____   Number of errors made: _____

Making Perfume

Lin loved lots of smells. She loved the smell of flowers. She loved the forest smell of pine needles. She loved the smell of oranges and lemons.

Lin wondered how people made perfumes. How did they get smells out of things in nature? Her mother took her to a perfume factory to see. A tour guide told them lots of things about perfumes.

The guide said that perfumes are made from oils. The oils once all came from nature. They came from flowers, leaves, fruits, roots, and seeds. Oils from these sources are still used. But scientists can now make many of the same smells in their labs. They also make new smells that are not in nature.

Lin watched people getting oils out of things. Some people squeezed them out. Some people boiled them out. Some people were putting flower petals on big, flat trays. They covered the petals with pork fat. The fat would pull out the sweet smells.

The guide said that as many as 300 different smells can go into one perfume. People who make perfumes must have a good sense of smell. They must know how to put different kinds of smells together.

Lin thought about her sense of smell. How good was it? She wondered if some day she might make perfumes.

1. What are some ways in which people get oils for perfumes?
2. Why is Lin interested in perfume?

© Macmillan/McGraw-Hill

Oral Fluency Record Sheet

Name _____ Date _____

Oral Reading Accuracy: _____%   Circle: **Fall Winter Spring**

Oral Reading Fluency Score: _____ words correct per minute

Prosody Rubric: (Circle Score) 1 2 3 4

Comprehension Question Responses

#1 _____

#2 _____

Making Perfume

	Lin loved lots of smells. She loved the smell of flowers.
11	She loved the forest smell of pine needles. She loved the smell of
24	oranges and lemons.
27	Lin wondered how people made perfumes. How did they
36	get smells out of things in nature? Her mother took her to a
49	perfume factory to see. A tour guide told them lots of things
61	about perfumes.
63	The guide said that perfumes are made from oils. The oils
74	once all came from nature. They came from flowers, leaves, fruits,
85	roots, and seeds. Oils from these sources are still used. But
96	scientists can now make many of the same smells in their labs.
108	They also make new smells that are not in nature.
118	Lin watched people getting oils out of things. Some people
128	squeezed them out. Some people boiled them out. Some people
138	were putting flower petals on big, flat trays. They covered the
149	petals with pork fat. The fat would pull out the sweet smells.
161	The guide said that as many as 300 different smells can go
173	into one perfume. People who make perfumes must have a good
184	sense of smell. They must know how to put different kinds of
196	smells together.
198	Lin thought about her sense of smell. How good was it?
209	She wondered if some day she might make perfumes. **218**

© Macmillan/McGraw-Hill

Number of words read: _____ Number of errors made: _____

Smokey the Bear

You may have seen Smokey the Bear. The National Forest Service uses him on many of its signs and anouncements. He teaches people about how to stop fires. But did you know that Smokey is based on a real bear?

In 1950 a big fire broke out in New Mexico. During the fire, some firefighters saw a little bear cub. It was walking along the fire line. It seemed to be looking for its mother. The men left it alone. They thought its mother would find it.

Later, the same men saw the cub again. It was high in a burned-out tree. Its legs and paws were burned. But it was still alive. The men got it down.

A rancher took the cub home. Then it was flown to a big city. An animal doctor took care of it. He treated the cub's burns.

News about the cub spread around the country. Pictures of the bear were in newspapers. People were interested in the bear's story. The Forest Service had a program about forest fires. It decided to use the bear in its program.

The little cub went to Washington, D.C. It lived in the zoo there for many years. There it became famous and known as Smokey the Bear.

1. Where did the firefighters see the little cub?
2. Why is the little cub a good symbol for fighting fires?

© Macmillan/McGraw-Hill

Oral Fluency Record Sheet

Name _____ Date _____

Oral Reading Accuracy: _____%   Circle: Fall Winter Spring

Oral Reading Fluency Score: _____ words correct per minute

Prosody Rubric: (Circle Score) 1 2 3 4

Comprehension Question Responses

#1 _____

#2 _____

Smokey the Bear

	You may have seen Smokey the Bear. The National Forest
10	Service uses him on many of its signs and announcements. He
21	teaches people about how to stop fires. But did you know that
33	Smokey is based on a real bear?
40	In 1950 a big fire broke out in New Mexico. During the
52	fire, some firefighters saw a little bear cub. It was walking along
64	the fire line. It seemed to be looking for its mother. The men left it
79	alone. They thought its mother would find it.
87	Later, the same men saw the cub again. It was high in a
100	burned-out tree. Its legs and paws were burned. But it was still
113	alive. The men got it down.
119	A rancher took the cub home. Then it was flown to a big
132	city. An animal doctor took care of it. He treated the cub's burns.
145	News about the cub spread around the country. Pictures of
155	the bear were in newspapers. People were interested in the bear's
166	story. The Forest Service had a program about forest fires. It
177	decided to use the bear in its program.
185	The little cub went to Washington, D.C. It lived in the zoo
197	there for many years. There it became famous and known as
208	Smokey the Bear. **211**

Number of words read: _____   Number of errors made: _____

The Robin

The robin is one of the most common birds in the United States. Robins go south in the winter. Then, in the spring, they are among the first birds to come back north. Toward the end of winter, many people watch for robins. They think the first robin is a sign of spring.

Robins are easy to spot because they have red chests. They often go back to the same place each year to build nests. They like to nest in trees. However, they also like to build nests on shelves and ledges.

Perhaps you have watched a robin catching a worm. It will tilt its head. Then it may reach down and tug a worm from the ground. The robin may look like it is listening when it tilts its head. In fact, this helps the robin see better. The robin's eyes are on the sides of its head. It needs to turn its head to see what is in front. Robins can find worms just by looking for the dirt around worm holes. They can also spot the tiniest part of an almost buried worm. Robins also eat fruit and beetles.

Robins are a special part of our landscape. Be sure to keep your eyes open for your next robin.

1. Tell two facts about robins from the passage.

2. Why do robins tilt their heads to catch worms?

© Macmillan/McGraw-Hill

Oral Fluency Record Sheet

Name _____ Date _____

Oral Reading Accuracy: _____% Circle: Fall Winter Spring

Oral Reading Fluency Score: _____ words correct per minute

Prosody Rubric: (Circle Score) 1 2 3 4

Comprehension Question Responses

#1 _____

#2 _____

The Robin

	The robin is one of the most common birds in the United
12	States. Robins go south in the winter. Then, in the spring, they are
25	among the first birds to come back north. Toward the end of
37	winter, many people watch for robins. They think the first robin is
49	a sign of spring.
53	Robins are easy to spot because they have red chests. They
64	often go back to the same place each year to build nests. They like
78	to nest in trees. However, they also like to build nests on
90	shelves and ledges.
93	Perhaps you have watched a robin catching a worm. It will
104	tilt its head. Then it may reach down and tug a worm from the
118	ground. The robin may look like it is listening when it tilts its head.
132	In fact, this helps the robin see better. The robin's eyes are on the
146	sides of its head. It needs to turn its head to see what is in front.
162	Robins can find worms just by looking for the dirt around worm
174	holes. They can also spot the tiniest part of an almost buried worm.
187	Robins also eat fruit and beetles.
193	Robins are a special part of our landscape. Be sure to keep
205	your eyes open for your next robin. 212

Number of words read: _____ Number of errors made: _____

A Great Save

Jack needed new clothes. His mom was taking him to the store. Meg would have to come, too. Meg was Jack's little sister. She was five. She didn't like shopping. But she couldn't stay home all alone.

The parking garage was crowded. Jack's mom drove around and around. There didn't seem to be any spots left. At last, she found a spot on the top level.

It was windy. The family headed for the store. The wind pulled at their clothes. It seemed to push them into the store.

The family went inside. Jack got new clothes. The family had some lunch. Then it was time to go.

The three got to the top level of the garage. Then Meg ran ahead. She reached the ledge and looked down. Jack and his mom walked behind, talking.

All of a sudden there was a cry for help.

"It's Meg!" cried Jack. He looked across the garage. Meg was hanging from the ledge. If she fell, she would drop four stories!

"Help!" Meg cried. "The wind! It pushed me over!"

Jack ran as fast as he could. He took hold of Meg's shirt just as Meg was about to let go. Then his mom reached them. She helped pull Meg up.

"You got to her fast!" said Jack's mom.

"I had to," said Jack. "She's my sister."

1. Why did Meg come with Jack and his mom to the store?
2. How did Jack save Meg?

Oral Fluency Record Sheet

Name _____   Date _____

Oral Reading Accuracy: _____%   Circle: Fall   Winter   Spring

Oral Reading Fluency Score: _____ words correct per minute

Prosody Rubric: (Circle Score) 1 2 3 4

Comprehension Question Responses

#1 _____

#2 _____

A Great Save

	Jack needed new clothes. His mom was taking him to the
11	store. Meg would have to come, too. Meg was Jack's little sister.
23	She was five. She didn't like shopping. But she couldn't stay home
35	all alone.
37	The parking garage was crowded. Jack's mom drove around
46	and around. There didn't seem to be any spots left. At last, she
59	found a spot on the top level.
66	It was windy. The family headed for the store. The wind
77	pulled at their clothes. It seemed to push them into the store.
89	The family went inside. Jack got new clothes. The family
99	had some lunch. Then it was time to go.
108	The three got to the top level of the garage. Then Meg ran
121	ahead. She reached the ledge and looked down. Jack and his mom
133	walked behind, talking.
136	All of a sudden there was a cry for help.
146	"It's Meg!" cried Jack. He looked across the garage. Meg
156	was hanging from the ledge. If she fell, she would drop four stories!
169	"Help!" Meg cried. "The wind! It pushed me over!"
178	Jack ran as fast as he could. He took hold of Meg's shirt
191	just as Meg was about to let go. Then his mom reached them. She
205	helped pull Meg up.
209	"You got to her fast!" said Jack's mom.
217	"I had to," said Jack. "She's my sister." **225**

Number of words read: _____   Number of errors made: _____

Where Are the Cookies?

Mrs. Ford was always in a hurry. She hurried to the store. She hurried to work. She hurried to get the laundry done. She hurried to cook dinner.

One night Mrs. Ford came home from the store. She had bought food and other things she needed for the house. Hurriedly she put everything away. The ice cream belonged in the freezer. The cookies belonged in the kitchen cabinet. The cat food belonged in the hall closet. The tissues belonged in the bathroom.

"It's time to get to my meeting," thought Mrs. Ford. "I need to take those nice cookies I bought."

Mrs. Ford looked in the cabinet. The cookies she had bought were not there. Instead, she found the tissues that belonged in the bathroom.

"That's strange," thought Mrs. Ford. She took the tissues out of the cabinet and walked to the bathroom. She opened the cabinet to put away the tissues and there was a container of ice cream.

"How odd," thought Mrs. Ford. She took the ice cream and put it away in the freezer. There she found the cat food.

"My goodness," thought Mrs. Ford. She took the cat food and put it into the hall closet. There she found the cookies.

"Perhaps, I should try to slow down and think next time," thought Mrs. Ford as she rushed out the door.

---

1. Why did Mrs. Ford put things in the wrong places?
2. Why do you think Mrs. Ford was always in a hurry?

Oral Fluency Record Sheet

Name _____ Date _____

Oral Reading Accuracy: _____%
Circle: Fall Winter Spring
Oral Reading Fluency Score: _____ words correct per minute
Prosody Rubric: (Circle Score) 1 2 3 4
Comprehension Question Responses
#1 _____
#2 _____

Where Are the Cookies?

	Mrs. Ford was always in a hurry. She hurried to the
11	store. She hurried to work. She hurried to get the laundry done.
23	She hurried to cook dinner.
28	One night Mrs. Ford came home from the store. She
38	had bought food and other things she needed for the house.
49	Hurriedly she put everything away. The ice cream belonged in
59	the freezer. The cookies belonged in the kitchen cabinet. The
69	cat food belonged in the hall closet. The tissues belonged
79	in the bathroom.
82	"It's time to get to my meeting," thought Mrs. Ford. "I
93	need to take those nice cookies I bought."
101	Mrs. Ford looked in the cabinet. The cookies she had
111	bought were not there. Instead, she found the tissues that
121	belonged in the bathroom.
125	"That's strange," thought Mrs. Ford. She took the tissues
134	out of the cabinet and walked to the bathroom. She
144	opened the cabinet to put away the tissues and there was a
156	container of ice cream.
160	"How odd," thought Mrs. Ford. She took the ice cream
170	and put it away in the freezer. There she found the cat food.
183	"My goodness," thought Mrs. Ford. She took the cat
192	food and put it into the hall closet. There she found the cookies.
205	"Perhaps, I should try to slow down and think next
215	time," thought Mrs. Ford as she rushed out the door. **225**

Number of words read: _____ Number of errors made: _____

Water Slides

They are fun. They are wet. They can make you scream.
What are they? They are water slides.

You may have gone on a water slide in a water park. What
goes into the design of one of these slides? First, the designer
thinks about safety. A good water slide thrills its riders. But it has
to be safe. The designer also thinks about how high the slide is
from top to bottom. He or she decides the number of curves, turns,
and drops. He or she figures out how much water flows down the
slide per minute.

Water slides are made in sections. Strong fiberglass is
molded into hundreds of pieces. The pieces are sent to the water
park. There they are put together.

On most slides, the rider never goes faster than 20 miles per
hour. In a car that would feel slow. On the slide it feels fast.
That's because the ride keeps changing. First, there may be a drop.
Then, you may hit a curve. Next, you may go into a banked curve
and feel like you are moving sideways. There may be a sudden, steep
drop. Finally, you splash into a pool at the bottom.

When you ride on a water slide, always go feet first. Stretch
out flat with your legs in front of you. Then go!

1. What is this passage mostly about?

2. Why does it feel like you are going very fast when you go downa
   water slide

Oral Fluency Record Sheet

Name _____ Date _____

Oral Reading Accuracy: _____%   Circle: Fall   Winter   Spring

Oral Reading Fluency Score: _____ words correct per minute

Prosody Rubric: (Circle Score) 1 2 3 4

Comprehension Question Responses

#1 _____

#2 _____

Water Slides

	They are fun. They are wet. They can make you scream.
11	What are they? They are water slides.
18	You may have gone on a water slide in a water park. What
31	goes into the design of one of these slides? First, the designer
43	thinks about safety. A good water slide thrills its riders. But it has
56	to be safe. The designer also thinks about how high the slide is
69	from top to bottom. He or she decides the number of curves, turns,
82	and drops. He or she figures out how much water flows down the
95	slide per minute.
98	Water slides are made in sections. Strong fiberglass is
107	molded into hundreds of pieces. The pieces are sent to the water
119	park. There they are put together.
125	On most slides, the rider never goes faster than 20 miles per
137	hour. In a car that would feel slow. On the slide it feels fast.
151	That's because the ride keeps changing. First, there may be a drop.
163	Then, you may hit a curve. Next, you may go into a banked curve
177	and feel like you are moving sideways. There may be a sudden, steep
190	drop. Finally, you splash into a pool at the bottom.
200	When you ride on a water slide, always go feet first. Stretch
212	out flat with your legs in front of you. Then go! **223**

Number of words read: _____   Number of errors made: _____

Up, Up, and Away

For thousands of years, people dreamed of flying. They tried many things. Nothing seemed to work.

Then in 1783, two brothers in France got a new idea. They were watching smoke. They noticed the way smoke moves up from a fire. It does not seem to come back down. The brothers filled paper bags with smoke. They watched as the smoke moved the bags into the air.

The brothers decided to make a big balloon. They filled it with smoke. When it was full, they let it go. Up, up it went.

Next, the brothers built another balloon. This time they attached a basket to the balloon. In September 1783, they were ready. They put a rooster, a duck, and a sheep in the basket. They filled the balloon with hot air and let it go. Up it went, this time with passengers. Then, high above the Earth, the warm air cooled. The balloon floated back to the ground. The three animals had taken a round-trip air flight.

Two other Frenchmen watched these events. They decided to become the first people to fly. They built a big blue and gold balloon. In November 1783, the balloon carried them over the city of Paris.

Today we take air travel for granted. But not too long ago, flight was still a mystery and a challenge.

1. What is this passage mainly about?
2. Explain what makes the balloons rise.

Oral Fluency Record Sheet

Name _____ Date _____

Oral Reading Accuracy: _____% Circle: Fall Winter Spring
Oral Reading Fluency Score: _____ words correct per minute
Prosody Rubric: (Circle Score) 1 2 3 4
Comprehension Question Responses
#1 _____
#2 _____

Up, Up, and Away

9	For thousands of years, people dreamed of flying. They tried many things. Nothing seemed to work.
16	
28	Then in 1783, two brothers in France got a new idea. They were watching smoke. They noticed the way smoke moves up
38	from a fire. It does not seem to come back down. The brothers
51	filled paper bags with smoke. They watched as the smoke moved
62	the bags into the air.
67	The brothers decided to make a big balloon. They filled it
78	with smoke. When it was full, they let it go. Up, up it went.
92	Next, the brothers built another balloon. This time they
101	attached a basket to the balloon. In September 1783, they were
112	ready. They put a rooster, a duck, and a sheep in the basket. They
126	filled the balloon with hot air and let it go. Up it went, this time
141	with passengers. Then, high above the Earth, the warm air cooled.
152	The balloon floated back to the ground. The three animals had
163	taken a round-trip air flight.
169	Two other Frenchmen watched these events. They decided
177	to become the first people to fly. They built a big blue and gold
191	balloon. In November 1783, the balloon carried them over the city
202	of Paris.
204	Today we take air travel for granted. But not too long ago,
216	flight was still a mystery and a challenge. **224**

© Macmillan/McGraw-Hill

Number of words read: _____ **Number of errors made:** _____

Munch Takes a Bus Ride

Munch the Mouse had never had a bus ride. It looked like fun. But Munch was short. How would he reach the first step?

Munch stood at the bus stop. Soon a man came and stood nearby. Munch thought, "I'll grab his pants leg. I'll hold on from behind. He won't even see me."

The bus pulled up. The man climbed on with Munch holding on to his pants leg. The driver asked for the fare. The man pulled out some coins. He put them into a box. Munch tried to tell the driver that he had no money. The driver didn't seem to hear him.

Munch wanted to get a better view of the bus. He climbed up a pole. He found a rack and sat there. He watched the people and the scenery. He thought to himself that this was fun. But then all of a sudden he heard a sharp cry. "It's a mouse!" screamed a little girl.

People started chasing Munch. He slid down the pole. He ran and hid far back under a seat. After a while, people stopped looking for him.

"He's gone," called the driver. The people finally settled back down.

"I don't think I'm welcome here," thought Munch. He moved over to the door. When it opened, he got out.

"That was interesting," thought Munch. "But I don't think I'll try it again."

1. Why did Munch climb up the pole?
2. Why do you think the bus driver did not answer Munch?

© Macmillan/McGraw-Hill

Oral Fluency Record Sheet

Name _____ Date _____

Oral Reading Accuracy: _____% Circle: Fall Winter Spring

Oral Reading Fluency Score: _____ words correct per minute

Prosody Rubric: (Circle Score) 1 2 3 4

Comprehension Question Responses

#1 _____

#2 _____

Munch Takes a Bus Ride

	Munch the Mouse had never had a bus ride. It looked like
12	fun. But Munch was short. How would he reach the first step?
24	Munch stood at the bus stop. Soon a man came and stood
36	nearby. Munch thought, "I'll grab his pants leg. I'll hold on from
48	behind. He won't even see me."
54	The bus pulled up. The man climbed on with Munch
64	holding on to his pants leg. The driver asked for the fare. The
77	man pulled out some coins. He put them into a box. Munch tried
90	to tell the driver that he had no money. The driver didn't seem to
104	hear him.
106	Munch wanted to get a better view of the bus. He climbed
118	up a pole. He found a rack and sat there. He watched the people
132	and the scenery. He thought to himself that this was fun. But then
145	all of a sudden he heard a sharp cry. "It's a mouse!" screamed a little girl.
161	People started chasing Munch. He slid down the pole. He
171	ran and hid far back under a seat. After a while, people stopped
184	looking for him.
187	"He's gone," called the driver. The people finally settled
196	back down.
198	"I don't think I'm welcome here," thought Munch. He
207	moved over to the door. When it opened, he got out.
218	"That was interesting," thought Munch. "But I don't think
227	I'll try it again." **231**

Number of words read: _____ Number of errors made: _____

Adventure on the River

Paco had never done anything like whitewater rafting. Even though he was a good swimmer who loved adventure, he knew this trip would be very different. Paco was feeling scared.

"Ready yet?" said his dad.

"Yes," said Paco. But he didn't look very sure.

Paco and his parents put on safety gear. Then they climbed into a small boat filled with air. This was the raft. Their guide handed them paddles. They began moving down the river. The waves were gentle here. Up ahead, though, things would be very different.

"Get ready," the guide said. Paco heard a loud roar. Around a bend, he saw big rolling waves. The water seemed to be turning white.

The guide steered through the waves. Water splashed into the boat. The waves threw them from side to side.

"Hold on!" shouted the guide.

Just then, they hit a wave hard. They took a big bounce. Paco seemed to fly up and out. Suddenly, he was in the water. For a moment, no one could see him. Time seemed to stand still. Where was he? Then his head popped up out of the water. The guide steered over to him. He pulled him on board.

"That was great!" laughed Paco. "This is fun!"

Everyone laughed. Now Paco knew he could handle the next big wave—and the next. He was having the time of his life.

1. What is this story mainly about?
2. What made Paco fall out of the raft?

© Macmillan/McGraw-Hill

Oral Fluency Record Sheet

Name _____ Date _____

Oral Reading Accuracy: _____%   Circle: Fall Winter Spring

Oral Reading Fluency Score: _____ words correct per minute

Prosody Rubric: (Circle Score) 1 2 3 4

Comprehension Question Responses

#1 _____

#2 _____

Adventure on the River

	Paco had never done anything like whitewater rafting.
8	Even though he was a good swimmer who loved adventure, he
19	knew this trip would be very different. Paco was feeling scared.
30	"Ready yet?" said his dad.
35	"Yes," said Paco. But he didn't look very sure.
44	Paco and his parents put on safety gear. Then they climbed
55	into a small boat filled with air. This was the raft. Their guide
68	handed them paddles. They began moving down the river. The
78	waves were gentle here. Up ahead, though, things would be
88	very different.
90	"Get ready," the guide said. Paco heard a loud roar.
100	Around a bend, he saw big rolling waves. The water seemed
111	to be turning white.
115	The guide steered through the waves. Water splashed into
124	the boat. The waves threw them from side to side.
134	"Hold on!" shouted the guide.
139	Just then, they hit a wave hard. They took a big bounce.
151	Paco seemed to fly up and out. Suddenly, he was in the water. For a
166	moment, no one could see him. Time seemed to stand still. Where
178	was he? Then his head popped up out of the water. The guide
191	steered over to him. He pulled him on board.
200	"That was great!" laughed Paco. "This is fun!"
208	Everyone laughed. Now Paco knew he could handle the
217	next big wave—and the next. He was having the time of
229	his life. **231**

© Macmillan/McGraw-Hill

Number of words read: _____   Number of errors made: _____

The Biggest Land Animal

The first thing you probably notice about elephants is that they are big. They are the biggest animals on land. Only some whales are bigger.

Elephants spend almost all day working on staying big. Each day elephants eat 300 to 500 pounds of food. They eat grass, leaves, water plants, fruit, branches, and bark. They wash this food down with as much as 50 gallons of water each day.

Elephants have thick skins. The skin of an adult is $1\frac{1}{2}$ inches thick. It weighs about 2,000 pounds.

Elephants do not sweat. They must cool off in other ways. Sometimes they flap their big ears. At other times, they spray water on themselves. They may also roll in mud. The mud dries on the skin. This layer protects the elephant from the sun.

A unique thing about the elephant is its trunk. The elephant breathes and smells with its trunk. It uses its trunk to carry food and water to its mouth. With its trunk, an elephant can pull up trees and dig for water. An elephant can pick up a 600-pound log with its trunk. It can also use the tip of its trunk to pick up something as small as a coin.

Experts today think that elephants are in danger. Hunters threaten them. People will need to work hard to make sure that elephants survive.

1. How do elephants keep themselves cool?
2. Why do elephants spend so much time eating and drinking?

Oral Fluency Record Sheet

Name _____ Date _____

Oral Reading Accuracy: _____% Circle: Fall Winter Spring

Oral Reading Fluency Score: _____ words correct per minute

Prosody Rubric: (Circle Score) 1 2 3 4

Comprehension Question Responses

#1 _____

#2 _____

The Biggest Land Animal

	The first thing you probably notice about elephants is that
10	they are big. They are the biggest animals on land. Only some
22	whales are bigger.
25	Elephants spend almost all day working on staying big.
34	Each day elephants eat 300 to 500 pounds of food. They eat grass,
47	leaves, water plants, fruit, branches, and bark. They wash this food
58	down with as much as 50 gallons of water each day.
69	Elephants have thick skins. The skin of an adult is $1\frac{1}{2}$
80	inches thick. It weighs about 2,000 pounds.
87	Elephants do not sweat. They must cool off in other ways.
98	Sometimes they flap their big ears. At other times, they spray water
110	on themselves. They may also roll in mud. The mud dries on the
123	skin. This layer protects the elephant from the sun.
132	A unique thing about the elephant is its trunk. The elephant
143	breathes and smells with its trunk. It uses its trunk to carry food
156	and water to its mouth. With its trunk, an elephant can pull up trees
170	and dig for water. An elephant can pick up a 600-pound log with
184	its trunk. It can also use the tip of its trunk to pick up something as
200	small as a coin.
204	Experts today think that elephants are in danger. Hunters
213	threaten them. People will need to work hard to make sure that
225	elephants survive. **228**

Number of words read: _____ Number of errors made: _____

The Great Wall of China

One of the wonders of the world stands in China. It is the Great Wall of China. The Great Wall is the longest structure ever built. It is about 4,600 miles long.

The Chinese built the wall as protection against enemies. It was started more than 2,500 years ago. Workers made big piles of dirt. They pounded the dirt until it was very hard. They would use this hard dirt to build the wall. Over time the wall crumbled. It was rebuilt again and again.

Often, the wall did not work. For example, in the 1200s, enemies climbed over it to conquer China.

Today, people see the wall that went up between 1368 and 1644. This wall went up during the Ming Dynasty. At first, the Ming built the old way. They piled and pounded dirt. But rain and wind destroyed these walls. The builders turned to stone and brick. These walls took longer to build. They cost more, too. But they lasted longer.

The new wall had towers. Soldiers lived in some of them. They sent signals from others. For signals, they built fires. They used smoke during the day. At night they used flames. People far away could get ready for an attack.

Today, the wall is crumbling. No one knows how much longer it will stand. Rain and wind break parts of the wall. Some people take bricks. Others write on the wall. The wall once protected China. Now China must protect the wall.

1. What is special about the Great Wall of China?

2. Why was the Great Wall built?

© Macmillan/McGraw-Hill

Oral Fluency Record Sheet

Name _____ Date _____

Oral Reading Accuracy: _____% 　　　　　Circle: Fall　Winter　Spring

Oral Reading Fluency Score: _____ words correct per minute

Prosody Rubric: (Circle Score) 1 2 3 4

Comprehension Question Responses

#1 _____

#2 _____

The Great Wall of China

	One of the wonders of the world stands in China. It is the
13	Great Wall of China. The Great Wall is the longest structure ever
25	built. It is about 4,600 miles long.
32	The Chinese built the wall as protection against enemies. It
42	was started more than 2,500 years ago. Workers made big piles of
54	dirt. They pounded the dirt until it was very hard. They would
66	use this hard dirt to build the wall. Over time the wall crumbled.
79	It was rebuilt again and again.
85	Often, the wall did not work. For example, in the 1200s,
96	enemies climbed over it to conquer China.
103	Today, people see the wall that went up between 1368
113	and 1644. This wall went up during the Ming Dynasty. At
124	first, the Ming built the old way. They piled and pounded dirt. But
137	rain and wind destroyed these walls. The builders turned to stone
148	and brick. These walls took longer to build. They cost more, too.
160	But they lasted longer.
164	The new wall had towers. Soldiers lived in some of them.
175	They sent signals from others. For signals, they built fires. They
186	used smoke during the day. At night they used flames. People far
198	away could get ready for an attack.
205	Today, the wall is crumbling. No one knows how much
215	longer it will stand. Rain and wind break parts of the wall. Some
228	people take bricks. Others write on the wall. The wall once
239	protected China. Now China must protect the wall. **247**

Number of words read: _____　　Number of errors made: _____

Name _____   Date _____

Babe and the Hot Cakes

Paul Bunyan was a big, strong man. He was so strong he could lift a bear by the tail. He was so tall he could see over a mountain. Paul and his men cleared many forests for farmland when the United States was an undeveloped country.

Paul had a blue ox named Babe. Babe was big and strong, too. If you stood at his head, you couldn't even see his tail. He could pull down mountains and dig lakes.

One day Babe got very sick. Here's what happened.

Paul had a big kitchen. In that kitchen was a big stove. You could cook one hundred hot cakes on that stove at one time. Hot cakes were Babe's favorite food.

One day, Paul's men found Babe lying on his side. Babe was moaning. Tears rolled down his face. The men decided to find out what was wrong.

"I will go down into Babe's belly," said one brave man. "The rest of you will lower me with ropes."

The man, carrying a lantern, went down into Babe's belly. There he discovered something big and black. The man tied a rope to it. The rest of the men pulled the thing up.

The big, black thing turned out to be the kitchen stove. Babe had eaten the hot cakes, stove and all.

Babe got well after that, but he never ate hot cakes—or stoves—again.

1. What made Babe sick?
2. How did the men find out what was making Babe sick?

© Macmillan/McGraw-Hill

Oral Fluency Record Sheet

Name _____ Date _____

Oral Reading Accuracy: _____%   Circle: Fall Winter Spring

Oral Reading Fluency Score: _____ words correct per minute

Prosody Rubric: (Circle Score) 1 2 3 4

Comprehension Question Responses

#1 _____

#2 _____

Babe and the Hot Cakes

	Paul Bunyan was a big, strong man. He was so strong he
12	could lift a bear by the tail. He was so tall he could see over a
28	mountain. Paul and his men cleared many forests for farmland
38	when the United States was an undeveloped country.
46	Paul had a blue ox named Babe. Babe was big and strong,
58	too. If you stood at his head, you couldn't even see his tail. He
72	could pull down mountains and dig lakes.
79	One day Babe got very sick. Here's what happened.
88	Paul had a big kitchen. In that kitchen was a big stove. You
101	could cook one hundred hot cakes on that stove at one time. Hot
114	cakes were Babe's favorite food.
119	One day, Paul's men found Babe lying on his side. Babe
130	was moaning. Tears rolled down his face. The men decided to find
142	out what was wrong.
146	"I will go down into Babe's belly," said one brave man.
157	"The rest of you will lower me with ropes."
166	The man, carrying a lantern, went down into Babe's belly.
176	There he discovered something big and black. The man tied a rope
188	to it. The rest of the men pulled the thing up.
199	The big, black thing turned out to be the kitchen stove.
210	Babe had eaten the hot cakes, stove and all.
219	Babe got well after that, but he never ate hot cakes—or
231	stoves—again. **233**

Number of words read: _____   Number of errors made: _____

Hero of the Flood

Rain had been pouring down for days. Now the river was starting to flood. Water was spilling over its banks. It was running through Kara's small town and carrying away houses, trees, and cars.

Most people had headed toward higher ground away from the river. They would be safe. But some people had climbed to the top of the highest hill at the center of town. The hill was not high enough. Soon the river would rise even more and cover the hill. Tall trees grew on the hill. The people had started to climb up to the tree tops.

Eighteen-year-old Kara had won many rowing contests at school. Now she would use her skill to save people. Today she had already taken her mother and grandmother to safety in her family's big rowboat. She had rowed them to safety on higher ground away from the river and the town.

News channels reported about the people who were stranded in town. Kara climbed into the rowboat and headed for the hill. The river was strong, but Kara was stronger. She rowed close to the trees and filled her boat with people. Then she rowed them to higher ground. Again and again, Kara rowed to the hill, filled her boat with people, and rowed them to safety.

The next day, newspapers were filled with stories about Kara. "I just did what I could do," said Kara. "I'm glad I was able to help."

1. What is this story mostly about?
2. What brave thing did Kara do?

Oral Fluency Record Sheet

Name _____ Date _____

Oral Reading Accuracy: _____%   Circle: Fall Winter Spring
Oral Reading Fluency Score: _____ words correct per minute
Prosody Rubric: (Circle Score) 1 2 3 4
Comprehension Question Responses
#1 _____
#2 _____

Hero of the Flood

	Rain had been pouring down for days. Now the river was
11	starting to flood. Water was spilling over its banks. It was
22	running through Kara's small town and carrying away houses,
31	trees, and cars.
34	Most people had headed toward higher ground away from
43	the river. They would be safe. But some people had climbed to
55	the top of the highest hill at the center of town. The hill was not
70	high enough. Soon the river would rise even more and cover the
82	hill. Tall trees grew on the hill. The people had started to climb up
96	to the tree tops.
100	Eighteen-year-old Kara had won many rowing contests at
110	school. Now she would use her skill to save people. Today she
122	had already taken her mother and grandmother to safety in her
133	family's big rowboat. She had rowed them to safety on higher
144	ground away from the river and the town.
152	News channels reported about the people who were stranded in
162	town. Kara climbed into the rowboat and headed for the hill. The
174	river was strong, but Kara was stronger. She rowed close to the
186	trees and filled her boat with people. Then she rowed them to
198	higher ground. Again and again, Kara rowed to the hill, filled her
210	boat with people, and rowed them to safety.
218	The next day, newspapers were filled with stories about
227	Kara. "I just did what I could do," said Kara. "I'm glad I was able
242	to help." **244**

© Macmillan/McGraw-Hill

Number of words read: _____   Number of errors made: _____

Name _____   Date _____

A New Game

It was summer. The days were long and hot. Toby had nothing to do. All his friends were off at camp. Toby had to stay home. His mother needed him to help care for his little sister. Toby spent most of his time at home watching television.

One sunny afternoon, his mother told him to go outside and play. For a while, Toby sat all alone on the front steps of his apartment building. Then he felt a tap on his shoulder. It was Mr. Blumberg. Mr. Blumberg lived upstairs. He was on his way to play chess in the park. Mr. Blumberg did this every day. He asked Toby if he wanted to learn the game.

Toby often watched Mr. Blumberg and his friends play chess. Toby had never thought of asking if he could join them. Toby said he would love to learn. Mr. Blumberg and Toby walked together to the park.

Toby met all of Mr. Blumberg's friends. Then Toby sat down. He was excited. He really wanted to learn this new game.

1. Why did Toby's mother tell him to go outside?
2. How did Toby feel about learning chess?

Oral Fluency Record Sheet

Name _____ Date _____

Oral Reading Accuracy: _____%   Circle: Fall Winter Spring

Oral Reading Fluency Score: _____ words correct per minute

Prosody Rubric: (Circle Score) 1 2 3 4

Comprehension Question Responses

#1 _____

#2 _____

A New Game

	It was summer. The days were long and hot. Toby
10	had nothing to do. All his friends were off at camp. Toby
22	had to stay home. His mother needed him to help care for
34	his little sister. Toby spent most of his time at home
45	watching television.
47	One sunny afternoon, his mother told him to go
56	outside and play. For a while, Toby sat all alone on the
68	front steps of his apartment building. Then he felt a tap
79	on his shoulder. It was Mr. Blumberg. Mr. Blumberg
88	lived upstairs. He was on his way to play chess in the
100	park. Mr. Blumberg did this every day. He asked Toby
110	if he wanted to learn the game.
117	Toby often watched Mr. Blumberg and his friends
125	play chess. Toby had never thought of asking if he could
136	join them. Toby said he would love to learn. Mr. Blumberg
147	and Toby walked together to the park.
154	Toby met all of Mr. Blumberg's friends. Then
162	Toby sat down. He was excited. He really wanted to learn
173	this new game. **176**

Number of words read: _____   Number of errors made: _____

The Little Brother

Anna thought her little brother was a real pest. He sat on her bed while she gossiped on the telephone. He watched her as she did her homework. He sat on the floor at her feet as she watched TV. Matt was three years old. Anna knew he loved her. She loved him, too, but enough was enough.

One afternoon, Anna was sitting at her tiny desk in the corner of the family room. She was trying to finish her math homework. Matt kept asking her questions about the spiral notebook she was using. He also wanted to know about the numbers that she was writing. And why, he asked, did she use her eraser so often? Finally, Anna pleaded with her mother for some help. She just wanted some peace and quiet.

 Anna's mother smiled. Then she asked Anna if she would like it if her friends always shooed her away. Anna suddenly saw that Matt was her friend, as well as her brother. She gave him a crayon and a piece of notebook paper. Then she made room for him at her desk.

1. What did Anna's little brother do to annoy her?
2. How did Anna's mother help her see her brother differently?

Oral Fluency Record Sheet

Name _____   Date _____

Oral Reading Accuracy: _____%   Circle: Fall Winter Spring
Oral Reading Fluency Score: _____ words correct per minute
Prosody Rubric: (Circle Score) 1 2 3 4
Comprehension Question Responses
#1 _____
#2 _____

The Little Brother

	Anna thought her little brother was a real pest. He sat on
12	her bed while she gossiped on the telephone. He watched her as
24	she did her homework. He sat on the floor at her feet as she
38	watched TV. Matt was three years old. Anna knew he loved her.
50	She loved him, too, but enough was enough.
58	One afternoon, Anna was sitting at her tiny desk in the
69	corner of the family room. She was trying to finish her math
81	homework. Matt kept asking her questions about the spiral
90	notebook she was using. He also wanted to know about the
101	numbers that she was writing. And why, he asked, did she use
113	her eraser so often? Finally, Anna pleaded with her mother for
124	some help. She just wanted some peace and quiet.
133	Anna's mother smiled. Then she asked Anna if she would
143	like it if her friends always shooed her away. Anna suddenly saw
155	that Matt was her friend, as well as her brother. She gave him a
169	crayon and a piece of notebook paper. Then she made room for
181	him at her desk. **185**

Number of words read: _____   Number of errors made: _____

Name _____ Date _____

Too Much Water

People need air, fire, and water to live. Yet these same elements can destroy life. Of these elements, water may be the most dangerous.

Many cultures have legends of great floods that covered the land. Since civilizations developed close to water, stories of flooding came naturally. Lakes and rivers do not flood any more often in our century than they did in the past. Today, however, floods seem to cause much more damage. This is because many more buildings are close to water. For example, people love to live on the beach. Yet they may suffer when a hurricane hits.

Many different weather conditions cause floods. Spring rain will quickly melt mountain snow causing it to race down into the valley. A raging rainstorm causes rivers to overflow. The high winds of a hurricane blow ocean water inland. Sudden storms cause flash floods in deserts where the water cannot sink into the ground. A volcanic eruption may also begin a flood. That is because the energy from the eruption causes huge waves to crash over nearby towns.

1. Why is the passage titled "Too Much Water"?
2. Name two conditions that cause floods.

Oral Fluency Record Sheet

Name _____ Date _____

Oral Reading Accuracy: _____%   Circle: Fall Winter Spring

Oral Reading Fluency Score: _____ words correct per minute

Prosody Rubric: (Circle Score) 1 2 3 4

Comprehension Question Responses

#1 _____

#2 _____

Too Much Water

	People need air, fire, and water to live. Yet these same
11	elements can destroy life. Of these elements, water may be
21	the most dangerous.
24	Many cultures have legends of great floods that covered
33	the land. Since civilizations developed close to water, stories of
43	flooding came naturally. Lakes and rivers do not flood any more
54	often in our century than they did in the past. Today, however,
66	floods seem to cause much more damage. This is because many
77	more buildings are close to water. For example, people love to
88	live on the beach. Yet they may suffer when a hurricane hits.
100	Many different weather conditions cause floods. Spring
107	rain will quickly melt mountain snow causing it to race down into
119	the valley. A raging rainstorm causes rivers to overflow. The high
130	winds of a hurricane blow ocean water inland. Sudden storms
140	cause flash floods in deserts where the water cannot sink into the
152	ground. A volcanic eruption may also begin a flood. That is
163	because the energy from the eruption causes huge waves to crash
174	over nearby towns. **177**

Number of words read: _____   **Number of errors made:** _____

Name _____   Date _____

Antlers

Male deer and moose have antlers that grow out of their
skulls. In fall and early winter, they shed their old antlers. These
animals grow new antlers. Some people collect the old antlers
that lie on the ground in many parks. They put them up over their
fireplaces. They make hat racks out of them. They even use them
to make fancy lamps.

In many parks, collecting antlers is against the law. There
is a good reason for this. Imagine if visitors could take home
whatever they found in the park. Pretty soon, there would be
nothing to look at and enjoy.

Another important reason to leave antlers alone is because
they are made of bone. Bone has lots of calcium. People need
calcium for strong bones and teeth. We get calcium from foods
such as milk, cheese, and green vegetables. Like people, animals
need calcium, too. They need it to grow. Small animals like mice
and chipmunks get calcium by chewing on animal bones. They
also chew on antlers. When people take antlers away, animals
lose a good way to get calcium.

1. What problem is discussed in this passage?
2. Why is it important to leave antlers where they are found?

Oral Fluency Record Sheet

Name _____ Date _____

Oral Reading Accuracy: _____%   Circle: Fall Winter Spring

Oral Reading Fluency Score: _____ words correct per minute

Prosody Rubric: (Circle Score) 1 2 3 4

Comprehension Question Responses

#1 _____

#2 _____

Antlers

	Male deer and moose have antlers that grow out of their
11	skulls. In fall and early winter, they shed their old antlers. These
23	animals grow new antlers. Some people collect the old antlers
33	that lie on the ground in many parks. They put them up over their
47	fireplaces. They make hat racks out of them. They even use them
59	to make fancy lamps.
63	In many parks, collecting antlers is against the law. There
73	is a good reason for this. Imagine if visitors could take home
85	whatever they found in the park. Pretty soon, there would be
96	nothing to look at and enjoy.
102	Another important reason to leave antlers alone is because
111	they are made of bone. Bone has lots of calcium. People need
123	calcium for strong bones and teeth. We get calcium from foods
134	such as milk, cheese, and green vegetables. Like people, animals
144	need calcium, too. They need it to grow. Small animals like mice
156	and chipmunks get calcium by chewing on animal bones. They
166	also chew on antlers. When people take antlers away, animals
176	lose a good way to get calcium. **183**

Number of words read: _____   Number of errors made: _____

Name _____   Date _____

A Big Decision

Although he was in fifth grade, Alex was small for his age. He was shorter than his sister, Donna, who was one year younger. When Alex told his sister he wanted to play a bass in the school orchestra, she laughed. "That bass is triple your size," said Donna, chuckling. When she suggested that he learn to play the violin because it was more his size, he ignored her.

Alex signed up for the orchestra the next day. The orchestra leader, Mrs. Higgins, was elated when he told her he wanted to play a bass. She introduced Alex to his fellow bass players who were all girls and petite in size.

"I will look like a giant in that row," Alex informed his mom that evening.

"Having this big beautiful instrument does not mean you will be able to play it," his mother reminded him. "You will have to practice every day."

Alex never missed a rehearsal. He practiced his part every day after school. He took excellent care of his bass and bow, rubbing down the warm wood. In fact, Alex became so good, that one of the girls in his row even asked him to help her.

1. What is the "big decision" in this story?
2. Why did Alex become so good at playing the bass?

Oral Fluency Record Sheet

Name _____ Date _____

Oral Reading Accuracy: _____%   Circle: Fall Winter Spring

Oral Reading Fluency Score: _____ words correct per minute

Prosody Rubric: (Circle Score) 1 2 3 4

Comprehension Question Responses

#1 _____

#2 _____

A Big Decision

	Although he was in fifth grade, Alex was small for his age.
12	He was shorter than his sister, Donna, who was one year
23	younger. When Alex told his sister he wanted to play a bass in the
37	school orchestra, she laughed. "That bass is triple your size," said
48	Donna, chuckling. When she suggested that he learn to play the
59	violin because it was more his size, he ignored her.
69	Alex signed up for the orchestra the next day. The orchestra
80	leader, Mrs. Higgins, was elated when he told her he wanted to
92	play a bass. She introduced Alex to his fellow bass players who
104	were all girls and petite in size.
111	"I will look like a giant in that row," Alex informed his mom
124	that evening.
126	"Having this big beautiful instrument does not mean you will
136	be able to play it," his mother reminded him. "You will have to
149	practice every day."
152	Alex never missed a rehearsal. He practiced his part every day
163	after school. He took excellent care of his bass and bow,
174	rubbing down the warm wood. In fact, Alex became so good, that
186	one of the girls in his row even asked him to help her. 199

Number of words read: _____   Number of errors made: _____

Name _____ Date _____

The Big Wave

Mark lived in the suburbs of Chicago. In the summertime, his family took trips to the beach, where he played in the waves. Sometimes he would ride a wave to the shore of the lake. He always looked forward to riding the waves, the bigger the better.

One summer, Mark went to visit his cousin in California. There, he was introduced to the Pacific Ocean. This was the first time Mark experienced anything besides the enormous lake in Chicago. He mistakenly believed that the lake and the ocean were the same in terms of power. When Mark's aunt told him to be careful, he laughed and assured her that he was an excellent swimmer. She cautioned him that the ocean was rough and perilous, but Mark just shrugged. He knew how to surf, didn't he?

Mark heard the gigantic wave before he saw it. He turned around and opened his mouth in horror. The wave was mammoth, and it was thundering directly toward him. Mark took a deep breath and cringed beneath the water. The wave crashed over him and carried him high onto shore. Mark gained a new respect for the ocean after that.

1. Why didn't Mark listen to his aunt?
2. What lesson did Mark learn about the ocean?

Oral Fluency Record Sheet

The Big Wave

	Mark lived in the suburbs of Chicago. In the summertime,
10	his family took trips to the beach, where he played in the
22	waves. Sometimes he would ride a wave to the shore of the
34	lake. He always looked forward to riding the waves, the bigger
45	the better.
47	One summer, Mark went to visit his cousin in California.
57	There, he was introduced to the Pacific Ocean. This was the first
69	time Mark experienced anything besides the enormous lake in
78	Chicago. He mistakenly believed that the lake and the ocean were
89	the same in terms of power. When Mark's aunt told him to be
102	careful, he laughed and assured her that he was an excellent
113	swimmer. She cautioned him that the ocean was rough and
123	perilous, but Mark just shrugged. He knew how to surf, didn't he?
135	Mark heard the gigantic wave before he saw it. He turned
146	around and opened his mouth in horror. The wave was mammoth,
157	and it was thundering directly toward him. Mark took a deep
168	breath and cringed beneath the water. The wave crashed over him
179	and carried him high onto shore. Mark gained a new respect for the
192	ocean after that. 195

Number of words read: _____   **Number of errors made:** _____

Inspiration

You win an award. You walk proudly onto the stage. You make a speech. You give the audience an idea of where you got your ideas. You talk about the people who helped you. You also tell where you got your inspiration.

A young Amelia Earhart attended a World's Fair where she saw an airplane fly high above her. Amelia always referred to that day as the start of her journey to become a pilot. In the same way, many writers will remember the first book that gripped their hearts. Sports stars can tell you everything about the first game they attended. Film directors remember every scene of the movie that made them buy their first camera.

This is the way many young people get an idea of what profession they would like to pursue. What has inspired you? Have you seen, read, or heard about anything that has given you ideas for your lifelong career? Have you met someone who has truly inspired you? You may have already made a decision about your future. If not, you can start to think about it!

1. What is this passage mostly about?

2. According to this passage, what are some things that inspire people?

Oral Fluency Record Sheet

Name _____ Date _____

Oral Reading Accuracy: _____%

Oral Reading Fluency Score: _____ words correct per minute

Circle: Fall Winter Spring

Prosody Rubric: (Circle Score) 1 2 3 4

Comprehension Question Responses

#1 _____

#2 _____

Inspiration

	You win an award. You walk proudly onto the stage. You
11	make a speech. You give the audience an idea of where you got
24	your ideas. You talk about the people who helped you. You also
36	tell where you got your inspiration.
42	A young Amelia Earhart attended a World's Fair where
51	she saw an airplane fly high above her. Amelia always referred
62	to that day as the start of her journey to become a pilot. In the
77	same way, many writers will remember the first book that
87	gripped their hearts. Sports stars can tell you everything about
97	the first game they attended. Film directors remember every
106	scene of the movie that made them buy their first camera.
117	This is the way many young people get an idea of what
129	profession they would like to pursue. What has inspired you?
139	Have you seen, read, or heard about anything that has given you
151	ideas for your lifelong career? Have you met someone who has
162	truly inspired you? You may have already made a decision about
173	your future. If not, you can start to think about it! 184

Number of words read: _____ Number of errors made: _____

Name _____   Date _____

Moons

Many years ago, Native Americans did not have calendars
to tell them what month or day it was. Instead, they had the moon.
By keeping track of the time it took for the moon to go from one
full moon phase to the next, they measured their days.

Each phase was called a moon, and each moon was about the
length of a month. They noted how cold the winds were and what
the Earth looked like around them. They observed what color
the rabbits' fur was, and if choke cherries were on the bushes.
Then they named that moon phase for what they saw and felt.

March might be the Moon of the Long Rains to a Native
American living in the Northeast. To a Native American in a dry
climate, March might be the Moon of the Desert Blooms. Moons
could also be named after feasts and ceremonies, such as the
moon of Summer Encampment. Children learned about the moons
from their elders, and looked forward to what each new moon
would bring.

1. How did Native Americans keep track of what month or day it was?

2. How did Native Americans decide what to name a moon phase?

Oral Fluency Record Sheet

Name _____ Date _____

Oral Reading Accuracy: _____%   Circle: Fall Winter Spring

Oral Reading Fluency Score: _____ words correct per minute

Prosody Rubric: (Circle Score) 1 2 3 4

Comprehension Question Responses

#1 _____

#2 _____

Moons

9	Many years ago, Native Americans did not have calendars to tell them what month or day it was. Instead, they had the moon.
23	By keeping track of the time it took for the moon to go from one
38	full moon phase to the next, they measured their days.
48	Each phase was called a moon, and each moon was about the
60	length of a month. They noted how cold the winds were and what
73	the Earth looked like around them. They observed what color
83	the rabbits' fur was, and if choke cherries were on the bushes.
95	Then they named that moon phase for what they saw and felt.
107	March might be the Moon of the Long Rains to a Native
119	American living in the Northeast. To a Native American in a dry
131	climate, March might be the Moon of the Desert Blooms. Moons
142	could also be named after feasts and ceremonies, such as the
153	moon of Summer Encampment. Children learned about the moons
162	from their elders, and looked forward to what each new moon
173	would bring. **175**

Number of words read: _____   **Number of errors made:** _____

Fingers and Toes

Lauren's dad told her she had to spend the weekend with her grandmother. Lauren had just moved to Kansas. She did not know her grandmother very well. She was worried she would be bored. She also worried that she would say or do something wrong. And she worried that her grandmother would be too busy to spend time with her.

Lauren was happily surprised. As soon as she arrived, Grandma asked what she wanted for lunch. Lauren asked for grilled cheese sandwiches. Grandma smiled and pulled out an old-fashioned grill. Lauren had never seen anything like it. Her dad made the sandwiches in a regular pan. Grandma also fixed a fresh fruit salad. The two had a good time eating and talking.

That night after a delicious omelet dinner, Granny asked Lauren what else she wanted to do. Lauren decided to be daring. She asked if they could paint their fingers and toes with nail polish. Granny smiled and left the living room. She came back with four different colors of nail polish. There was pink, orange, light red, and dark red. Lauren picked orange. By bedtime, she and Grandma had very interesting-looking fingers and toes!

1. How would you describe Grandma?
2. How did Lauren's feelings change during the story?

Oral Fluency Record Sheet

Name _____ Date _____

Oral Reading Accuracy: _____%   Circle: Fall Winter Spring

Oral Reading Fluency Score: _____ words correct per minute

Prosody Rubric: (Circle Score) 1 2 3 4

Comprehension Question Responses

#1 _____

#2 _____

Fingers and Toes

	Lauren's dad told her she had to spend the weekend with
11	her grandmother. Lauren had just moved to Kansas. She did not
22	know her grandmother very well. She was worried she would be
33	bored. She also worried that she would say or do something wrong.
45	And she worried that her grandmother would be too busy to spend
57	time with her.
60	Lauren was happily surprised. As soon as she arrived,
69	Grandma asked what she wanted for lunch. Lauren asked for
79	grilled cheese sandwiches. Grandma smiled and pulled out an old-
89	fashioned grill. Lauren had never seen anything like it. Her dad
100	made the sandwiches in a regular pan. Grandma also fixed a fresh
112	fruit salad. The two had a good time eating and talking.
123	That night after a delicious omelet dinner, Granny asked
132	Lauren what else she wanted to do. Lauren decided to be daring.
144	She asked if they could paint their fingers and toes with nail polish.
157	Granny smiled and left the living room. She came back with four
169	different colors of nail polish. There was pink, orange, light red,
180	and dark red. Lauren picked orange. By bedtime, she and Grandma
191	had very interesting-looking fingers and toes! 198

Number of words read: _____   Number of errors made: _____

A New Home

Anna could not sleep. It was her last night in Aunt Cara's house. Her sister slept quietly near her in her crib. Tomorrow was moving day. Life was about to change.

Mom and Dad had good jobs now. They just rented their own house near a playground. The new house had a big bedroom for Anna's parents. It had a smaller one for Anna. It even had a tiny room for the baby. Anna and her dad planned to make the backyard beautiful. They would weed it. Then they would plant some colorful flowers.

It all sounded better than living with Aunt Cara. Aunt Cara's house was small. Everyone felt crowded. People got grumpy all of the time.

"But I will miss Aunt Cara," thought Anna. Every evening she and Anna read together. They used to read picture books. Now they were reading a chapter book about two sisters and two brothers. The girl named Randy was Anna's favorite character.

Suddenly Anna thought about the book. Randy's family moved, too. At first, Randy missed her old house. Later on, she loved the new one. Aunt Cara would not be far away. She would still see her often. Thinking of this, Anna fell asleep.

1. Why would the new house be an improvement?
2. Why would Anna miss Aunt Cara?

Oral Fluency Record Sheet

Name _____   Date _____

Oral Reading Accuracy: _____%   Circle: Fall Winter Spring
Oral Reading Fluency Score: _____ words correct per minute
Prosody Rubric: (Circle Score) 1 2 3 4
Comprehension Question Responses
#1 _____
#2 _____

A New Home

	Anna could not sleep. It was her last night in Aunt Cara's
12	house. Her sister slept quietly near her in her crib. Tomorrow was
24	moving day. Life was about to change.
31	Mom and Dad had good jobs now. They just rented their
42	own house near a playground. The new house had a big bedroom
54	for Anna's parents. It had a smaller one for Anna. It even had a tiny
69	room for the baby. Anna and her dad planned to make the
81	backyard beautiful. They would weed it. Then they would plant
91	some colorful flowers.
94	It all sounded better than living with Aunt Cara. Aunt Cara's
105	house was small. Everyone felt crowded. People got grumpy
114	all of the time.
118	"But I will miss Aunt Cara," thought Anna. Every evening
128	she and Anna read together. They used to read picture books. Now
140	they were reading a chapter book about two sisters and two
151	brothers. The girl named Randy was Anna's favorite character.
160	Suddenly Anna thought about the book. Randy's family
168	moved, too. At first, Randy missed her old house. Later on, she
180	loved the new one. Aunt Cara would not be far away. She would
193	still see her often. Thinking of this, Anna fell asleep. **203**

Number of words read: _____   Number of errors made: _____

Backyard Memorial

A memorial is a lasting reminder of someone or something important from the past. Most people think of something like the Lincoln Memorial when they hear the word. But memorials do not have to be for national heroes or events only.

For example, my friend has a pear tree in his backyard. My friend planted the tree in memory of his father. The pears get ripe in the summer. My friend gives the pears to neighbors on the street. Each time we eat one of those pears, we think fondly of his father. The pear tree is his father's memorial.

In another neighbor's kitchen sits a photograph of her mother. Two candles stand in front of her mother's picture. My neighbor lights these candles every evening. The photo and the candles are a miniature memorial.

In my backyard is a small stone painted white. Underneath lies my old pet hamster. Each time I see the stone, I think of Tootsie and what a good companion she was. Though it is a memorial to a hamster, it is still a memorial. Whatever makes you stop and remember can be called a memorial.

1. What is a memorial?
2. Why aren't memorials just for national heroes?

Oral Fluency Record Sheet

Name _____   Date _____

Oral Reading Accuracy: _____%   Circle: Fall Winter Spring
tOral Reading Fluency Score: _____ words correct per minute
Prosody Rubric: (Circle Score) 1 2 3 4
Comprehension Question Responses
#1 _____
#2 _____

Backyard Memorial

	A memorial is a lasting reminder of someone or
9	something important from the past. Most people think of
18	something like the Lincoln Memorial when they hear the
27	word. But memorials do not have to be for national heroes
38	or events only.
41	For example, my friend has a pear tree in his backyard. My
53	friend planted the tree in memory of his father. The pears get ripe
66	in the summer. My friend gives the pears to neighbors on the
78	street. Each time we eat one of those pears, we think fondly of his
92	father. The pear tree is his father's memorial.
100	In another neighbor's kitchen sits a photograph of her mother.
110	Two candles stand in front of her mother's picture. My
120	neighbor lights these candles every evening. The photo and the
130	candles are a miniature memorial.
135	In my backyard is a small stone painted white. Underneath
145	lies my old pet hamster. Each time I see the stone, I think of
159	Tootsie and what a good companion she was. Though it is a
171	memorial to a hamster, it is still a memorial. Whatever makes
182	you stop and remember can be called a memorial. 191

Number of words read: _____   Number of errors made: _____

Name _____ Date _____

Without a Trace

Life on the open seas can be very risky. You never know what may lie ahead when you set sail. A calm sea can turn dark and stormy without much warning. Occasionally, ships are found abandoned with no sign of life. Others sink after catastrophic accidents and debris from these ships later floats to the surface. Still others have vanished without a trace. With these ships, not even a plank of wood or a lifejacket is ever found.

The British ship *Waratah* weighed 16,800 tons. It was last spotted on July 27, 1909. Some said the ship seemed top-heavy, when trying to explain her disappearance. This might have caused her to turn over and sink in heavy seas. There were 211 people on board, none of whom were ever found.

The mystery of the missing *Cyclops* is also disturbing. This American ship, weighing 19,000 tons, was last heard from in March 1918, on her way from the West Indies to the port of Baltimore, Maryland. Our Navy has never found a sign of the missing ship or the 309 passengers she had on board, and the file on this missing ship is still open.

1. To what does the title "Without a Trace" refer?
2. What might have caused the *Waratah* to sink?

Oral Fluency Record Sheet

Name _____ Date _____

Oral Reading Accuracy: _____%   Circle: Fall Winter Spring

Oral Reading Fluency Score: _____ words correct per minute

Prosody Rubric: (Circle Score) 1 2 3 4

Comprehension Question Responses

#1 _____

#2 _____

Without a Trace

	Life on the open seas can be very risky. You never know
12	what may lie ahead when you set sail. A calm sea can turn dark
26	and stormy without much warning. Occasionally, ships are found
35	abandoned with no sign of life. Others sink after catastrophic
45	accidents and debris from these ships later floats to the surface.
56	Still others have vanished without a trace. With these ships, not
67	even a plank of wood or a lifejacket is ever found.
78	The British ship *Waratah* weighed 16,800 tons. It was
87	last spotted on July 27, 1909. Some said the ship seemed top-
99	heavy, when trying to explain her disappearance. This might
108	have caused her to turn over and sink in heavy seas. There were
121	211 people on board, none of whom were ever found.
131	The mystery of the missing *Cyclops* is also disturbing.
140	This American ship, weighing 19,000 tons, was last heard from
150	in March 1918, on her way from the West Indies to the port of
164	Baltimore, Maryland. Our Navy has never found a sign of the
175	missing ship or the 309 passengers she had on board, and the
187	file on this missing ship is still open. 195

Number of words read: _____   Number of errors made: _____

Before and Now

You do not have to be Columbus to be interested
in traveling to new places. Many people living today are just
as curious as Columbus once was. These brave people leave
their beloved homelands behind and move to new countries
to live. These people are called *immigrants,* and they show
extraordinary courage! Try to imagine leaving everything
you know and love behind, and moving to a place you have
never even seen before. Perhaps your parents or grandparents
did just that. Maybe you are an immigrant yourself.

But what about the countries left behind? What did
they look like? If you know any immigrants, ask them if they
have any old photographs you can look at. What would you
see in those photos? What would the automobiles look like,
the buildings, even the clothes the people wore? What would
these things tell you about the other place the person had
lived? If you do not know anyone who has moved to this
country, or you do not have any photos to look at, you can
go to your local library. Look up travel books and videos.
If you are extremely lucky, you may know someone who
kept a diary or journal describing what life was like where
he or she came from. This type of keepsake will help bring
the old country and the new one together.

1. What is this passage mostly about?

2. Why might people move to a new country?

Oral Fluency Record Sheet

Name _____ Date _____

Oral Reading Accuracy: _____%   Circle: Fall Winter Spring

Oral Reading Fluency Score: _____ words correct per minute

Prosody Rubric: (Circle Score) 1 2 3 4

Comprehension Question Responses

#1 _____

#2 _____

Before and Now

	You do not have to be Columbus to be interested
10	in traveling to new places. Many people living today are just
21	as curious as Columbus once was. These brave people leave
31	their beloved homelands behind and move to new countries
40	to live. These people are called *immigrants*, and they show
50	extraordinary courage! Try to imagine leaving everything
57	you know and love behind, and moving to a place you have
69	never even seen before. Perhaps your parents or grandparents
78	did just that. Maybe you are an immigrant yourself.
87	But what about the countries left behind? What did
96	they look like? If you know any immigrants, ask them if they
108	have any old photographs you can look at. What would you
119	see in those photos? What would the automobiles look like,
129	the buildings, even the clothes the people wore? What would
139	these things tell you about the other place the person had
150	lived? If you do not know anyone who has moved to this
162	country, or you do not have any photos to look at, you can
175	go to your local library. Look up travel books and videos.
186	If you are extremely lucky, you may know someone who
196	kept a diary or journal describing what life was like where
207	he or she came from. This type of keepsake will help bring
219	the old country and the new one together. **227**

© Macmillan/McGraw-Hill

Number of words read: _____ Number of errors made: _____

Name _____ Date _____

Why Winter Comes

Centuries ago, people noticed that Earth was warm
and green some of the time and bitter cold at other times.
This was a cycle that repeated itself over and over. To explain
these changes, ancient people told stories. There were myths
to explain just about every cycle in nature. Some stories
explained why the sun disappeared each night and reappeared
each morning. Other myths told what caused the moon to
wax and wane.

Why winter arrived each year is explained in one myth about
a Greek goddess named Demeter. The myth said that Demeter
had a beautiful daughter named Persephone. Hades, the god of
the underworld, snatched Persephone and brought her to his
kingdom. Demeter was so depressed by her daughter's sudden
disappearance that she caused Earth to become cold and
barren. Nothing grew during the time that Persephone was
in the underworld.

Demeter begged Hades to return her daughter. Eventually,
Hades gave in and allowed the girl to return to her
mother. But Demeter had to promise that Persephone would spend
part of every year with him. When she saw Persephone again,
Demeter was overjoyed, and she allowed plants to grow again.

This was an early explanation of why winter arrived each
year. Winter was the time that Persephone had to go back to
the underworld.

1. What is the author's purpose for writing this passage?

2. According to this myth, what causes winter?

Oral Fluency Record Sheet

Name _____ Date _____

Oral Reading Accuracy: _____%   Circle: Fall Winter Spring
Oral Reading Fluency Score: _____ words correct per minute
Prosody Rubric: (Circle Score) 1 2 3 4
Comprehension Question Responses
#1 _____
#2 _____

Why Winter Comes

8	Centuries ago, people noticed that Earth was warm
20	and green some of the time and bitter cold at other times.
32	This was a cycle that repeated itself over and over. To explain
41	these changes, ancient people told stories. There were myths
51	to explain just about every cycle in nature. Some stories
60	explained why the sun disappeared each night and reappeared
70	each morning. Other myths told what caused the moon to
73	wax and wane.
84	Why winter arrived each year is explained in one myth about
94	a Greek goddess named Demeter. The myth said that Demeter
104	had a beautiful daughter named Persephone. Hades, the god of
113	the underworld, snatched Persephone and brought her to his
122	kingdom. Demeter was so depressed by her daughter's sudden
131	disappearance that she caused Earth to become cold and
140	barren. Nothing grew during the time that Persephone was
143	in the underworld.
151	Demeter begged Hades to return her daughter. Eventually,
162	Hades gave in and allowed the girl to return to her
172	mother. But Demeter had to promise that Persephone would spend
183	part of every year with him. When she saw Persephone again,
193	Demeter was overjoyed, and she allowed plants to grow again.
203	This was an early explanation of why winter arrived each
215	year. Winter was the time that Persephone had to go back to
	the underworld. **217**

© Macmillan/McGraw-Hill

Number of words read: _____   Number of errors made: _____

Hometown Hero

What makes a hero? This question can be answered in many ways. Courage in the face of danger is one attribute. Unselfish leadership for the good of the community is another. Yet there are many heroes who never face danger and cannot be called leaders.

These noble people go about their lives helping others for no reward other than knowing it is the right thing to do. They do not take a day off and they put their own needs last. Unfortunately, their heroic actions are mostly unnoticed. Maybe there is a hero like this living in your house.

What makes people do heroic things? The heroes that we study in school often found themselves in history-making situations. Courage in wartime is an example. Other people are natural leaders who inspire their followers to make important changes in society.

Perhaps at this time in your life, you have not met any heroes. If not, try to be one in your own life each day. Put the needs of others first. Be kind and helpful to your friends and family. It is not easy to be a hero, but it is a daily possibility.

---

1. What is "Hometown Hero" mostly about?

2. What can you do in your daily life to become a hero?

Oral Fluency Record Sheet

Name _____ Date _____

Oral Reading Accuracy: _____% Circle: Fall Winter Spring
Oral Reading Fluency Score: _____ words correct per minute
Prosody Rubric: (Circle Score) 1 2 3 4
Comprehension Question Responses
#1 _____
#2 _____

Hometown Hero

	What makes a hero? This question can be answered in
10	many ways. Courage in the face of danger is one attribute.
21	Unselfish leadership for the good of the community is another.
31	Yet there are many heroes who never face danger and
44	cannot be called leaders.
45	These noble people go about their lives helping others
54	for no reward other than knowing it is the right thing to do. They
68	do not take a day off and they put their own needs last.
81	Unfortunately, their heroic actions are mostly unnoticed. Maybe
89	there is a hero like this living in your house.
99	What makes people do heroic things? The heroes that we
109	study in school often found themselves in history-making
118	situations. Courage in wartime is an example. Other people are
128	natural leaders who inspire their followers to make important
137	changes in society.
140	Perhaps at this time in your life, you have not met any
152	heroes. If not, try to be one in your own life each day. Put the
167	needs of others first. Be kind and helpful to your friends and
179	family. It is not easy to be a hero, but it is a daily possibility. 194

Number of words read: _____ Number of errors made: _____

Perfect Preservation

A hard, transparent lump of amber sells for over $20,000. Its gold coloring is pretty but why does it sell for so much? Take a closer look, and you will see the reason. A 30-million-year-old lizard is trapped inside the lump.

Amber is fossilized resin. It is sap from ancient trees. Over millions of years, the sap has turned rock hard. It is golden brown and beautiful. It is also hard to damage. That is why artists use it to make jewelry. Some amber pieces contain items such as leaves, insects, or reptiles. These once living things were trapped in the sap millions of years ago. When the sap hardened, the objects were preserved.

Picture a tree trunk sticky with resin. An insect lands on the sticky trunk. The unlucky bug tries to get free, but its feet are glued to the tree. Another flow of resin moves down the tree. This time the sap covers the bug all over. Over millions of years the resin slowly turns to amber. Inside the amber case, the insect's body dries out. Although it is long dead, the bug looks just like it did when it was alive.

1. What is the passage mostly about?
2. What is amber?

Oral Fluency Record Sheet

Name _____   Date _____

Oral Reading Accuracy: _____%   Circle: Fall Winter Spring

Oral Reading Fluency Score: _____ words correct per minute

Prosody Rubric: (Circle Score) 1 2 3 4

Comprehension Question Responses

#1 _____

#2 _____

Perfect Preservation

	A hard, transparent lump of amber sells for over $20,000.
10	Its gold coloring is pretty but why does it sell for so much? Take
24	a closer look, and you will see the reason. A 30-million-year-old
38	lizard is trapped inside the lump.
44	Amber is fossilized resin. It is sap from ancient trees.
54	Over millions of years, the sap has turned rock hard. It is golden
67	brown and beautiful. It is also hard to damage. That is why artists
80	use it to make jewelry. Some amber pieces contain items such
91	as leaves, insects, or reptiles. These once living things were
101	trapped in the sap millions of years ago. When the sap hardened,
113	the objects were preserved.
117	Picture a tree trunk sticky with resin. An insect lands on
128	the sticky trunk. The unlucky bug tries to get free, but its feet are
142	glued to the tree. Another flow of resin moves down the tree.
154	This time the sap covers the bug all over. Over millions of years
167	the resin slowly turns to amber. Inside the amber case, the
178	insect's body dries out. Although it is long dead, the bug looks
190	just like it did when it was alive. **198**

Number of words read: _____   Number of errors made: _____

New Pathways

If you cannot get from one place to another, maybe you
need a bridge, tunnel, or road. A person trained as a special kind
of engineer can help you. Civil engineers design and construct
highways, harbors, bridges, and tunnels. These engineers have
specialized training in physics and math. Frequently, they are also
talented architects.

Most people think of bridges as structures that cross
waterways. But bridges have been built to go across wide spaces
as well. Centuries ago, bridges were usually made of wood
and rope. They were built to help people cross deep canyons between
mountains. Now bridges are often constructed in large cities.
They allow people to cross between buildings and tall skyscrapers.
Engineers build bridges primarily for cars, trucks, and trains.
Sometimes several levels are built, one for cars and trucks and
one for trains. Cars and trucks may be routed through different
levels. But what about people? They deserve a pathway across
a bridge, too. People like to stroll, ride bikes, and even jog
across bridges. Many bridges now have designated pathways
just for people without automobiles.

Civil engineers also build tunnels. Recently, a tunnel
was built beneath the English Channel that connects England
and France. For the first time in history, people can drive their
automobiles from the United Kingdom to the mainland of Europe.

1. What are bridges used for?

2. Why do bridges need special pathways?

Oral Fluency Record Sheet

Name _____ Date _____

Oral Reading Accuracy: _____% Circle: Fall Winter Spring

Oral Reading Fluency Score: _____ words correct per minute

Prosody Rubric: (Circle Score) 1 2 3 4

Comprehension Question Responses

#1 _____

#2 _____

New Pathways

	If you cannot get from one place to another, maybe you
11	need a bridge, tunnel, or road. A person trained as a special kind
24	of engineer can help you. Civil engineers design and construct
34	highways, harbors, bridges, and tunnels. These engineers have
42	specialized training in physics and math. Frequently, they are also
52	talented architects.
54	Most people think of bridges as structures that cross
63	waterways. But bridges have been built to go across wide spaces
74	as well. Centuries ago, bridges were usually made of wood
84	and rope. They were built to help people cross deep canyons between
96	mountains. Now bridges are often constructed in large cities.
105	They allow people to cross between buildings and tall skyscrapers.
115	Engineers build bridges primarily for cars, trucks, and trains.
124	Sometimes several levels are built, one for cars and trucks and
135	one for trains. Cars and trucks may be routed through different
146	levels. But what about people? They deserve a pathway across
156	a bridge, too. People like to stroll, ride bikes, and even jog
168	across bridges. Many bridges now have designated pathways
176	just for people without automobiles.
181	Civil engineers also build tunnels. Recently, a tunnel
189	was built beneath the English Channel that connects England
198	and France. For the first time in history, people can drive their
210	automobiles from the United Kingdom to the mainland of Europe. **220**

Number of words read: _____ Number of errors made: _____

Special Eyes

Tim and his family are raising a special puppy named Luke. Luke is a German shepherd. He was born at the guide dog center. With his three brothers and sisters, he will become a guide dog. He will learn how to help blind people.

Guide dogs help blind people cross busy streets. They help them walk inside stores and buy groceries. They help them in restaurants and on buses.

Luke's brothers and sisters are named Lark, Lisa, and Len. Why do all the names begin with the same letter? It helps the center keep track of Luke and the group.

Luke will grow up with Tim and his family. He will learn about riding in cars and living with people. When he is fourteen months old, he will go back to the center. There he will learn to obey commands. He will learn words such as "left," "right," and "sit." He will also learn to keep his mind on his work. Most dogs are distracted by sounds, smells, and other animals. Luke will learn to concentrate on leading his partner.

At Luke's graduation, Tim will meet Luke's new partner. Tim will be sad to say good-bye. But he will be happy for Luke. Luke will be a loving helper. His eyes will become special eyes for someone who needs him.

1. What is the role of Tim and his family in Luke's life?

2. What is a guide dog's job mostly about?

Oral Fluency Record Sheet

Name _____ Date _____

Oral Reading Accuracy: _____%   Circle: **Fall Winter Spring**

Oral Reading Fluency Score: _____ words correct per minute

Prosody Rubric: (Circle Score) 1 2 3 4

Comprehension Question Responses

#1 _____

#2 _____

Special Eyes

	Tim and his family are raising a special puppy named
10	Luke. Luke is a German shepherd. He was born at the guide dog
23	center. With his three brothers and sisters, he will become a
34	guide dog. He will learn how to help blind people.
44	Guide dogs help blind people cross busy streets. They
53	help them walk inside stores and buy groceries. They help them
64	in restaurants and on buses.
69	Luke's brothers and sisters are named Lark, Lisa, and Len.
79	Why do all the names begin with the same letter? It helps the
92	center keep track of Luke and the group.
100	Luke will grow up with Tim and his family. He will learn
112	about riding in cars and living with people. When he is fourteen
124	months old, he will go back to the center. There he will learn to
138	obey commands. He will learn words such as "left," "right," and
149	"sit." He will also learn to keep his mind on his work. Most dogs
163	are distracted by sounds, smells, and other animals. Luke will
173	learn to concentrate on leading his partner.
180	At Luke's graduation, Tim will meet Luke's new partner.
189	Tim will be sad to say good-bye. But he will be happy for Luke.
204	Luke will be a loving helper. His eyes will become special eyes
216	for someone who needs him. **221**

Number of words read: _____ **Number of errors made:** _____

Natural Protection

Most crabs have hard shells. Their shells protect them like suits of armor. When a crab's shell gets too tight, it pulls itself out. Under the old shell, a new one has already grown.

A hermit crab has hard front claws, but it has a soft shell in back. For protection, a hermit crab moves into another creature's shell. For example, after a sea snail dies, the empty shell it leaves behind makes a perfect home for a hermit crab. The crab squeezes right into the shape of the snail's shell. The crab's head, legs, and pincers poke out of the opening. When it grows too large in this borrowed shell, it finds a larger one. Leaving the old shell behind, it moves into a new one.

A hermit crab's shell may not always protect it. If an octopus comes along, for instance, it can stick one of its eight arms into the shell's opening. Then it can pluck the crab out. Some hermit crabs have extra protection. They have creatures called sea anemones sticking to the outsides of their shells. Anemones have many tentacles. Their tentacles have stinging cells. An octopus may not even approach a hermit crab's home when a stinging watchdog guards it.

1. Why is a crab's shell like a suit of armor?

2. What extra protection does a hermit crab have?

Oral Fluency Record Sheet

Name _____ Date _____

Oral Reading Accuracy: _____%   Circle: Fall Winter Spring
Oral Reading Fluency Score: _____ words correct per minute
Prosody Rubric: (Circle Score) 1 2 3 4
Comprehension Question Responses
#1 _____
#2 _____

Natural Protection

	Most crabs have hard shells. Their shells protect them
9	like suits of armor. When a crab's shell gets too tight, it pulls
22	itself out. Under the old shell, a new one has already grown.
34	A hermit crab has hard front claws, but it has a soft shell
47	in back. For protection, a hermit crab moves into another
57	creature's shell. For example, after a sea snail dies, the empty
68	shell it leaves behind makes a perfect home for a hermit crab.
80	The crab squeezes right into the shape of the snail's shell. The
92	crab's head, legs, and pincers poke out of the opening. When it
104	grows too large in this borrowed shell, it finds a larger one.
116	Leaving the old shell behind, it moves into a new one.
127	A hermit crab's shell may not always protect it. If an
138	octopus comes along, for instance, it can stick one of its eight
150	arms into the shell's opening. Then it can pluck the crab out.
162	Some hermit crabs have extra protection. They have creatures
171	called sea anemones sticking to the outsides of their shells.
181	Anemones have many tentacles. Their tentacles have stinging
189	cells. An octopus may not even approach a hermit crab's home
200	when a stinging watchdog guards it. **206**

Number of words read: _____ Number of errors made: _____

Manatees

Manatees are slow, gentle mammals that live in water.
Some people call them sea cows. They breathe air and can stay
underwater for 20 minutes at a time. Usually, though, they come
up for air every five minutes or so.

An adult manatee has gray skin. It is about 10 feet long and
weighs up to 1,800 pounds. The manatee is related to the elephant
but is shaped more like a walrus. It has a flat tail and two flippers.
It also has a box-shaped snout with whiskers.

Manatees live near coastlines or in rivers in warm, shallow
water. Many live in South America and spend winters in Florida.
They eat water plants. An adult can eat up to 150 pounds of food a
day. This is very hard on its teeth. Manatees grow new teeth when
their old ones wear out.

It is important for manatees to have many babies because
they are endangered. They have no animal predators, but people
like to hunt them. A female manatee is pregnant for one year. Then
she gives birth to just one baby. Baby manatees are called calves.
The calf is about 3 feet long at birth and weighs 60 pounds. That is
bigger than most six-year-old children!

1. How often do manatees come up for air?

2. Why are manatees endangered?

Oral Fluency Record Sheet

Name _____ Date _____

Oral Reading Accuracy: _____%   Circle: Fall Winter Spring

Oral Reading Fluency Score: _____ words correct per minute

Prosody Rubric: (Circle Score) 1 2 3 4

Comprehension Question Responses

#1 _____

#2 _____

Manatees

	Manatees are slow, gentle mammals that live in water.
9	Some people call them sea cows. They breathe air and can stay
21	underwater for 20 minutes at a time. Usually, though, they come
32	up for air every five minutes or so.
40	An adult manatee has gray skin. It is about 10 feet long and
53	weighs up to 1,800 pounds. The manatee is related to the elephant
65	but is shaped more like a walrus. It has a flat tail and two flippers.
80	It also has a box-shaped snout with whiskers.
89	Manatees live near coastlines or in rivers in warm, shallow
99	water. Many live in South America and spend winters in Florida.
110	They eat water plants. An adult can eat up to 150 pounds of food a
125	day. This is very hard on its teeth. Manatees grow new teeth when
138	their old ones wear out.
143	It is important for manatees to have many babies because
153	they are endangered. They have no animal predators, but people
163	like to hunt them. A female manatee is pregnant for one year. Then
176	she gives birth to just one baby. Baby manatees are called calves.
188	The calf is about 3 feet long at birth and weighs 60 pounds. That is
203	bigger than most six-year-old children! **210**

Number of words read: _____   Number of errors made: _____

A Question of Time

Jason used to spend Saturday afternoons with his Uncle Robert. His parents both worked in a restaurant downtown, and on Saturdays they were busy all day long.

Then a few weeks ago, Uncle Robert told Jason that he had become a volunteer at an organization called Second Harvest. This was a place where local restaurants gave away food they didn't use. The volunteers packed up the food, and then they distributed it to people who needed it.

"You're a big kid now," said Uncle Robert. "You can stay with your cousins on Saturdays. Instead, I will see you on the weekdays."

"But I want to go to the museum with you, and baseball games, and movies. Why do you have to ruin our Saturdays packing fruit?" Jason whined.

"Your dad worked on this with the city council. He hates throwing away perfectly edible food. It is a good program, and I want to get involved."

"My dad set it up?" Jason asked. He was surprised. His parents had not told him anything about it.

"Yes. Your mom helped, too," said Uncle Robert. "It's a family thing."

"Well, if it's a family thing, then I should be there," said Jason. "I can spend time with you, be a part of my parents' program, and help people, all at the same time!"

---

1. What did Jason like to do with his uncle on Saturdays?

2. Why did Jason change his mind about the food program?

Oral Fluency Record Sheet

Name _____ Date _____

Oral Reading Accuracy: _____%   Circle: Fall Winter Spring

Oral Reading Fluency Score: _____ words correct per minute

Prosody Rubric: (Circle Score) 1 2 3 4

Comprehension Question Responses

#1 _____

#2 _____

A Question of Time

	Jason used to spend Saturday afternoons with his Uncle
9	Robert. His parents both worked in a restaurant downtown, and on
20	Saturdays they were busy all day long.
27	Then a few weeks ago, Uncle Robert told Jason that he had
39	become a volunteer at an organization called Second Harvest. This
49	was a place where local restaurants gave away food they didn't use.
61	The volunteers packed up the food, and then they distributed it to
73	people who needed it.
77	"You're a big kid now," said Uncle Robert. "You can stay
88	with your cousins on Saturdays. Instead, I will see you on
99	the weekdays."
101	"But I want to go to the museum with you, and baseball
113	games, and movies. Why do you have to ruin our Saturdays
124	packing fruit?" Jason whined.
128	"Your dad worked on this with the city council. He hates
139	throwing away perfectly edible food. It is a good program, and I
151	want to get involved."
155	"My dad set it up?" Jason asked. He was surprised. His
166	parents had not told him anything about it.
174	"Yes. Your mom helped, too," said Uncle Robert. "It's a
184	family thing."
186	"Well, if it's a family thing, then I should be there," said
198	Jason. "I can spend time with you, be a part of my parents'
211	program, and help people, all at the same time!" **220**

Number of words read: _____ Number of errors made: _____

Name _____ Date _____

The Soldier

Marisa had a social studies project due first thing Monday morning. Her class was studying the lives of interesting people in modern history. Her teacher said that there were people who had lived through interesting events all around them.

Marisa moaned to her grandmother, "I have to write a composition. I have to interview somebody about his or her life. But this town is so boring. I can't think of anyone who has ever done anything interesting."

Her grandmother smiled. "Everybody has a story to tell," she said. "You just have to ask."

Marisa stared blankly at her grandmother. She had never seen Grandma do anything interesting. But she had never asked Grandma questions about her life either. Grandma had lived with the family for as long as Marisa could recall. She bought food, fixed lunches, and cleaned up around the house. But Marisa didn't know much about what Grandma did before she came to live with the family.

"Tell me about your life before you got married," said Marisa.

"Well," said Grandma, "I was a soldier."

Grandmother, a soldier? Could it be true? Suddenly, Marisa saw Grandma in an entirely new light. "Where were you a soldier? Did you wear a uniform?" Marisa began firing questions.

"Just get a pencil and paper and prepare yourself for a fascinating story," said Grandma.

1. In what way did Grandma surprise Marisa?

2. What lesson do you think Marisa learned by doing this project?

Oral Fluency Record Sheet

Name _____   Date _____

Oral Reading Accuracy: _____%   Circle: Fall Winter Spring

Oral Reading Fluency Score: _____ words correct per minute

Prosody Rubric: (Circle Score) 1 2 3 4

Comprehension Question Responses

#1 _____

#2 _____

The Soldier

	Marisa had a social studies project due first thing Monday
10	morning. Her class was studying the lives of interesting people in
21	modern history. Her teacher said that there were people who had
32	lived through interesting events all around them.
39	Marisa moaned to her grandmother, "I have to write a
49	composition. I have to interview somebody about his or her life.
60	But this town is so boring. I can't think of anyone who has ever
74	done anything interesting."
77	Her grandmother smiled. "Everybody has a story to tell,"
86	she said. "You just have to ask."
93	Marisa stared blankly at her grandmother. She had never
102	seen Grandma do anything interesting. But she had never asked
112	Grandma questions about her life either. Grandma had lived with
122	the family for as long as Marisa could recall. She bought food,
134	fixed lunches, and cleaned up around the house. But Marisa didn't
145	know much about what Grandma did before she came to live with
157	the family.
159	"Tell me about your life before you got married,"
168	said Marisa.
170	"Well," said Grandma, "I was a soldier."
177	Grandmother, a soldier? Could it be true? Suddenly, Marisa
186	saw Grandma in an entirely new light. "Where were you a soldier?
198	Did you wear a uniform?" Marisa began firing questions.
207	"Just get a pencil and paper and prepare yourself for a
218	fascinating story," said Grandma. **222**

© Macmillan/McGraw-Hill

Number of words read: _____   Number of errors made: _____

Dolphins at Play

One time, a young boy fell from a fishing boat. A dolphin happened to be nearby. It was surfing the waves made by the boat as it moved through the water. When the boy splashed into the sea, the dolphin's nose was right there. The dolphin scooped him up and tossed him into the air. The boy landed in his father's arms.

Similar stories about dolphins are heard everywhere. That is why many scientists study these animals. Some scientists think that when dolphins save people, it is not because they love them. It is because dolphins are playful. Dolphins love to play with toys, such as balls and hoops. For fun, they sometimes tow large objects, such as mattresses, to shore. Scientists think dolphins that save drowning people are really just playing with them, as if they were toys.

Dolphins are so playful that sometimes they make their own toys. A dolphin dives deep into the ocean. Then it blows an air ring into the water. It swims through the ring or tries to keep it from rising.

Dolphins love swimming fast and jumping high into the air. After jumping up, they often twist on the way back down into the water. This action creates a loud splash that the dolphins seem to enjoy.

---

1. What is this passage mostly about?

2. Why do dolphins save humans from drowning?

Oral Fluency Record Sheet

Name _____   Date _____

Oral Reading Accuracy: _____%   Circle: Fall Winter Spring
Oral Reading Fluency Score: _____ words correct per minute
Prosody Rubric: (Circle Score) 1 2 3 4
Comprehension Question Responses
#1 _____
#2 _____

Dolphins at Play

12	One time, a young boy fell from a fishing boat. A dolphin
25	happened to be nearby. It was surfing the waves made by the boat
38	as it moved through the water. When the boy splashed into the sea,
49	the dolphin's nose was right there. The dolphin scooped him up
62	and tossed him into the air. The boy landed in his father's arms.
70	Similar stories about dolphins are heard everywhere. That
80	is why many scientists study these animals. Some scientists think
93	that when dolphins save people, it is not because they love them. It
104	is because dolphins are playful. Dolphins love to play with toys,
116	such as balls and hoops. For fun, they sometimes tow large objects,
126	such as mattresses, to shore. Scientists think dolphins that save
137	drowning people are really just playing with them, as if they
139	were toys.
148	Dolphins are so playful that sometimes they make their
161	own toys. A dolphin dives deep into the ocean. Then it blows an
176	air ring into the water. It swims through the ring or tries to keep it
178	from rising.
188	Dolphins love swimming fast and jumping high into the air.
201	After jumping up, they often twist on the way back down into the
212	water. This action creates a loud splash that the dolphins seem
	to enjoy. **214**

© Macmillan/McGraw-Hill

Number of words read: _____   Number of errors made: _____

Crossing the Seas

Ships are one of the oldest and most important forms of transportation. Giant tankers carry oil and other liquids. Refrigerator ships carry fresh fruits, meats, and vegetables. People traveled across the ocean on ships before airplanes became widely used. Now people take vacations on cruise ships.

Throughout history, nations became rich and powerful by taking control of the seas. When they lost that control, they also often lost their power.

Probably the earliest "ship" was a log that someone used to cross a lake or river. Later people tied logs together to create rafts and discovered how to use trees to make canoes. In places where wood was scarce, people made boats out of animal skins. They sewed the skins into a bag, filled the bag with air, and used the bag as a float.

By about 3000 B.C., the Egyptians had discovered how to use sails to move boats. They also learned how to make boats out of planks of wood. For the next 5,000 years, shipbuilders focused on building bigger and bigger ships with better sails.

A big change in shipbuilding came in the 1800s. People began to use steam instead of wind power to move ships. These ships were fueled by coal. Later people began using heavy oil instead of coal. Today people even use nuclear power to move large ships.

1. What was probably the earliest ship?
2. According to the article, why was controlling the seas important long ago?

Oral Fluency Record Sheet

Name _____ Date _____

Oral Reading Accuracy: _____%   Circle: Fall Winter Spring

Oral Reading Fluency Score: _____ words correct per minute

Prosody Rubric: (Circle Score) 1 2 3 4

Comprehension Question Responses

#1 _____

#2 _____

Crossing the Seas

11	Ships are one of the oldest and most important forms of transportation. Giant tankers carry oil and other liquids.
19	Refrigerator ships carry fresh fruits, meats, and vegetables. People
28	traveled across the ocean on ships before airplanes became widely
38	used. Now people take vacations on cruise ships.
46	Throughout history, nations became rich and powerful by
54	taking control of the seas. When they lost that control, they also
66	often lost their power.
70	Probably the earliest "ship" was a log that someone used to
81	cross a lake or river. Later people tied logs together to create rafts
94	and discovered how to use trees to make canoes. In places where
106	wood was scarce, people made boats out of animal skins. They
117	sewed the skins into a bag, filled the bag with air, and used the bag
132	as a float.
135	By about 3000 B.C., the Egyptians had discovered how to
145	use sails to move boats. They also learned how to make boats out
158	of planks of wood. For the next 5,000 years, shipbuilders focused
169	on building bigger and bigger ships with better sails.
178	A big change in shipbuilding came in the 1800s. People
188	began to use steam instead of wind power to move ships. These
200	ships were fueled by coal. Later people began using heavy oil
211	instead of coal. Today people even use nuclear power to move
222	large ships. **224**

Number of words read: _____   Number of errors made: _____

Name _____ Date _____

Officer Jenson and the Tool Prints

It was a dark night. Two men broke into a jewelry store and robbed the safe. They knocked the dial off the safe door and drilled holes into it. Then they opened the door using a heavy screwdriver.

Officer Jim Jenson was put on the case. At the store, he found no fingerprints or other clues. But he saw scrape marks on the door. He decided to take the safe door to the crime lab. He had used the marks left by tools to solve cases before.

The woman at the lab could tell that a screwdriver had made the marks on the door. Jim knew that no two tools leave the same marks. Each tool has its own special bumps and dents.

The next day, another officer mentioned that he had stopped a suspicious truck the night before. The men inside seemed nervous. And they had a toolbox. The officer had found nothing wrong, but he took the men's names before they drove off.

Jim got the names and then he got a search warrant to take the toolbox from the men's house. The woman at the lab made marks on metal with the screwdriver from the toolbox. The marks matched the ones on the safe door. This screwdriver had been used in the robbery. Jim and the tool prints helped convict the men of the crime.

1. What did Jim Jenson use to solve the crime?
2. What did the robbers do to try to get away with the crime?

Oral Fluency Record Sheet

Name _____ Date _____

Oral Reading Accuracy: _____%   Circle: Fall Winter Spring

Oral Reading Fluency Score: _____ words correct per minute

Prosody Rubric: (Circle Score) 1 2 3 4

Comprehension Question Responses

#1 _____

#2 _____

Officer Jenson and the Tool Prints

	It was a dark night. Two men broke into a jewelry store and
13	robbed the safe. They knocked the dial off the safe door and
25	drilled holes into it. Then they opened the door using a
36	heavy screwdriver.
38	Officer Jim Jenson was put on the case. At the store, he
50	found no fingerprints or other clues. But he saw scrape marks on
62	the door. He decided to take the safe door to the crime lab.
75	He had used the marks left by tools to solve cases before.
87	The woman at the lab could tell that a screwdriver had
98	made the marks on the door. Jim knew that no two tools leave the
112	same marks. Each tool has its own special bumps and dents.
123	The next day, another officer mentioned that he had
132	stopped a suspicious truck the night before. The men inside
142	seemed nervous. And they had a toolbox. The officer had found
153	nothing wrong, but he took the men's names before they drove off.
165	Jim got the names and then he got a search warrant to take
178	the toolbox from the men's house. The woman at the lab made
190	marks on metal with the screwdriver from the toolbox. The marks
201	matched the ones on the safe door. This screwdriver had been used
213	in the robbery. Jim and the tool prints helped convict the men of
226	the crime. **228**

Number of words read: _____   Number of errors made: _____

The Frequent Biker's Program

"One big problem today is car emissions," said Mr. Bing, the history teacher. He was talking to the class about problems in the environment. "If people drove less, and used their bikes more, there would be much less pollution."

After class Pedro stopped to chat with Sandy. "Air pollution is really a problem. Sometimes when I get up, I can see the dirt in the air. When it's warm, we use our bikes to get into town. I wonder if there's a way we could get adults to use bikes instead of cars to go into town."

Sandy had an idea. "We could give people a reward every time they rode a bike to town. We could call it our Frequent Biker's Program. Maybe after people got a certain number of points they could use their points to buy things."

Pedro liked the idea and suggested it to Mr. Bing. With Mr. Bing's help, the boys got the town to support their idea. Many stores agreed to give people points for biking to their stores and to let people use their points for discounts to buy things. The town would try the plan for a month. If it worked, they would think about continuing it.

Pedro, Sandy, and the other kids from school put up posters all over town. Lots of people liked the idea, and soon there were more bicycles than cars in the downtown area. The program was a great success!

1. What problem did Pedro and Sandy want to help change?

2. What solution did the boys suggest in the story?

Oral Fluency Record Sheet

Name _____ Date _____

Oral Reading Accuracy: _____%   Circle: Fall Winter Spring

Oral Reading Fluency Score: _____ words correct per minute

Prosody Rubric: (Circle Score) 1 2 3 4

Comprehension Question Responses

#1 _____

#2 _____

The Frequent Biker's Program

	"One big problem today is car emissions," said Mr. Bing,
10	the history teacher. He was talking to the class about problems in
22	the environment. "If people drove less, and used their bikes
32	more, there would be much less pollution."
39	After class Pedro stopped to chat with Sandy. "Air pollution
49	is really a problem. Sometimes when I get up, I can see the dirt in
64	the air. When it's warm, we use our bikes to get into town. I
78	wonder if there's a way we could get adults to use bikes instead of
92	cars to go into town."
97	Sandy had an idea. "We could give people a reward every
108	time they rode a bike to town. We could call it our Frequent
121	Biker's Program. Maybe after people got a certain number of
131	points they could use their points to buy things."
140	Pedro liked the idea and suggested it to Mr. Bing. With Mr.
152	Bing's help, the boys got the town to support their idea. Many
164	stores agreed to give people points for biking to their stores and to
177	let people use their points for discounts to buy things. The town
189	would try the plan for a month. If it worked, they would think
202	about continuing it.
205	Pedro, Sandy, and the other kids from school put up posters
216	all over town. Lots of people liked the idea, and soon there were
229	more bicycles than cars in the downtown area. The program
239	was a great success! **243**

Number of words read: _____   Number of errors made: _____

Name _____ Date _____

Teamwork Is Key

Alaska has a famous dogsled race every year. Sled drivers, called mushers, race from Anchorage to Nome, a distance of about 1,049 miles. The race is long and difficult. Not all the mushers and their dogsled teams are able to finish the race.

Finding the right dogs for the dogsled team is not easy. The dogs must be strong and healthy, but they must also obey orders. Each dog must be willing to share the work. They must get along and work together as a team. Sled dogs are usually about 2 feet tall at the shoulders. They usually weigh 40 to 80 pounds. They have a protective outer coat of fur as well as an undercoat. They shed the undercoat in the summer, but in winter it allows the dogs to sleep in very cold temperatures.

The lead dog or dogs on the team must be smart because leaders often have to make decisions on their own. Being in front, lead dogs usually see problems before anyone else.

The dogs behind the leaders are called swing dogs. Swing dogs are very strong. Their job is to help move the whole team around turns or curves.

The dogs right in front of the sled are called wheel dogs. These dogs must pull the sled out and around corners or trees. All of the other dogs in the team are called team dogs. In dogsled racing, teamwork is key.

1. How do sled dogs work together as a team?

2. Why should the lead dog be the smartest dog of all?

Oral Fluency Record Sheet

Name _____ Date _____

Oral Reading Accuracy: _____%   Circle: Fall Winter Spring
Oral Reading Fluency Score: _____ words correct per minute
Prosody Rubric: (Circle Score) 1 2 3 4
Comprehension Question Responses
#1 _____
#2 _____

Teamwork Is Key

10	Alaska has a famous dogsled race every year. Sled drivers,
21	called mushers, race from Anchorage to Nome, a distance of about
34	1,049 miles. The race is long and difficult. Not all the mushers and
43	their dogsled teams are able to finish the race.
55	Finding the right dogs for the dogsled team is not easy. The
67	dogs must be strong and healthy, but they must also obey orders.
80	Each dog must be willing to share the work. They must get along
93	and work together as a team. Sled dogs are usually about 2 feet
105	tall at the shoulders. They usually weigh 40 to 80 pounds. They
118	have a protective outer coat of fur as well as an undercoat. They
131	shed the undercoat in the summer, but in winter it allows the dogs
137	to sleep in very cold temperatures.
149	The lead dog or dogs on the team must be smart because
161	leaders often have to make decisions on their own. Being in front,
169	lead dogs usually see problems before anyone else.
179	The dogs behind the leaders are called swing dogs. Swing
192	dogs are very strong. Their job is to help move the whole team
196	around turns or curves.
208	The dogs right in front of the sled are called wheel dogs.
221	These dogs must pull the sled out and around corners or trees. All
234	of the other dogs in the team are called team dogs. In dogsled
	racing, teamwork is key. **238**

Number of words read: _____   Number of errors made: _____

Name _____ Date _____

Peace and Quiet

Everybody knows that air pollution can be dangerous. Many people are also concerned about water pollution and poisons in the soil. But there is another kind of pollution—noise pollution.

Jet planes make a lot of noise. City planners try to build airports far from local neighborhoods. This reduces the noise. However, sometimes it makes the airports harder to get to.

The sounds of jackhammers are also unpleasant and quite harmful. People who work these machines wear earplugs. These protect them from the loud noise.

But there is one kind of noise that may damage your hearing without disturbing you at all. That noise is loud music. Do you turn the volume all the way up? Do you blast everyone nearby? You may be harming the delicate organs of your ears. Month by month, hearing damage builds. Over time it becomes hearing loss.

Many people exercise to loud music. They exercise to stay healthy. They do not think about the harm the loud music may cause.

The personal CD player did nothing to reduce the effects of loud music. Even though others are protected, you may still be hurting your own ears.

What can you do about this kind of pollution? Turn down the volume on your personal music players. If you go to a concert, think about wearing earplugs. Some people are wearing them to movie theaters, too. And get your hearing checked. It's better to be safe than sorry.

1. What is the author's purpose for writing this passage?

2. According to the author, what may be the most damaging type of noise pollution?

Oral Fluency Record Sheet

Name _____ Date _____

Oral Reading Accuracy: _____%   Circle: Fall   Winter   Spring

Oral Reading Fluency Score: _____ words correct per minute

Prosody Rubric: (Circle Score) 1 2 3 4

Comprehension Question Responses

#1 _____

#2 _____

Peace and Quiet

	Everybody knows that air pollution can be dangerous.
8	Many people are also concerned about water pollution and poisons
18	in the soil. But there is another kind of pollution—noise pollution.
30	Jet planes make a lot of noise. City planners try to build
42	airports far from local neighborhoods. This reduces the noise.
51	However, sometimes it makes the airports harder to get to.
61	The sounds of jackhammers are also unpleasant and quite
70	harmful. People who work these machines wear earplugs. These
79	protect them from the loud noise.
85	But there is one kind of noise that may damage your
96	hearing without disturbing you at all. That noise is loud
106	music. Do you turn the volume all the way up? Do you blast
119	everyone nearby? You may be harming the delicate organs of your
130	ears. Month by month, hearing damage builds. Over time it
140	becomes hearing loss.
143	Many people exercise to loud music. They exercise to stay
153	healthy. They do not think about the harm the loud music may cause.
166	The personal CD player did nothing to reduce the effects of
177	loud music. Even though others are protected, you may still be
188	hurting your own ears.
192	What can you do about this kind of pollution? Turn down
203	the volume on your personal music players. If you go to a concert,
216	think about wearing earplugs. Some people are wearing them to
226	movie theaters, too. And get your hearing checked. It's better to be
238	safe than sorry. 241

Number of words read: _____   Number of errors made: _____

Name _____ Date _____

The Kite Contest

Jed and his little brother Tom were at the park for the kite
contest. The contestant whose kite stayed up the longest would win.

The boys waited to hear their numbers. Kites swooped and
soared above them. Some stayed up for a long time. Others dropped
to the grass almost immediately. Finally the boys' numbers were
called. Jed raced to the open field, but Tom stood still.

"I can't," he mumbled as he dropped his kite.

Jed thought for a moment. Then he went over and picked
up Tom's kite. "I'll fly both of them," he said.

Jed began to run, and both kites soared into the sky. Then
unexpectedly the wind jerked at Jed's kite, and the kite ripped. "My
kite can't fly now," thought Jed. He dropped the string to his kite,
and the kite fell to the ground. But he still had Tom's kite. He kept
on running.

Suddenly the whistle blew. The contest was over. The boys
met near the judge's stand to hear who had won.

"There are three winners," the judge announced. "First
place goes to number 21. Second place goes to number 9. Third
place goes to number 35."

"Number 35!" Jed shouted. "That's me." He
jumped up and ran quickly to the judge.

"You're the one who flew two kites," the judge said. "Great
job!" He handed him a green ribbon.

"It was really my brother's kite," Jed said shyly. "I'm going
to share this prize with him."

---

1. What did a contestant need to do to win the contest?

2. What was unusual about the way Jed won his ribbon?

Oral Fluency Record Sheet

Name _____ Date _____

Oral Reading Accuracy: _____%   Circle: Fall Winter Spring

Oral Reading Fluency Score: _____ words correct per minute

Prosody Rubric: (Circle Score) 1 2 3 4

Comprehension Question Responses

#1 _____

#2 _____

The Kite Contest

	Jed and his little brother Tom were at the park for the kite
13	contest. The contestant whose kite stayed up the longest would win.
24	The boys waited to hear their numbers. Kites swooped and
34	soared above them. Some stayed up for a long time. Others dropped
46	to the grass almost immediately. Finally the boys' numbers were
56	called. Jed raced to the open field, but Tom stood still.
67	"I can't," he mumbled as he dropped his kite.
76	Jed thought for a moment. Then he went over and picked
87	up Tom's kite. "I'll fly both of them," he said.
97	Jed began to run, and both kites soared into the sky. Then
109	unexpectedly the wind jerked at Jed's kite, and the kite ripped. "My
121	kite can't fly now," thought Jed. He dropped the string to his kite,
134	and the kite fell to the ground. But he still had Tom's kite. He kept
149	on running.
151	Suddenly the whistle blew. The contest was over. The boys
161	met near the judge's stand to hear who had won.
171	"There are three winners," the judge announced. "First
179	place goes to number 21. Second place goes to number 9. Third
191	place goes to number 35."
196	"Number 35!" Jed shouted. "That's me." He
203	jumped up and ran quickly to the judge.
211	"You're the one who flew two kites," the judge said. "Great
222	job!" He handed him a green ribbon.
229	"It was really my brother's kite," Jed said shyly. "I'm going
240	to share this prize with him." **246**

Number of words read: _____   Number of errors made: _____

The Big Game

Jimmy Glen played first base for the Larks. His team was leading 3 to 2 in the last game of the season. If the Larks could hold on, they would win the championship. The other team, the Macros, had two outs and two runners on base. A hit could win the game for them.

Jimmy could hear his father shouting from the stands. Jimmy's father had been a major league baseball player. Jimmy wanted to make his dad proud of him.

The pitcher, Joe Lee, sent a ball flying low to the batter. The batter swung and hit a ground ball to first base. It looked like an easy catch, but then the ball took a bad bounce and jumped away from Jimmy's mitt. The two Macros players on base slid into home. The Macros had won.

None of the other Larks would look at Jimmy. Jimmy walked over to the water fountain. "Tough luck," called his father, running up to him.

"Everyone hates me," said Jimmy. "I'm just no good."

"Come on home," said his dad. "I want to show you something."

When they got home, Jimmy's dad pulled out an old clipping. The headline read: **Glen Strikes Out with Bases Loaded, Loses Big Game.**

"That was my last game in high school," said Mr. Glen.

"But you were a star!" said Jimmy.

Mr. Glen grinned. "Jimmy, even stars make mistakes. I messed up in my big game. But I didn't let it stop me. Life goes on. You have a whole future ahead of you."

1. Why wouldn't Jimmy's teammates look at him?

2. What does Jimmy's father do to make him feel better?

Oral Fluency Record Sheet

Name _____ Date _____

Oral Reading Accuracy: _____%   Circle: Fall Winter Spring
Oral Reading Fluency Score: _____ words correct per minute
Prosody Rubric: (Circle Score) 1 2 3 4
Comprehension Question Responses
#1 _____
#2 _____

The Big Game

	Jimmy Glen played first base for the Larks. His team was
11	leading 3 to 2 in the last game of the season. If the Larks could
26	hold on, they would win the championship. The other team, the
37	Macros, had two outs and two runners on base. A hit could win the
51	game for them.
54	Jimmy could hear his father shouting from the stands.
63	Jimmy's father had been a major league baseball player. Jimmy
73	wanted to make his dad proud of him.
81	The pitcher, Joe Lee, sent a ball flying low to the batter.
93	The batter swung and hit a ground ball to first base. It looked like
107	an easy catch, but then the ball took a bad bounce and jumped
120	away from Jimmy's mitt. The two Macros players on base slid into
132	home. The Macros had won.
137	None of the other Larks would look at Jimmy. Jimmy
147	walked over to the water fountain. "Tough luck," called his father,
158	running up to him.
162	"Everyone hates me," said Jimmy. "I'm just no good."
171	"Come on home," said his dad. "I want to show you something."
183	When they got home, Jimmy's dad pulled out an old clipping.
194	The headline read: **Glen Strikes Out with Bases Loaded, Loses**
204	**Big Game.**
206	"That was my last game in high school," said Mr. Glen.
217	"But you were a star!" said Jimmy.
224	Mr. Glen grinned. "Jimmy, even stars make mistakes. I
233	messed up in my big game. But I didn't let it stop me. Life goes on.
249	You have a whole future ahead of you." **257**

Number of words read: _____   Number of errors made: _____

The Garden

Nancy decided one day that she wanted to grow a garden. She lived in an apartment, though, so she was not quite sure how she might do this. Nancy stood at her bedroom window and looked longingly out into the courtyard that was formed by the two L-shaped buildings of the apartment complex. Then suddenly she had an idea.

Nancy went to the superintendent of her building. She asked if the patch of dirt in the center of the courtyard was being used for any purpose. Mr. Hernandez informed Nancy that in the decade since he had begun managing the buildings, nothing had ever been done to that area.

With Mr. Hernandez's assistance, Nancy got permission from the landlord to start a garden. The landlord told her that as long as she took care of whatever she planted, she was free to plant anything she liked.

Nancy arranged a family meeting that night. She gave each of her sisters an assignment. One sister went to the library and borrowed books on growing flowers and vegetables. Another sister e-mailed their grandmother on the Internet, asking her how to grow tomatoes. The third sister accompanied Nancy to a store where they purchased seeds for flowers and vegetables.

A few months later, Nancy and her family were eating tomatoes from the courtyard garden. And a vase of fresh asters looked gorgeous in the center of the table.

1. What is this passage mostly about?

2. How would you describe Nancy?

Oral Fluency Record Sheet

Name _____ Date _____

Oral Reading Accuracy: _____%   Circle: Fall Winter Spring

Oral Reading Fluency Score: _____ words correct per minute

Prosody Rubric: (Circle Score) 1 2 3 4

Comprehension Question Responses

#1 _____

#2 _____

The Garden

	Nancy decided one day that she wanted to grow a garden.
11	She lived in an apartment, though, so she was not quite sure how
24	she might do this. Nancy stood at her bedroom window and looked
36	longingly out into the courtyard that was formed by the two
47	L-shaped buildings of the apartment complex. Then suddenly she had
58	an idea.
60	Nancy went to the superintendent of her building. She
69	asked if the patch of dirt in the center of the courtyard was being
83	used for any purpose. Mr. Hernandez informed Nancy that in the
94	decade since he had begun managing the buildings, nothing had
104	ever been done to that area.
110	With Mr. Hernandez's assistance, Nancy got permission
117	from the landlord to start a garden. The landlord told her that as
130	long as she took care of whatever she planted, she was free to plant
144	anything she liked.
147	Nancy arranged a family meeting that night. She gave each
157	of her sisters an assignment. One sister went to the library and
169	borrowed books on growing flowers and vegetables. Another sister
178	e-mailed their grandmother on the Internet, asking her how to grow
190	tomatoes. The third sister accompanied Nancy to a store where
200	they purchased seeds for flowers and vegetables.
207	A few months later, Nancy and her family were eating
217	tomatoes from the courtyard garden. And a vase of fresh asters
228	looked gorgeous in the center of the table. **236**

Number of words read: _____   Number of errors made: _____

When You Snooze, You Lose

Carlos detested getting up in the morning. He rarely felt awake until sometime in the afternoon. By dinnertime, he was prepared for anything. By bedtime, he was unbelievably energized. Unfortunately for Carlos, school starts in the morning.

Carlos's dad resented having to wake him up ten times each morning. So his parents bought Carlos an alarm clock that had an especially loud buzz for an alarm. They informed him that getting up was now his responsibility.

The first morning, the buzz was deafening. Carlos woke up terrified. Then he realized it was simply his new alarm clock. He decided that he did not need such an earsplitting signal. Happily, he lowered the sound level.

The next morning, Carlos continued sleeping through the quiet buzz. He missed breakfast, missed the bus, and had to hustle off to school on his own two legs.

It was raining, but Carlos forgot to close his backpack. His homework got drenched and fell apart in his hands. He also forgot his lunch money as he sprinted out of the apartment. So Carlos had no lunch and then stayed after school to redo his homework. He missed the bus again and plodded home in the drizzling rain.

As soon as Carlos entered his apartment, he raced to his room and turned up the volume on his alarm. Sleeping late was just not worth it.

1. Why did Carlos's parents get him an alarm clock?

2. What lesson did Carlos learn?

Oral Fluency Record Sheet

Name _____   Date _____

Oral Reading Accuracy: _____%   Circle: Fall Winter Spring
Oral Reading Fluency Score: _____ words correct per minute
Prosody Rubric: (Circle Score) 1 2 3 4
Comprehension Question Responses
#1 _____
#2 _____

When You Snooze, You Lose

	Carlos detested getting up in the morning. He rarely
9	felt awake until sometime in the afternoon. By dinnertime, he was
20	prepared for anything. By bedtime, he was unbelievably energized.
29	Unfortunately for Carlos, school starts in the morning.
37	Carlos's dad resented having to wake him up ten times
47	each morning. So his parents bought Carlos an alarm clock that had
59	an especially loud buzz for an alarm. They informed him that
70	getting up was now his responsibility.
76	The first morning, the buzz was deafening. Carlos woke up
86	terrified. Then he realized it was simply his new alarm clock. He
98	decided that he did not need such an earsplitting signal. Happily, he
110	lowered the sound level.
114	The next morning, Carlos continued sleeping through the
122	quiet buzz. He missed breakfast, missed the bus, and had to hustle
134	off to school on his own two legs.
142	It was raining, but Carlos forgot to close his backpack. His
153	homework got drenched and fell apart in his hands. He also forgot
165	his lunch money as he sprinted out of the apartment. So Carlos had
178	no lunch and then stayed after school to redo his homework. He
190	missed the bus again and plodded home in the drizzling rain.
201	As soon as Carlos entered his apartment, he raced to his
212	room and turned up the volume on his alarm. Sleeping late was just
225	not worth it. **228**

© Macmillan/McGraw-Hill

Number of words read: _____   Number of errors made: _____

Name _____ Date _____

Break the Cycle

A *cycle* is a pattern that is repeated over and over. Cycles work in two ways. They can have positive results or they can have negative ones. An example of a cycle with positive results is physical exercise. When you exercise, you feel healthier and get stronger. The next time you exercise, you build on those positive effects. As exercise becomes a regular habit, you are able to do it for a longer time. You have more energy and you feel mentally better about yourself.

An example of a cycle with negative results is not studying. Because you fail to study, you create a poor foundation on which to build the next time you study. Your knowledge base becomes thin and incomplete. It seems that you will never be able to learn what you want.

Another example of a cycle with negative results affects your health. When you do not exercise your muscles each day, they become weaker and weaker. Each hour you spend sitting in front of a monitor, computer, or television is an hour your muscles are not used as they should be.

You may eventually decide to get more active. But it will be difficult. You have allowed your body to become weak.

It is not hard to turn these cycles around, though. The key is to do a little each day. Study a little each day. Exercise for a short period of time each day. Your mind and body will benefit greatly from regular activity.

1. What is a cycle?
2. How can you turn around a negative cycle?

© Macmillan/McGraw-Hill

Oral Fluency Record Sheet

Name _____ Date _____

Oral Reading Accuracy: _____%   Circle: Fall Winter Spring

Oral Reading Fluency Score: _____ words correct per minute

Prosody Rubric: (Circle Score) 1 2 3 4

Comprehension Question Responses

#1 _____

#2 _____

Break the Cycle

12	A *cycle* is a pattern that is repeated over and over. Cycles
25	work in two ways. They can have positive results or they can have
36	negative ones. An example of a cycle with positive results is
46	physical exercise. When you exercise, you feel healthier and get
57	stronger. The next time you exercise, you build on those positive
70	effects. As exercise becomes a regular habit, you are able to do it
82	for a longer time. You have more energy and you feel mentally
85	better about yourself.
96	An example of a cycle with negative results is not studying.
108	Because you fail to study, you create a poor foundation on which
119	to build the next time you study. Your knowledge base becomes
132	thin and incomplete. It seems that you will never be able to learn
135	what you want.
144	Another example of a cycle with negative results affects
155	your health. When you do not exercise your muscles each day,
166	they become weaker and weaker. Each hour you spend sitting in
178	front of a monitor, computer, or television is an hour your muscles
185	are not used as they should be.
196	You may eventually decide to get more active. But it will
206	be difficult. You have allowed your body to become weak.
219	It is not hard to turn these cycles around, though. The key is
235	to do a little each day. Study a little each day. Exercise for a short period
246	of time each day. Your mind and body will benefit greatly
	from regular activity. **249**

© Macmillan/McGraw-Hill

Number of words read: _____   Number of errors made: _____

Wordwatches

When Pablo was eleven years old, he thought of a concept for a product called the Wordwatch. Pablo needed his uncle's assistance to create this invention because he needed the help of a computer programmer. Programming was Uncle Tim's job. Pablo and his uncle figured out how to make Wordwatches.

Like most watches, a Wordwatch shows the time. However, unlike other watches, the Wordwatch also shows a word. It displays a different word every day. If you look at the watch on Monday, you might see the word *artificial*. On Tuesday, you might see the word *concentrate*. The same word appears on the watch throughout the day. If you press one button, you see a definition for the word. If you press a different button, the word is used in a sentence. If you're awake at midnight, the Wordwatch reveals a different word.

Pablo and Uncle Tim employed a teacher to research which words should be used in the Wordwatch. She generated different lists of words for different ages. The watch for nine-year-olds has simpler words than the one for high-school students. After a year, a Wordwatch owner may send the watch back to the factory. The staff there will reprogram it with new vocabulary.

Pablo's invention helps kids learn to spell many difficult words and read better. He and Uncle Tim are not millionaires yet, but Wordwatches appear to be selling very well.

1. What is a Wordwatch?
2. Why is Pablo's invention useful for children in school?

© Macmillan/McGraw-Hill

Oral Fluency Record Sheet

Name _____ Date _____

Oral Reading Accuracy: _____%   Circle: Fall Winter Spring

Oral Reading Fluency Score: _____ words correct per minute

Prosody Rubric: (Circle Score) 1 2 3 4

Comprehension Question Responses

#1 _____

#2 _____

Wordwatches

	When Pablo was eleven years old, he thought of a concept
11	for a product called the Wordwatch. Pablo needed his uncle's
21	assistance to create this invention because he needed the help of a
33	computer programmer. Programming was Uncle Tim's job. Pablo
41	and his uncle figured out how to make Wordwatches.
50	Like most watches, a Wordwatch shows the time.
58	However, unlike other watches, the Wordwatch also shows a word.
68	It displays a different word every day. If you look at the watch on
82	Monday, you might see the word *artificial*. On Tuesday, you
92	might see the word *concentrate*. The same word appears on the
103	watch throughout the day. If you press one button, you see a
115	definition for the word. If you press a different button, the word is
128	used in a sentence. If you're awake at midnight, the Wordwatch
139	reveals a different word.
143	Pablo and Uncle Tim employed a teacher to research which
153	words should be used in the Wordwatch. She generated different
163	lists of words for different ages. The watch for nine-year-olds has
176	simpler words than the one for high-school students. After a year, a
189	Wordwatch owner may send the watch back to the factory. The
200	staff there will reprogram it with new vocabulary.
208	Pablo's invention helps kids learn to spell many difficult
217	words and read better. He and Uncle Tim are not millionaires yet,
229	but Wordwatches appear to be selling very well. **237**

Number of words read: _____   Number of errors made: _____

Mr. Lazy-Bones

Matt Kroger was incredibly lazy. He was so lazy that sometimes at dinnertime he would still be lounging in his pajamas. Putting on regular clothes was too much work, and so was tying shoes, combing hair, or striding up a one-story flight of stairs instead of taking the elevator. Matt focused on avoiding any kind of activity. But Matt loved money, so when Mrs. Tinsley asked him to walk her dog Coco, Matt grabbed the opportunity. Five dollars for a ten-minute walk was a terrific deal.

When he asked me to accompany him, I thought, "Why not? I have nothing better to do anyway."

One dog eventually led to two, because Matt discovered that walking a second pooch was like getting paid double for an identical amount of work. Then we were asked to walk a third and a fourth dog.

While strolling with the dogs, we thought, "Why not take on a paper route as well?"

"It would be like free money," Matt declared. "It won't take us any more time because we have to go around the neighborhood every day anyway."

That's right. We delivered newspapers while we walked the four dogs. Never mind that our ten-minute walk now required an investment of more than an hour. The laziest kid in the universe had become the hardest-working one of all.

1. Why did Matt decide to start walking dogs?

2. What lesson did Matt learn in this story?

Oral Fluency Record Sheet

Name _____ Date _____

Oral Reading Accuracy: _____%   Circle: Fall Winter Spring

Oral Reading Fluency Score: _____ words correct per minute

Prosody Rubric: (Circle Score) 1 2 3 4

Comprehension Question Responses

#1 _____

#2 _____

Mr. Lazy-Bones

	Matt Kroger was incredibly lazy. He was so lazy that
10	sometimes at dinnertime he would still be lounging in his pajamas.
21	Putting on regular clothes was too much work, and so was tying
33	shoes, combing hair, or striding up a one-story flight of stairs
45	instead of taking the elevator. Matt focused on avoiding any
55	kind of activity. But Matt loved money, so when Mrs.
65	Tinsley asked him to walk her dog Coco, Matt grabbed the
76	opportunity. Five dollars for a ten-minute walk was a terrific deal.
88	When he asked me to accompany him, I thought, "Why
98	not? I have nothing better to do anyway."
106	One dog eventually led to two, because Matt discovered
115	that walking a second pooch was like getting paid double for an
127	identical amount of work. Then we were asked to walk a third
139	and a fourth dog.
143	While strolling with the dogs, we thought, "Why not take
153	on a paper route as well?"
159	"It would be like free money," Matt declared. "It won't take
170	us any more time because we have to go around the neighborhood
182	every day anyway."
185	That's right. We delivered newspapers while we walked the
194	four dogs. Never mind that our ten-minute walk now required an
206	investment of more than an hour. The laziest kid in the universe
218	had become the hardest-working one of all. **226**

Number of words read: _____   Number of errors made: _____

The Rains

I had just relocated to Florida from the deserts of the Southwest. The dry air, the beige landscape, the burning sun of my native Arizona—all these things I loved and knew I would miss. However, since Florida is also in the southern part of the United States, I imagined that in some ways it would be very similar.

To my surprise, everything in Florida looked strange and wondrous. Everything was green. Flowers seemed to bloom everywhere. The air was humid, almost too wet to breathe. There was so much humidity to adjust to. But the thing that disturbed me the most was the rain.

I could endure the humidity and I actually had affection for the alligators. The rain, however, was scary. I experienced my first Florida rainstorm when I was coming home from my first day of school. I sat next to the window, gawking out as the rain pelted our big, bulky bus. The road appeared to be a raging river. I thought it was the end of the world.

I glanced around, expecting my classmates to do what I wanted to do—jump up in terror. But no one moved or even seemed to notice. Everyone else had probably already gone through rainstorms much worse than this one. The bus driver simply turned on the windshield wipers and kept driving, just a fraction more slowly.

1. How were Florida and Arizona different?
2. Why was the rainstorm frightening to the narrator in this story?

© Macmillan/McGraw-Hill

Oral Fluency Record Sheet

Name _____ Date _____

Oral Reading Accuracy: _____%   Circle: Fall Winter Spring

Oral Reading Fluency Score: _____ words correct per minute

Prosody Rubric: (Circle Score) 1 2 3 4

Comprehension Question Responses

#1 _____

#2 _____

The Rains

	I had just relocated to Florida from the deserts of the
11	Southwest. The dry air, the beige landscape, the burning sun of my
23	native Arizona—all these things I loved and knew I would miss.
35	However, since Florida is also in the southern part of the United
47	States, I imagined that in some ways it would be very similar.
59	To my surprise, everything in Florida looked strange and
68	wondrous. Everything was green. Flowers seemed to bloom
76	everywhere. The air was humid, almost too wet to breathe. There
87	was so much humidity to adjust to. But the thing that disturbed me
100	the most was the rain.
105	I could endure the humidity and I actually had affection for
116	the alligators. The rain, however, was scary. I experienced my first
127	Florida rainstorm when I was coming home from my first day of
139	school. I sat next to the window, gawking out as the rain pelted our
153	big, bulky bus. The road appeared to be a raging river. I thought it
167	was the end of the world.
173	I glanced around, expecting my classmates to do what I
183	wanted to do—jump up in terror. But no one moved or even
196	seemed to notice. Everyone else had probably already gone
205	through rainstorms much worse than this one. The bus driver simply
216	turned on the windshield wipers and kept driving, just a fraction
227	more slowly. **229**

Number of words read: _____   Number of errors made: _____

The Eyes of El Greco

El Greco was a great painter. Born in 1541, El Greco developed an unusual painting style. All the people in his paintings are long and thin. This gives his paintings a strange beauty. Was El Greco's style a result of a problem with his eyesight?

People first suggested that El Greco's style was nothing more than a vision problem in 1913. Although healthy eyeballs are round and shaped like basketballs, El Greco's eyes were shaped like footballs. The shape of El Greco's eyes affected the way he saw the world. Because of this, everything that he saw appeared to be long and thin. This suggests that El Greco painted things the way he actually saw them.

Many experts, though, reject this idea. They agree that El Greco might have seen objects as long. But they believe he would have known their actual shapes. He could have drawn them as they really were if he wanted to.

To understand this argument, imagine that you are colorblind. You see red as blue. Through your eyes, a ripe tomato appears blue. But you know that tomatoes are really red. When you paint one, you use red paint. In any case, art experts point out that, in many cases, El Greco painted figures that looked normal. This suggests that El Greco used his unique style because he liked the way it looked.

1. What did people first think about El Greco's style of painting?

2. Why does the author include the reference to colorblindness in the passage?

Oral Fluency Record Sheet

Name _____   Date _____

Oral Reading Accuracy: _____%   Circle: Fall Winter Spring
Oral Reading Fluency Score: _____ words correct per minute
Prosody Rubric: (Circle Score) 1 2 3 4
Comprehension Question Responses
#1 _____
#2 _____

The Eyes of El Greco

	El Greco was a great painter. Born in 1541, El Greco
11	developed an unusual painting style. All the people in his paintings
22	are long and thin. This gives his paintings a strange beauty.
33	Was El Greco's style a result of a problem with his eyesight?
45	People first suggested that El Greco's style was nothing
54	more than a vision problem in 1913. Although healthy eyeballs are
65	round and shaped like basketballs, El Greco's eyes were shaped like
76	footballs. The shape of El Greco's eyes affected the way he saw
88	the world. Because of this, everything that he saw appeared to
99	be long and thin. This suggests that El Greco painted things the
111	way he actually saw them.
116	Many experts, though, reject this idea. They agree that El
126	Greco might have seen objects as long. But they believe he would
138	have known their actual shapes. He could have drawn them as they
150	really were if he wanted to.
156	To understand this argument, imagine that you are colorblind.
165	You see red as blue. Through your eyes, a ripe tomato appears blue. But
179	you know that tomatoes are really red. When you paint one, you use red
193	paint. In any case, art experts point out that, in many cases, El Greco
207	painted figures that looked normal. This suggests that El Greco used his
219	unique style because he liked the way it looked. **228**

Number of words read: _____   Number of errors made: _____

Looking at Clouds

How are clouds formed? To understand cloud formation, you need to remember two basic laws. First, warm air is somewhat lighter than cool air. Second, warm air holds more water than cool air. On a clear day, the sun heats the ground unevenly. Pockets of warm air, called thermals, are light, and they rise like bubbles into the sky. Since they are warm, these thermals hold more water than the surrounding atmosphere. As they rise, the surrounding air gets colder, so the thermals soon cool off. Since cool air holds less moisture than warm air, the water in a thermal will drop out and form a puffy white cloud. Small clouds may last no longer than twenty minutes. But occasionally they may merge to form a larger cloud that lasts a great deal longer, maybe even for an hour or so.

Some thermals are bigger, warmer, and wetter than others, and they rise higher into colder air levels. There they consolidate with other thermals to form a large rain cloud or thundercloud. These massive clouds can last for nine hours or so, before hurling their moisture toward the ground as precipitation.

A large thundercloud can reach great heights, as much as ten miles up into the sky. Ice crystals inside of a thundercloud swirl furiously, smashing into one another. This smashing tends to create an electrical charge at the bottom of the cloud. If this charge grows big enough, it will discharge, resulting in a bolt of lightning that impacts the ground.

1. What process is explained in this passage?
2. Why do thermals hold more water than the surrounding atmosphere?

© Macmillan/McGraw-Hill

Oral Fluency Record Sheet

Name _____ Date _____

Oral Reading Accuracy: _____% Circle: Fall Winter Spring

Oral Reading Fluency Score: _____ words correct per minute

Prosody Rubric: (Circle Score) 1 2 3 4

Comprehension Question Responses

#1 _____

#2 _____

Looking at Clouds

	How are clouds formed? To understand cloud formation,
8	you need to remember two basic laws. First, warm air is
19	somewhat lighter than cool air. Second, warm air holds more
29	water than cool air. On a clear day, the sun heats the ground
42	unevenly. Pockets of warm air, called thermals, are light, and
52	they rise like bubbles into the sky. Since they are warm, these
64	thermals hold more water than the surrounding atmosphere. As
73	they rise, the surrounding air gets colder, so the thermals soon
84	cool off. Since cool air holds less moisture than warm air, the
96	water in a thermal will drop out and form a puffy white cloud.
109	Small clouds may last no longer than twenty minutes. But
119	occasionally they may merge to form a larger cloud that lasts
130	a great deal longer, maybe even for an hour or so.
141	Some thermals are bigger, warmer, and wetter than
149	others, and they rise higher into colder air levels. There they
160	consolidate with other thermals to form a large rain cloud
170	or thundercloud. These massive clouds can last for nine hours
180	or so, before hurling their moisture toward the ground
189	as precipitation.
191	A large thundercloud can reach great heights, as much as
201	ten miles up into the sky. Ice crystals inside of a thundercloud
213	swirl furiously, smashing into one another. This smashing tends
223	to create an electrical charge at the bottom of the cloud. If this
235	charge grows big enough, it will discharge, resulting in a bolt
246	of lightning that impacts the ground. **252**

Number of words read: _____ Number of errors made: _____

Malik's Project

Malik had an interesting idea for a science project, but he couldn't carry out the project without some special equipment. His idea was to track warbler migrations in his hometown. Warblers are small singing birds. There are many different species that migrate south in the fall and north in the spring. Malik wanted to spend six weekends in each season recording warbler movements in and out of his area. The only problem was that warblers are very small. To be able to tell one kind from another, Malik would need a pair of expensive binoculars.

Malik thought long and hard about how he might get what he needed. He had heard of a bird-watching organization with many chapters nationwide. Using the Internet at school, he discovered a chapter in his town. Malik called the local chapter and talked with Mrs. Simpson, the president. He told her about his idea and also about his problem.

"Well, Malik," Mrs. Simpson said, "our group counts birds every spring and fall. Our members know a lot about warblers. But some of them are elderly people who can't see very well, even with their binoculars. We certainly would appreciate having your strong, young eyes to help us. I'm sure someone would be delighted to lend you a pair of binoculars, if you promise to come with us the next time we go out to count birds."

1. What was Malik's science project mostly about?
2. How did Malik find a bird-watching group in his hometown?

Oral Fluency Record Sheet

Name _____   Date _____

Oral Reading Accuracy: _____%   Circle: Fall Winter Spring
Oral Reading Fluency Score: _____ words correct per minute
Prosody Rubric: (Circle Score) 1 2 3 4
Comprehension Question Responses
#1 _____
#2 _____

Malik's Project

	Malik had an interesting idea for a science project, but he
11	couldn't carry out the project without some special equipment. His
21	idea was to track warbler migrations in his hometown. Warblers
31	are small singing birds. There are many different species that
41	migrate south in the fall and north in the spring. Malik wanted to
54	spend six weekends in each season recording warbler movements
63	in and out of his area. The only problem was that warblers are very
77	small. To be able to tell one kind from another, Malik would need
90	a pair of expensive binoculars.
95	Malik thought long and hard about how he might get what
106	he needed. He had heard of a bird-watching organization with
117	many chapters nationwide. Using the Internet at school, he
126	discovered a chapter in his town. Malik called the local chapter and
138	talked with Mrs. Simpson, the president. He told her about his idea
150	and also about his problem.
155	"Well, Malik," Mrs. Simpson said, "our group counts birds
164	every spring and fall. Our members know a lot about warblers. But
176	some of them are elderly people who can't see very well, even with
189	their binoculars. We certainly would appreciate having your
197	strong, young eyes to help us. I'm sure someone would be
208	delighted to lend you a pair of binoculars, if you promise to come
221	with us the next time we go out to count birds." **232**

© Macmillan/McGraw-Hill

Number of words read: _____   Number of errors made: _____

Hannah's Story

Hannah was discouraged. She had an assignment for class
to write a story about how she had accomplished a goal. But
no matter how hard she tried, she could not think of anything to
write about.

"I'd better make a list of ideas," she told herself. She jotted
down some notes about the time she helped her father reorganize
his carpentry tools in the woodshed. She started another
page and made a chart and diagram showing what her aunt had
taught her about growing tulips. Neither of these ideas inspired her.

"Maybe it would be worthwhile just to try writing down
every single word that pops into my head," she thought. She sat at
her desk in suspense, waiting for some words to come, but nothing
came to her. Suddenly the process of developing an idea seemed
completely beyond her.

Hannah's father gave her some good advice. "Why don't
you postpone working on the assignment for a few minutes, take a
short walk, and entirely clear your mind," he said.

Hannah went out and walked around the block. "Writing
this story is one goal I just cannot seem to accomplish," she
mused. Then something clicked. The ideal topic had been hidden
within her imagination the whole time, and she had finally found
it. What you are reading is the story Hannah wrote, and I
am Hannah.

1. What were some things that Hannah did to help think of a writing
   idea?

2. How did Hannah solve her writing problem?

Oral Fluency Record Sheet

Hannah's Story

	Hannah was discouraged. She had an assignment for class
9	to write a story about how she had accomplished a goal. But
21	no matter how hard she tried, she could not think of anything to
34	write about.
36	"I'd better make a list of ideas," she told herself. She jotted
48	down some notes about the time she helped her father reorganize
59	his carpentry tools in the woodshed. She started another
68	page and made a chart and diagram showing what her aunt had
80	taught her about growing tulips. Neither of these ideas inspired her.
91	"Maybe it would be worthwhile just to try writing down
101	every single word that pops into my head," she thought. She sat at
114	her desk in suspense, waiting for some words to come, but nothing
126	came to her. Suddenly the process of developing an idea seemed
137	completely beyond her.
140	Hannah's father gave her some good advice. "Why don't
149	you postpone working on the assignment for a few minutes, take a
161	short walk, and entirely clear your mind," he said.
170	Hannah went out and walked around the block. "Writing
179	this story is one goal I just cannot seem to accomplish," she
191	mused. Then something clicked. The ideal topic had been hidden
201	within her imagination the whole time, and she had finally found
212	it. What you are reading is the story Hannah wrote, and I
224	am Hannah. **226**

© Macmillan/McGraw-Hill

Number of words read: _____   **Number of errors made: _____**

The Trial of John Peter Zenger

John Peter Zenger was a courageous man who won an
important victory for freedom of the press. In 1732, he was the
editor of a New York City newspaper. At that time, the country
was still a collection of British colonies.

The governor of New York carried out British policies. He
did not care whether or not the people approved of these policies.
Most newspapers kept quiet about the governor. Zenger's
newspaper, however, printed many articles that criticized him.

In those days, just printing stories that criticized the
government was against the law. It did not matter whether the
stories were true or not.

Sure enough, Zenger was arrested and sent to prison. He
spent ten months there. His newspaper was shut down and went
out of business. But Zenger believed he had done the right thing.
He met with a lawyer named Andrew Hamilton. Hamilton agreed
to take his case.

At the trial, Hamilton argued that people should have the
right to print and speak the truth. Hamilton also said that the law
Zenger broke was a bad one. The editor should be given his
freedom. The jury agreed with Hamilton and freed Zenger.

At the time, few people knew about the Zenger trial.
However, as time went on, freedom of the press came to be seen as
an important right.

1. What was John Peter Zenger tried for?

2. What conclusion did the jury reach at the end of the trial?

© Macmillan/McGraw-Hill

Oral Fluency Record Sheet

Name _____ Date _____

Oral Reading Accuracy: _____% Circle: Fall Winter Spring

Oral Reading Fluency Score: _____ words correct per minute

Prosody Rubric: (Circle Score) 1 2 3 4

Comprehension Question Responses

#1 _____

#2 _____

The Trial of John Peter Zenger

	John Peter Zenger was a courageous man who won an
10	important victory for freedom of the press. In 1732, he was the
22	editor of a New York City newspaper. At that time, the country
34	was still a collection of British colonies.
41	The governor of New York carried out British policies. He
51	did not care whether or not the people approved of these policies.
63	Most newspapers kept quiet about the governor. Zenger's
71	newspaper, however, printed many articles that criticized him.
79	In those days, just printing stories that criticized the
88	government was against the law. It did not matter whether the
99	stories were true or not.
104	Sure enough, Zenger was arrested and sent to prison. He
114	spent ten months there. His newspaper was shut down and went
125	out of business. But Zenger believed he had done the right thing.
137	He met with a lawyer named Andrew Hamilton. Hamilton agreed
147	to take his case.
151	At the trial, Hamilton argued that people should have the
161	right to print and speak the truth. Hamilton also said that the law
174	Zenger broke was a bad one. The editor should be given his
186	freedom. The jury agreed with Hamilton and freed Zenger.
195	At the time, few people knew about the Zenger trial.
205	However, as time went on, freedom of the press came to be seen as
219	an important right. **222**

© Macmillan/McGraw-Hill

Number of words read: _____ Number of errors made: _____

Harriet Beecher Stowe Takes a Stand

In 1852, Harriet Beecher Stowe was a young woman living in a little town in Maine. She had been concerned for a long time about slavery. She believed it was immoral, and she couldn't understand why everyone else did not agree with her. Over the years, she had gone to many lectures about the need to give slaves their freedom. She had read many newspaper articles saying the same thing. But the lectures and articles always annoyed her. They were dry and hard to read, using complex legal arguments.

"Why couldn't someone write a good, readable story?" she asked herself. "Why couldn't a writer show, in dramatic fashion, how terrible slavery is? Why couldn't a clever author show exactly what was going on?" She finally decided to do it herself. She vowed that her story would catch the attention of everybody in the country.

Finally, she finished her book, *Uncle Tom's Cabin*. It not only told about the slaves' struggles but it showed them in vivid detail. The book caused quite a disturbance throughout the country. People who had been against slavery without taking action suddenly became active and voiced their objections to it.

The Civil War broke out a few years after the book was published. During the war, President Abraham Lincoln met Harriet Beecher Stowe. He looked at Stowe and smiled. "So you are the woman who wrote the book that made this great war," Lincoln said with a wide grin.

1. What caused Harriet Beecher Stowe to write *Uncle Tom's Cabin*?
2. What effect did Harriet's book have on the country?

Oral Fluency Record Sheet

Name _____ Date _____

Oral Reading Accuracy: _____%   Circle: Fall Winter Spring

Oral Reading Fluency Score: _____ words correct per minute

Prosody Rubric: (Circle Score) 1 2 3 4

Comprehension Question Responses

#1 _____

#2 _____

Harriet Beecher Stowe Takes a Stand

	In 1852, Harriet Beecher Stowe was a young woman living
10	in a little town in Maine. She had been concerned for a long time
24	about slavery. She believed it was immoral, and she couldn't
34	understand why everyone else did not agree with her. Over the
45	years, she had gone to many lectures about the need to give slaves
58	their freedom. She had read many newspaper articles saying the
68	same thing. But the lectures and articles always annoyed her. They
79	were dry and hard to read, using complex legal arguments.
89	"Why couldn't someone write a good, readable story?" she
98	asked herself. "Why couldn't a writer show, in dramatic fashion,
108	how terrible slavery is? Why couldn't a clever author show exactly
119	what was going on?" She finally decided to do it herself. She vowed
132	that her story would catch the attention of everybody in the country.
144	Finally, she finished her book, *Uncle Tom's Cabin*. It not only told
156	about the slaves' struggles but it showed them in vivid detail. The
168	book caused quite a disturbance throughout the country. People who
178	had been against slavery without taking action suddenly became active
188	and voiced their objections to it.
194	The Civil War broke out a few years after the book was
206	published. During the war, President Abraham Lincoln met Harriet
215	Beecher Stowe. He looked at Stowe and smiled. "So you are the
227	woman who wrote the book that made this great war," Lincoln
238	said with a wide grin. **243**

Number of words read: _____ Number of errors made: _____

Alicia's Dilemma

Alicia had a dog, a miniature schnauzer named Rosie. She had gotten Rosie when both she and the dog were babies, and they had grown up together. Now Alicia had a little sister, Marta, who also loved the dog. But Marta was always sick. She had red, itchy eyes and a runny nose daily. Lately, she was getting ear infections.

"I am afraid that your sister is allergic to your pooch," Dr. Hurtago said to Alicia one day when her mom had taken Marta to the doctor's office.

"But Marta loves Rosie!" cried Alicia.

"That may be so, but the dog is making your sister very ill. She is more uncomfortable than you realize, and it is bad for her to have these constant ear infections."

"Rosie is a member of our family," said Alicia's mom. "What can we do?"

The girls went home and embraced Rosie. Then Marta started sniffling all over again.

The next day after school, Alicia walked over to the office of Rosie's veterinarian. She explained the problem she was having.

"I love Rosie, but I know she can't stay with us. I wish I could find her another home, someplace where I could visit her," she said.

The vet looked thoughtful. "You know," she said, "my sister loves schnauzers and she just moved into town. She has been thinking about getting a dog. This may work out perfectly."

Alicia's face brightened. "And could I visit Rosie and take her for walks?" she asked.

"I'm sure you could," smiled the vet.

1. Who told Alicia that Marta was allergic to Rosie?

2. What is Alicia's dilemma?

Oral Fluency Record Sheet

Name _____ Date _____

Oral Reading Accuracy: _____% Circle: Fall Winter Spring
Oral Reading Fluency Score: _____ words correct per minute
Prosody Rubric: (Circle Score) 1 2 3 4
Comprehension Question Responses
#1 _____
#2 _____

Alicia's Dilemma

	Alicia had a dog, a miniature schnauzer named Rosie. She
10	had gotten Rosie when both she and the dog were babies, and they
23	had grown up together. Now Alicia had a little sister, Marta, who
35	also loved the dog. But Marta was always sick. She had red, itchy
48	eyes and a runny nose daily. Lately, she was getting ear infections.
60	"I am afraid that your sister is allergic to your pooch," Dr.
72	Hurtago said to Alicia one day when her mom had taken Marta to
85	the doctor's office.
88	"But Marta loves Rosie!" cried Alicia.
94	"That may be so, but the dog is making your sister very ill.
107	She is more uncomfortable than you realize, and it is bad for her to
121	have these constant ear infections."
126	"Rosie is a member of our family," said Alicia's mom.
136	"What can we do?"
140	The girls went home and embraced Rosie. Then Marta
149	started sniffling all over again.
154	The next day after school, Alicia walked over to the office
165	of Rosie's veterinarian. She explained the problem she was having.
175	"I love Rosie, but I know she can't stay with us. I wish I could
190	find her another home, someplace where I could visit her," she said.
202	The vet looked thoughtful. "You know," she said, "my sister
212	loves schnauzers and she just moved into town. She has been thinking
224	about getting a dog. This may work out perfectly."
233	Alicia's face brightened. "And could I visit Rosie and take her
244	for walks?" she asked.
248	"I'm sure you could," smiled the vet. **255**

© Macmillan/McGraw-Hill

Number of words read: _____ Number of errors made: _____

Name _____ Date _____

The New Neighbor

Sara Benito moved directly across the street in December. We hit it off immediately, and I thought here was someone I could cherish as a best friend. At school, I introduced Sara to dozens of acquaintances, and she was instantly popular. That first day, Astrid invited both of us over to try a new computer game even though Astrid had never invited me to anything before. The next day Trisha and Becky invited Sara and me to go ice-skating, which I had never done with them before either.

Shortly afterwards, Marisole asked us to go to the aquarium on the weekend. I already had plans, so I asked Marisole if we could postpone the trip. Marisole informed me that it did not matter, that she and Sara would go anyway. Instantly, it hit me that all of the invitations were not really for me. They were for Sara, and I didn't really need to be available.

Meanwhile, Sara kept getting invited to birthday parties, trips to the mall, excursions to the seashore with somebody and her parents, you name it. After a while, I seldom saw Sara anymore, so I sort of discarded the idea that she could be my best friend.

Then, one Friday afternoon, she came knocking at my door, and I asked what was wrong. "Don't you have any parties, films, or concerts to go to?" I asked.

Sara told me that she would prefer to spend the weekend with her best friend, which meant me. Sara and I were best friends after all.

1. What is this story mostly about?

2. Why do you think Sara preferred spending the weekend with her best friend?

Oral Fluency Record Sheet

Name _____ Date _____

Oral Reading Accuracy: _____%   Circle: Fall Winter Spring
Oral Reading Fluency Score: _____ words correct per minute
Prosody Rubric: (Circle Score) 1 2 3 4
Comprehension Question Responses
#1 _____
#2 _____

The New Neighbor

	Sara Benito moved directly across the street in December.
9	We hit it off immediately, and I thought here was someone I
21	could cherish as a best friend. At school, I introduced Sara to
33	dozens of acquaintances, and she was instantly popular. That
42	first day, Astrid invited both of us over to try a new computer
55	game even though Astrid had never invited me to anything
65	before. The next day Trisha and Becky invited Sara and me to
77	go ice-skating, which I had never done with them before either.
89	Shortly afterwards, Marisole asked us to go to the aquarium
99	on the weekend. I already had plans, so I asked Marisole if we
112	could postpone the trip. Marisole informed me that it did not
123	matter, that she and Sara would go anyway. Instantly, it hit me
135	that all of the invitations were not really for me. They were for
148	Sara, and I didn't really need to be available.
157	Meanwhile, Sara kept getting invited to birthday parties,
165	trips to the mall, excursions to the seashore with somebody and
176	her parents, you name it. After a while, I seldom saw Sara
188	anymore, so I sort of discarded the idea that she could be my
201	best friend.
203	Then, one Friday afternoon, she came knocking at my door,
213	and I asked what was wrong. "Don't you have any parties, films,
225	or concerts to go to?" I asked.
232	Sara told me that she would prefer to spend the weekend
243	with her best friend, which meant me. Sara and I were best
255	friends after all. **258**

Number of words read: _____ Number of errors made: _____

Making a Home in a New Place

Every year, millions of people move to the United States from other countries. To move from one country to another is called *immigration*. Immigrants come from all over the world, and they have many different reasons for packing up their belongings and seeking a home in a new country. They may be looking for better jobs, or they may be fleeing from a land where their freedom was denied. Natural disasters may have forced them to leave. Maybe they are looking for the chance to have a better education. Whatever their reasons, they leave behind friends, a way of life, and many memories.

After an immigrant family moves to the United States, they may decide not to stay in the same city they first arrived at. Many immigrants first try to establish themselves near other family members who had immigrated earlier. Sooner or later, the new immigrants may discover that they would have better opportunities elsewhere. They might prefer living in another town, or even another state.

At the beginning of the last century, for instance, many immigrants came from Europe on vessels that landed in New York City. Quite a few of them remained there. But millions of them headed elsewhere, traveling by train, boat, or car.

Today, a family may travel conveniently by plane. However, they still face the same old-fashioned challenge of making a home in a strange place. A family may move a number of times before they eventually find an appropriate place to live.

1. Why do people immigrate?
2. What are some of the decisions new immigrants need to make?

© Macmillan/McGraw-Hill

Oral Fluency Record Sheet

Name _____ Date _____

Oral Reading Accuracy: _____%   Circle: Fall Winter Spring

Oral Reading Fluency Score: _____ words correct per minute

Prosody Rubric: (Circle Score) 1 2 3 4

Comprehension Question Responses

#1 _____

#2 _____

Making a Home in a New Place

11	Every year, millions of people move to the United States from other countries. To move from one country to another is called
22	*immigration.* Immigrants come from all over the world, and they have
33	many different reasons for packing up their belongings and seeking
43	a home in a new country. They may be looking for better jobs, or they
58	may be fleeing from a land where their freedom was denied. Natural
70	disasters may have forced them to leave. Maybe they are looking for the
83	chance to have a better education. Whatever their reasons, they leave
94	behind friends, a way of life, and many memories.
103	After an immigrant family moves to the United States, they
113	may decide not to stay in the same city they first arrived at.
126	Many immigrants first try to establish themselves near other family
136	members who had immigrated earlier. Sooner or later, the new
146	immigrants may discover that they would have better opportunities
155	elsewhere. They might prefer living in another town, or even
165	another state.
167	At the beginning of the last century, for instance, many
177	immigrants came from Europe on vessels that landed in New York
188	City. Quite a few of them remained there. But millions of them
200	headed elsewhere, traveling by train, boat, or car.
208	Today, a family may travel conveniently by plane. However,
217	they still face the same old-fashioned challenge of making a home in
230	a strange place. A family may move a number of times before they
243	eventually find an appropriate place to live. **250**

Number of words read: _____ Number of errors made: _____

Job Moves

The work that you do can determine how frequently you change your home address. If you are a migrant worker, for instance, you must follow agricultural crops to make a living. Your employment depends on what is being cultivated and harvested in a farm during a particular season. Of course, your family goes where you go.

If circus performing is your specialty, your job may sound exciting, but circuses travel from town to town all over the country annually. You have to learn how to get in and out of a location quickly because the next arena is waiting.

If you work for the military, you are also frequently asked to change locations. Suddenly, you may be stationed in a foreign country, thousands of miles away from your current residence.

Being a physician often does not keep you in one place either. You may have to work in various hospitals while you finish your internship. It may be exciting for you because you can look forward to expanding your knowledge in a new institution, but how would your family feel about moving again?

How about research scientists, you might inquire? Surely you can get a job at a great laboratory and your projects might be paid for by the government or by big corporations. But sometimes, your project may last for only a year or two, and not be renewed. Then you just find another project somewhere else. Of course, as a consequence, your family will have to pack up and say good-bye to their friends.

1. How might the kind of job you have affect where you live?

2. Why would it be difficult for a family to keep moving to different locations?

© Macmillan/McGraw-Hill

Oral Fluency Record Sheet

Name _____   Date _____

Oral Reading Accuracy: _____%

Oral Reading Fluency Score: _____ words correct per minute

Prosody Rubric: (Circle Score) 1 2 3 4

Comprehension Question Responses

#1 _____

#2 _____

Job Moves

	The work that you do can determine how frequently you
10	change your home address. If you are a migrant worker, for
21	instance, you must follow agricultural crops to make a living. Your
32	employment depends on what is being cultivated and harvested in
42	a farm during a particular season. Of course, your family goes
53	where you go.
56	If circus performing is your specialty, your job may sound
66	exciting, but circuses travel from town to town all over the country
78	annually. You have to learn how to get in and out of a location
92	quickly because the next arena is waiting.
99	If you work for the military, you are also frequently asked
110	to change locations. Suddenly, you may be stationed in a foreign
121	country, thousands of miles away from your current residence.
130	Being a physician often does not keep you in one place
141	either. You may have to work in various hospitals while you finish
153	your internship. It may be exciting for you because you can look
165	forward to expanding your knowledge in a new institution, but
175	how would your family feel about moving again?
183	How about research scientists, you might inquire? Surely
191	you can get a job at a great laboratory and your projects might be
205	paid for by the government or by big corporations. But sometimes,
216	your project may last for only a year or two, and not be renewed.
230	Then you just find another project somewhere else. Of course, as a
242	consequence, your family will have to pack up and say good-bye to
255	their friends. **257**

Number of words read: _____   Number of errors made: _____

The Good Old Days

Jada was helping Ms. Funes dig a space for a new porch. "Be careful," Ms. Funes said. "There used to be a library on this site, about 100 years ago, and we might discover some books buried underground."

"It would be amazing to unearth real books!" Jada exclaimed. She had learned about them in school in her twenty-first century culture class, but to actually experience a real book would be absolutely astonishing. Suddenly, Jada felt a large object that had pages and seemed to be made of paper. "Is this what you call a book?" Jada asked, and Ms. Funes nodded. The title of the book was *A Guide to Collecting Postage Stamps*. Completely intrigued, Jada looked at the photographs and wondered what postage stamps were. Ms. Funes explained that they were things people used to put on letters. Letters were an ancient form of writing that people used to communicate.

"Why didn't they just communicate by mental telepathy, like we do?" Jada asked.

"Their technology was very ancient," Ms. Funes responded. An instant later, Jada felt something much bigger than the book. The two amateur archaeologists spent several minutes unearthing something that had a large viewing screen and a keyboard.

"It is one of the first computers ever created!" Ms. Funes cried.

"But why," Jada asked, "would they make a computer so immense?" Ms. Funes tried to explain. "They must have appreciated things that were massive and solid. It is hard to comprehend, isn't it?"

1. What is this story mostly about?
2. Why didn't Jada know what a real book was?

Oral Fluency Record Sheet

Name _____   Date _____

Oral Reading Accuracy: _____%   Circle: Fall Winter Spring
Oral Reading Fluency Score: _____ words correct per minute
Prosody Rubric: (Circle Score) 1 2 3 4
Comprehension Question Responses
#1 _____
#2 _____

The Good Old Days

	Jada was helping Ms. Funes dig a space for a new porch. "Be
13	careful," Ms. Funes said. "There used to be a library on this site, about
27	100 years ago, and we might discover some books buried underground."
38	"It would be amazing to unearth real books!" Jada exclaimed. She
49	had learned about them in school in her twenty-first century culture class,
62	but to actually experience a real book would be absolutely astonishing.
73	Suddenly, Jada felt a large object that had pages and seemed to be made
87	of paper. "Is this what you call a book?" Jada asked, and Ms. Funes
101	nodded. The title of the book was *A Guide to Collecting Postage Stamps*.
114	Completely intrigued, Jada looked at the photographs and wondered what
124	postage stamps were. Ms. Funes explained that they were things people
135	used to put on letters. Letters were an ancient form of writing that people
149	used to communicate.
152	"Why didn't they just communicate by mental telepathy, like we
162	do?" Jada asked.
165	"Their technology was very ancient," Ms. Funes responded. An
174	instant later, Jada felt something much bigger than the book. The two
186	amateur archaeologists spent several minutes unearthing something that
194	had a large viewing screen and a keyboard.
202	"It is one of the first computers ever created!" Ms. Funes cried.
214	"But why," Jada asked, "would they make a computer so immense?"
225	Ms. Funes tried to explain. "They must have appreciated things that
236	were massive and solid. It is hard to comprehend, isn't it?" **247**

Number of words read: _____   Number of errors made: _____

The Soccer Hog

Henry was the town's soccer superstar. His dad had started him on lessons in how to run, kick, and score with a soccer ball when he was very young. Henry was kicking a soccer ball before he could speak. No one was surprised when Henry was chosen to be the team captain. No one was astonished when Henry scored all the goals. No one was astounded when Henry played like a team of one on the soccer field.

No one was surprised, astonished, or astounded, but no one was delighted either. Henry had become a soccer hog. His teammates never got to do fancy tricks with the ball and never had an opportunity to score.

Henry's dad was the team coach. He saw that a lot of the other players were grumbling about the situation. He realized that they had good reason to grumble. Henry was helping them to win almost all their games, but he was taking a lot of the fun out of winning.

Henry's dad sat Henry down and told him he had coached him well, but he had created a selfish athlete. He told his son that even though he was probably the best player on the team, he had to allow the other players time with the ball.

Henry was not happy, but he knew his dad was right. After that, he made sure to set his teammates up to score some goals, too. After that, the team seemed to play even better than before, and the team victories were now a lot more satisfying.

1. Why was Henry called a soccer hog?
2. What did Henry's dad ask him to do?

Oral Fluency Record Sheet

Name _____   Date _____

Oral Reading Accuracy: _____%   Circle: Fall Winter Spring

Oral Reading Fluency Score: _____ words correct per minute

Prosody Rubric: (Circle Score) 1 2 3 4

Comprehension Question Responses

#1 _____

#2 _____

The Soccer Hog

	Henry was the town's soccer superstar. His dad had started
10	him on lessons in how to run, kick, and score with a soccer ball
24	when he was very young. Henry was kicking a soccer ball before
36	he could speak. No one was surprised when Henry was chosen to
48	be the team captain. No one was astonished when Henry scored all
60	the goals. No one was astounded when Henry played like a team of
73	one on the soccer field.
78	No one was surprised, astonished, or astounded, but no one
88	was delighted either. Henry had become a soccer hog. His
98	teammates never got to do fancy tricks with the ball and never had
111	an opportunity to score.
115	Henry's dad was the team coach. He saw that a lot of the
128	other players were grumbling about the situation. He realized that
138	they had good reason to grumble. Henry was helping them to win
150	almost all their games, but he was taking a lot of the fun out of winning.
166	Henry's dad sat Henry down and told him he had coached
177	him well, but he had created a selfish athlete. He told his son that
191	even though he was probably the best player on the team, he had to
205	allow the other players time with the ball.
213	Henry was not happy, but he knew his dad was right. After
225	that, he made sure to set his teammates up to score some goals, too.
239	After that, the team seemed to play even better than before, and the
252	team victories were now a lot more satisfying. **260**

Number of words read: _____   Number of errors made: _____

Name _____   Date _____

Pompeii Yesterday and Today

Pompeii was an ancient city in southern Italy that disappeared after a nearby volcano erupted in A.D. 79. The city lay buried under layers of cinders, ashes, and stone for hundreds of years before it was rediscovered in the 1700s. Now more than three quarters of the city has been uncovered, and much of the city looks just as it did in ancient times.

During the disaster, lava and mud flowed into a nearby city but not into Pompeii. Instead, the city was showered with hot, wet ashes and cinders. When the ashes and cinders dried, they covered and sealed up much of the city. Only the tops of walls and columns could be seen. Later, other eruptions completely buried the city.

Many wealthy Romans lived in ancient Pompeii. The weather in Pompeii was warm and sunny, and Romans built large villas there to take advantage of the good climate. Many of the buildings near the center of the city had two stories. The city was surrounded by a great wall with seven gates and had a theater, many temples, a gladiator's court, and three large public baths.

During the eruption of A.D. 79, the air was filled with poisonous gases. Many people were able to get away, but many others died in their homes or as they fled.

Today visitors can walk in and out of houses and up and down narrow lanes, just as people did long ago. The eruption took place while the city was having an election. Visitors can still see election slogans on many walls.

1. Why was Pompeii so well preserved?
2. Why is finding Pompeii an important discovery?

Oral Fluency Record Sheet

Name _____ Date _____

Oral Reading Accuracy: _____% Circle: Fall Winter Spring

Oral Reading Fluency Score: _____ words correct per minute

Prosody Rubric: (Circle Score) 1 2 3 4

Comprehension Question Responses

#1 _____

#2 _____

Pompeii Yesterday and Today

	Pompeii was an ancient city in southern Italy that
9	disappeared after a nearby volcano erupted in A.D. 79. The city lay
21	buried under layers of cinders, ashes, and stone for hundreds of
32	years before it was rediscovered in the 1700s. Now more than
43	three quarters of the city has been uncovered, and much of the city
56	looks just as it did in ancient times.
64	During the disaster, lava and mud flowed into a nearby city
75	but not into Pompeii. Instead, the city was showered with hot, wet
87	ashes and cinders. When the ashes and cinders dried, they covered
98	and sealed up much of the city. Only the tops of walls and columns
112	could be seen. Later, other eruptions completely buried the city.
122	Many wealthy Romans lived in ancient Pompeii. The
130	weather in Pompeii was warm and sunny, and Romans built large
141	villas there to take advantage of the good climate. Many of the
153	buildings near the center of the city had two stories. The city was
166	surrounded by a great wall with seven gates and had a theater,
178	many temples, a gladiator's court, and three large public baths.
188	During the eruption of A.D. 79, the air was filled with
199	poisonous gases. Many people were able to get away, but many
210	others died in their homes or as they fled.
219	Today visitors can walk in and out of houses and up and
231	down narrow lanes, just as people did long ago. The eruption took
243	place while the city was having an election. Visitors can still see
255	election slogans on many walls. **260**

Number of words read: _____ Number of errors made: _____

The Last Frontier

Many people claim that space is the last frontier. By this they mean that every country on Earth has already been discovered and explored. To be true explorers, they say, we must journey to distant planets.

While it may be true that space is an open frontier, plenty of frontier still exists here on our planet. This is because the deepest spots of our planet, deep areas beneath the oceans, are still unexplored. The average depth of the world's oceans is 12,200 feet, but parts of the ocean plunge much deeper. The deepest known spot is in the western Pacific and is 36,198 feet below sea level.

Divers can go only so far with the deep sea breathing equipment we have today. To really reach the ocean's depths, people need to travel in special vehicles especially built for underwater exploration. Only a handful of people have done that.

We know that plant life is rare deep below the ocean's surface. That's because sunlight is necessary for plant survival and solar rays can penetrate only about 660 feet below the surface of the water. Deeper than that, the waters are completely dark and plants are unable to survive. Many sea creatures depend on plants for food. What can we assume then about animal activity in the deep water?

We know that some animals have adapted to life in the dark by becoming luminous, giving off a glow. Other creatures have become scavengers, feeding on whatever drops to the ocean floor. But these are just scattered pieces of information. Perhaps one day you will become an underwater explorer and uncover even more secrets of the deep sea.

1. In the author's opinion, what really is the last frontier?
2. Why don't we know more about life at the bottom of the ocean?

Oral Fluency Record Sheet

Name _____   Date _____

Oral Reading Accuracy: _____%   Circle: Fall Winter Spring

Oral Reading Fluency Score: _____ words correct per minute

Prosody Rubric: (Circle Score) 1 2 3 4

Comprehension Question Responses

#1 _____

#2 _____

The Last Frontier

	Many people claim that space is the last frontier. By this
11	they mean that every country on Earth has already been discovered
22	and explored. To be true explorers, they say, we must journey to
34	distant planets.
36	While it may be true that space is an open frontier, plenty
48	of frontier still exists here on our planet. This is because the
60	deepest spots of our planet, deep areas beneath the oceans, are still
72	unexplored. The average depth of the world's oceans is 12,200 feet,
83	but parts of the ocean plunge much deeper. The deepest known
94	spot is in the western Pacific and is 36,198 feet below sea level.
107	Divers can go only so far with the deep sea breathing
118	equipment we have today. To really reach the ocean's depths,
128	people need to travel in special vehicles especially built for
138	underwater exploration. Only a handful of people have done that.
148	We know that plant life is rare deep below the ocean's
159	surface. That's because sunlight is necessary for plant survival and
169	solar rays can penetrate only about 660 feet below the surface of
181	the water. Deeper than that, the waters are completely dark and
192	plants are unable to survive. Many sea creatures depend on plants
203	for food. What can we assume then about animal activity in the
215	deep water?
217	We know that some animals have adapted to life in the dark
229	by becoming luminous, giving off a glow. Other creatures have
239	become scavengers, feeding on whatever drops to the ocean floor.
249	But these are just scattered pieces of information. Perhaps one day
260	you will become an underwater explorer and uncover even more
270	secrets of the deep sea. **275**

Number of words read: _____   Number of errors made: _____

Name _____ Date _____

The Trojan Horse

Many of the great legends of ancient Greece were about the Trojan Wars. Troy and Greece had been fighting each other for more than 10 years. Neither side was winning. The Greek army was outside of the walls of Troy. It had been trying to get into the city, but the Greek leaders could not figure out a way to get through Troy's walls. All their attempts had failed.

Odysseus was the most resourceful of the Greek leaders. Finally, he came up with an idea. The Greeks would build an immense wooden horse. It would have a huge hollow compartment inside. Odysseus and the best of the Greek warriors would hide inside the horse. The horse would be given to the Trojans as a peace offering. If the plan worked, the Trojans themselves would let the horse with the Greek warriors inside into the city.

Odysseus ordered the rest of the Greeks to sail away. Only one Greek seemed to be left behind, a man named Sinon.

Sinon went to the city gates and told a wondrous tale. The Greeks had departed, leaving the horse as a gift. The horse would bring good fortune to Troy.

The Trojans believed Sinon. They carried the horse past the walls and into the city. That night, as the Trojans slept, the Greek army turned its ships around and sailed back to Troy. The soldiers inside the horse crept out. They opened the city gates for the rest of the army. The Greeks killed the Trojans and burned their city. The wars were over.

1. What problem did the Greeks face in trying to conquer Troy?

2. What solution did Odysseus invent for the Greek warriors?

Oral Fluency Record Sheet

Name _____ Date _____

Oral Reading Accuracy: _____%   Circle: Fall Winter Spring

Oral Reading Fluency Score: _____ words correct per minute

Prosody Rubric: (Circle Score) 1 2 3 4

Comprehension Question Responses

#1 _____

#2 _____

The Trojan Horse

11	Many of the great legends of ancient Greece were about the
	Trojan Wars. Troy and Greece had been fighting each other for
22	more than 10 years. Neither side was winning. The Greek army
33	was outside of the walls of Troy. It had been trying to get into the
48	city, but the Greek leaders could not figure out a way to get
61	through Troy's walls. All their attempts had failed.
69	Odysseus was the most resourceful of the Greek leaders.
78	Finally, he came up with an idea. The Greeks would build an
90	immense wooden horse. It would have a huge hollow compartment
100	inside. Odysseus and the best of the Greek warriors would hide
111	inside the horse. The horse would be given to the Trojans as a
124	peace offering. If the plan worked, the Trojans themselves would
134	let the horse with the Greek warriors inside into the city.
145	Odysseus ordered the rest of the Greeks to sail away. Only
156	one Greek seemed to be left behind, a man named Sinon.
167	Sinon went to the city gates and told a wondrous tale. The
179	Greeks had departed, leaving the horse as a gift. The horse would
191	bring good fortune to Troy.
196	The Trojans believed Sinon. They carried the horse past
205	the walls and into the city. That night, as the Trojans slept, the
218	Greek army turned its ships around and sailed back to Troy. The
230	soldiers inside the horse crept out. They opened the city gates for
242	the rest of the army. The Greeks killed the Trojans and burned
254	their city. The wars were over. **260**

Number of words read: _____   Number of errors made: _____

Odysseus and the Sirens

Odysseus was a distinguished Greek hero celebrated in many legends. One of these legends tells about an adventure Odysseus had while sailing home from Troy.

Odysseus knew that he and his crew would have to pass perilously close to the island of the Sirens. The Sirens were a dangerous group of singers whose voices were extremely beautiful. Every time a ship got close to the island, the Sirens would deliberately stand on a hilltop, waving and singing rhythmically. The ship's crew would forget about steering and head directly for the beautiful melody. Before long, their boat would crash and break against the rocky shore.

Odysseus was a man with common sense. He did not want his boat to be destroyed by the Sirens. He came up with a good plan. He instructed his crew to plug their ears with wax while the ship was steering past the island. Then the crew would not be able to hear the song, and the boat would be safe.

But Odysseus yearned to hear the Sirens' song. So he thought of another scheme. He had the crew strap him tightly to the mast. Then, as the crew rowed near the island, Odysseus listened to the most beautiful music imaginable. He struggled in vain to get free, to throw himself into the water and swim toward the Sirens. Finally, the boat passed the island. The sailors took the wax out of their ears and loosened the knots tying Odysseus. He was exhausted, but safe.

1. What danger did Odysseus face near the island of the Sirens?
2. Why did the crew tie Odysseus to the mast?

© Macmillan/McGraw-Hill

Oral Fluency Record Sheet

Name _____ Date _____

Oral Reading Accuracy: _____% Circle: Fall Winter Spring

Oral Reading Fluency Score: _____ words correct per minute

Prosody Rubric: (Circle Score) 1 2 3 4

Comprehension Question Responses

#1 _____

#2 _____

Odysseus and the Sirens

	Odysseus was a distinguished Greek hero celebrated in
8	many legends. One of these legends tells about an adventure
18	Odysseus had while sailing home from Troy.
25	Odysseus knew that he and his crew would have to pass
36	perilously close to the island of the Sirens. The Sirens were a
48	dangerous group of singers whose voices were extremely beautiful.
57	Every time a ship got close to the island, the Sirens would
69	deliberately stand on a hilltop, waving and singing rhythmically.
78	The ship's crew would forget about steering and head directly for
89	the beautiful melody. Before long, their boat would crash and
99	break against the rocky shore.
104	Odysseus was a man with common sense. He did not want
115	his boat to be destroyed by the Sirens. He came up with a good
129	plan. He instructed his crew to plug their ears with wax while the
142	ship was steering past the island. Then the crew would not be able
155	to hear the song, and the boat would be safe.
165	But Odysseus yearned to hear the Sirens' song. So he
175	thought of another scheme. He had the crew strap him tightly to
187	the mast. Then, as the crew rowed near the island, Odysseus
198	listened to the most beautiful music imaginable. He struggled in
208	vain to get free, to throw himself into the water and swim toward
221	the Sirens. Finally, the boat passed the island. The sailors took the
233	wax out of their ears and loosened the knots tying Odysseus. He
245	was exhausted, but safe. **249**

Number of words read: _____ Number of errors made: _____

Name _____ Date _____

Egyptian Writing

Egyptian picture writing, or hieroglyphics, began almost
5,000 years ago. At first, the Egyptians just drew pictures to stand
for objects. For example, the sun was a circle with a dot in it. A
house was a small rectangle. Over time, it became too difficult to
come up with a new picture for each word. So the Egyptians began
to combine words to make sounds. For example, the Egyptian
word for "go out" sounds like the words for "house" and "sun."
Writers just combined these two pictures when they needed to write
the word that means "go out."

Over the centuries, the ability to understand Egyptian
writing was lost. Experts puzzled over Egyptian texts without any
idea of what they meant. Then, in 1799, an officer in the French
army found the Rosetta Stone in Egypt. The strange black stone
had three sections of writing carved into it. The first section was a
story in Greek. The other two sections were translations of the
same story into Egyptian picture writing. Using these translations,
experts quickly decoded the Rosetta Stone. Using what they
deciphered, they soon solved the puzzle of Egyptian hieroglyphics.

Picture writing was used for thousands of years. But by
1000 B.C., the Phoenicians, a people who also lived in the Middle
East, created a less clumsy writing system. Instead of combining
pictures to make sounds, they developed an alphabet. Each letter in
the alphabet stood for a sound. To form words, several sounds
were blended together. The alphabet that we use today comes from
the original Phoenician alphabet.

1. How is ancient Egyptian writing different from the way we write?

2. What is the importance of the Rosetta Stone?

Oral Fluency Record Sheet

Name _____ Date _____

Oral Reading Accuracy: _____%   Circle: Fall Winter Spring

Oral Reading Fluency Score: _____ words correct per minute

Prosody Rubric: (Circle Score) 1 2 3 4

Comprehension Question Responses

#1 _____

#2 _____

Egyptian Writing

	Egyptian picture writing, or hieroglyphics, began almost
7	5,000 years ago. At first, the Egyptians just drew pictures to stand
19	for objects. For example, the sun was a circle with a dot in it. A
34	house was a small rectangle. Over time, it became too difficult to
46	come up with a new picture for each word. So the Egyptians began
59	to combine words to make sounds. For example, the Egyptian
69	word for "go out" sounds like the words for "house" and "sun."
81	Writers just combined these two pictures when they needed to write
92	the word that means "go out."
98	Over the centuries, the ability to understand Egyptian
106	writing was lost. Experts puzzled over Egyptian texts without any
116	idea of what they meant. Then, in 1799, an officer in the French
129	army found the Rosetta Stone in Egypt. The strange black stone
140	had three sections of writing carved into it. The first section was a
153	story in Greek. The other two sections were translations of the
164	same story into Egyptian picture writing. Using these translations,
173	experts quickly decoded the Rosetta Stone. Using what they
182	deciphered, they soon solved the puzzle of Egyptian hieroglyphics.
191	Picture writing was used for thousands of years. But by
201	1000 B.C., the Phoenicians, a people who also lived in the Middle
213	East, created a less clumsy writing system. Instead of combining
223	pictures to make sounds, they developed an alphabet. Each letter in
234	the alphabet stood for a sound. To form words, several sounds
245	were blended together. The alphabet that we use today comes from
256	the original Phoenician alphabet. **260**

Number of words read: _____   Number of errors made: _____

Dr. Seuss

What was the title of the first book you read by yourself from cover to cover? Was it one of the many books by Dr. Seuss?

Dr. Seuss's last name was not really Seuss, and Dr. Seuss was not really a doctor. His real name was Theodor Seuss Geisel. His friends called him Ted. Ted did not start out writing children's books. Instead, after he graduated from college, he drew pictures for ads. Many of these pictures were funny cartoons.

One company he worked for sold an insecticide called Flit. Flit came in big spray guns. For Flit ads, Ted drew many funny cartoons of big, strange-looking bugs. His ads became famous. Ted signed them all with the name Dr. Seuss.

Ted got the idea for his first children's book during a trip on an ocean liner. The ship's engine made a *ka chunka, ka chunka* sound. The engine's sounds made a simple rhyme pop into Ted's head. It went, "And that is a story that no one can beat. And to think that I saw it on Mulberry Street." Dr. Seuss's first children's book was called *And to Think That I Saw It on Mulberry Street*.

One of Dr. Seuss's most famous books is *The Cat in the Hat*. In this story, two children find themselves home alone with a very strange cat. Children love this story about a cat and his very bad manners. Another of his famous books is *Green Eggs and Ham*. The book tells its story with a vocabulary of just 50 words.

1. What is Dr. Seuss known for?

2. What inspired the first children's book that Dr. Seuss wrote?

© Macmillan/McGraw-Hill

Oral Fluency Record Sheet

Name _____ Date _____

Oral Reading Accuracy: _____%   Circle: Fall Winter Spring

Oral Reading Fluency Score: _____ words correct per minute

Prosody Rubric: (Circle Score) 1 2 3 4

Comprehension Question Responses

#1 _____

#2 _____

Dr. Seuss

	What was the title of the first book you read by yourself
12	from cover to cover? Was it one of the many books by Dr. Seuss?
26	Dr. Seuss's last name was not really Seuss, and Dr. Seuss
37	was not really a doctor. His real name was Theodor Seuss Geisel.
49	His friends called him Ted. Ted did not start out writing children's
61	books. Instead, after he graduated from college, he drew pictures
71	for ads. Many of these pictures were funny cartoons.
80	One company he worked for sold an insecticide called Flit.
90	Flit came in big spray guns. For Flit ads, Ted drew many funny
103	cartoons of big, strange-looking bugs. His ads became famous. Ted
114	signed them all with the name Dr. Seuss.
122	Ted got the idea for his first children's book during a trip on
135	an ocean liner. The ship's engine made a *ka chunka, ka chunka*
147	sound. The engine's sounds made a simple rhyme pop into Ted's
158	head. It went, "And that is a story that no one can beat. And to
173	think that I saw it on Mulberry Street." Dr. Seuss's first children's
185	book was called *And to Think That I Saw It on Mulberry Street*.
198	One of Dr. Seuss's most famous books is *The Cat in the*
210	*Hat*. In this story, two children find themselves home alone with a
222	very strange cat. Children love this story about a cat and his very
235	bad manners. Another of his famous books is *Green Eggs and*
246	*Ham*. The book tells its story with a vocabulary of just
257	50 words. **259**

Number of words read: _____ Number of errors made: _____

Max Delivers

Walter's dog, a retriever named Max, went everywhere with him. He followed him to the playground, to school, and to friends' homes. But today Walter did not care if Max followed him. He was so angry that he did not even want to look at Max. Max had ruined Walter's homework, a report on the history of fireworks. Walter had left his report on the kitchen table next to his lunch, a meatball sandwich. Max ripped open the paper bag and spilled tomato sauce all over the report. Walter couldn't take the report to school, and he didn't have time to make another copy.

Walter trudged to school with Max plodding along behind him. What should he do? He had no report to present to the class. When Walter reached the school yard, Max waited for him outside, the way he always did. When an orange tabby cat walked by, Max growled. Walter ignored Max and walked into class.

It was a hot day. All the windows in the classroom were open. Promptly at nine, the class reports began. First, Jenny gave a talk about the geography of China. Then Raj gave a report about ancient inventions. Eventually, the teacher called on Walter.

Suddenly, something orange came hurtling in through the open window. It was the cat from the playground. Max had chased it and was barking ferociously outside. The commotion lasted for a while. By the time the custodian came to take the cat out of the building, it was too late for Walter's report. For tomorrow, Walter could make a fresh copy of the report. For now, Max had saved him. What a terrific dog!

1. Why was Walter upset on the way to school?

2. What does the title "Max Delivers" mean?

Oral Fluency Record Sheet

Name _____ Date _____

Oral Reading Accuracy: _____%

Circle: Fall Winter Spring

Oral Reading Fluency Score: _____ words correct per minute

Prosody Rubric: (Circle Score) 1 2 3 4

Comprehension Question Responses

#1 _____

#2 _____

Max Delivers

	Walter's dog, a retriever named Max, went everywhere
8	with him. He followed him to the playground, to school, and to
20	friends' homes. But today Walter did not care if Max followed him.
32	He was so angry that he did not even want to look at Max. Max
47	had ruined Walter's homework, a report on the history of
57	fireworks. Walter had left his report on the kitchen table next to his
70	lunch, a meatball sandwich. Max ripped open the paper bag and
81	spilled tomato sauce all over the report. Walter couldn't take the
92	report to school, and he didn't have time to make another copy.
104	Walter trudged to school with Max plodding along behind
113	him. What should he do? He had no report to present to the class.
127	When Walter reached the school yard, Max waited for him outside,
138	the way he always did. When an orange tabby cat walked by, Max
151	growled. Walter ignored Max and walked into class.
159	It was a hot day. All the windows in the classroom were open.
172	Promptly at nine, the class reports began. First, Jenny gave a talk
184	about the geography of China. Then Raj gave a report about ancient
196	inventions. Eventually, the teacher called on Walter.
203	Suddenly, something orange came hurtling in through the open
212	window. It was the cat from the playground. Max had chased it and
225	was barking ferociously outside. The commotion lasted for a while.
235	By the time the custodian came to take the cat out of the building, it
250	was too late for Walter's report. For tomorrow, Walter could make a
262	fresh copy of the report. For now, Max had saved him. What a
275	terrific dog! **277**

© Macmillan/McGraw-Hill

Number of words read: _____ Number of errors made: _____

A Rare Find

Maria and Todd discovered an old vinyl record while looking through the attic. "Thelma Cross!" Maria cried. "I read about her in a magazine. This could be worth millions!" As it turned out, the record was not worth quite that much. However, it was a very rare recording, one of the few original Thelma Cross recordings left.

Mr. Sanchez, an executive at an auction company, told Maria and Todd that it could be worth thousands. He thought they should think about selling it. Todd thought this was a good idea. Maria, however, didn't want to do anything until she found out more about Thelma Cross.

At the library, they listened to tapes of her songs. They also saw photographs of her that were decades old and looked through a biography about the singer's life and music. They also found an article on the Internet about what Thelma had been doing recently. She still worked occasionally as a performer because she needed the money. Although Thelma originally earned good money for her work, she never owned the copyrights to her songs. That meant that while other people still profited from her old songs, she no longer earned a penny from them.

"That's not fair!" Todd cried.

A few minutes later, Maria called Mr. Sanchez. "We still want to sell the record," she told him. "But we want the money to go to Thelma Cross. Can you help us do that?"

"I sure can," said Mr. Sanchez. Then he added, "You two are doing a commendable thing."

1. What is this story mostly about?

2. Why did Todd and Maria decide to give away the money?

Oral Fluency Record Sheet

Name _____ Date _____

Oral Reading Accuracy: _____%   Circle: Fall Winter Spring

Oral Reading Fluency Score: _____ words correct per minute

Prosody Rubric: (Circle Score) 1 2 3 4

Comprehension Question Responses

#1 _____

#2 _____

A Rare Find

9	Maria and Todd discovered an old vinyl record while looking through the attic. "Thelma Cross!" Maria cried. "I read
19	about her in a magazine. This could be worth millions!" As it
31	turned out, the record was not worth quite that much. However, it
43	was a very rare recording, one of the few original Thelma Cross
55	recordings left.
57	Mr. Sanchez, an executive at an auction company, told Maria
67	and Todd that it could be worth thousands. He thought they should think
80	about selling it. Todd thought this was a good idea. Maria, however,
92	didn't want to do anything until she found out more about
103	Thelma Cross.
105	At the library, they listened to tapes of her songs. They also
117	saw photographs of her that were decades old and looked through a
129	biography about the singer's life and music. They also found an
140	article on the Internet about what Thelma had been doing recently.
151	She still worked occasionally as a performer because she needed
161	the money. Although Thelma originally earned good money for her
171	work, she never owned the copyrights to her songs. That meant
182	that while other people still profited from her old songs, she no
194	longer earned a penny from them.
200	"That's not fair!" Todd cried.
205	A few minutes later, Maria called Mr. Sanchez. "We still
215	want to sell the record," she told him. "But we want the money to
229	go to Thelma Cross. Can you help us do that?"
239	"I sure can," said Mr. Sanchez. Then he added, "You two
250	are doing a commendable thing." **255**

© Macmillan/McGraw-Hill

Number of words read: _____   Number of errors made: _____

Grade 6 • Fluency Assessment • **353**

New Pearls

With its deep white luster, the beauty of a pearl is beyond
compare. Yet pearls start out as nothing more than tiny bits of
matter. A grain of sand gets inside the shell of an oyster or clam.
The animal then covers the sand with layers of shell-like
material called mother-of-pearl. In time, a beautiful round
pearl forms.

Oyster pearls are definitely the most popular pearls
because of their roundness and deep white color. But other
mollusks, animals with shells, also make pearls. In fact, pearls
come in a wide variety of shapes, sizes, and colors. The
Caribbean conch produces dazzling pink pearls. Blue, black,
and yellow pearls are highly prized because they are rare.

Some pearls are valued at thousands of dollars. This price
reflects how fascinating they are. It also shows how rare it is to
find a natural pearl. Pearl divers discover a good pearl only once
in about a thousand attempts.

But where there is a will, there is a way. Japanese pearl
collectors grew tired of depending on fortune alone to find pearls.
So, they invented a process to encourage oysters to make pearls
faster. They deposited a particle into the body of an oyster, and in
three to five years, a decent-size cultured pearl was almost sure
to form.

The invention of cultured pearls opened up a new market
for pearls. Previously, only very wealthy people could afford a string
of natural pearls. Now, pearls are available to everyone. Each year
some 500 million cultured pearls are made. They cost less than a
natural pearl but are almost as attractive.

1. How are cultured pearls and natural pearls different?

2. Why are pearls more affordable now than they were in the past?

© Macmillan/McGraw-Hill

Oral Fluency Record Sheet

Name _____ Date _____

Oral Reading Accuracy: _____% Circle: Fall Winter Spring

Oral Reading Fluency Score: _____ words correct per minute

Prosody Rubric: (Circle Score) 1 2 3 4

Comprehension Question Responses

#1 _____

#2 _____

New Pearls

	With its deep white luster, the beauty of a pearl is beyond
12	compare. Yet pearls start out as nothing more than tiny bits of
24	matter. A grain of sand gets inside the shell of an oyster or clam.
38	The animal then covers the sand with layers of shell-like
49	material called mother-of-pearl. In time, a beautiful round
59	pearl forms.
61	Oyster pearls are definitely the most popular pearls
69	because of their roundness and deep white color. But other
79	mollusks, animals with shells, also make pearls. In fact, pearls
89	come in a wide variety of shapes, sizes, and colors. The
100	Caribbean conch produces dazzling pink pearls. Blue, black,
108	and yellow pearls are highly prized because they are rare.
118	Some pearls are valued at thousands of dollars. This price
128	reflects how fascinating they are. It also shows how rare it is to
141	find a natural pearl. Pearl divers discover a good pearl only once
153	in about a thousand attempts.
158	But where there is a will, there is a way. Japanese pearl
170	collectors grew tired of depending on fortune alone to find pearls.
181	So, they invented a process to encourage oysters to make pearls
192	faster. They deposited a particle into the body of an oyster, and in
205	three to five years, a decent-size cultured pearl was almost sure
217	to form.
219	The invention of cultured pearls opened up a new market
229	for pearls. Previously, only very wealthy people could afford a string
240	of natural pearls. Now, pearls are available to everyone. Each year
251	some 500 million cultured pearls are made. They cost less than a
263	natural pearl but are almost as attractive. **270**

Number of words read: _____ Number of errors made: _____

Centuries of Whaling

When Vikings roamed the Atlantic Ocean long ago, one of the greatest prizes they sought was whales. Way back in the 1100s, the struggle between whale and sailor was a fairly even one, but over time, whaling methods grew more and more advanced. By the mid-1800s, whaling had become a big business.

Norwegian whalers, the modern relatives of the Vikings, were among the leaders in whaling technology. In 1863, a Norwegian sea captain created a new type of whaling ship. The 82-foot-long boat was sleek and swift, fast enough to catch up with even the fastest swimming whale. It also had bomb harpoons. These harpoons were tipped with bombs that would explode inside the whale. They caused death much sooner than ordinary harpoons. Suddenly, the seas were even more dangerous than ever for whales.

By the late 1800s, many whale species were endangered. The numbers of both the right whale and the bowhead whale dropped sharply. Because these whales were slower than the new boats, they were easy to kill. Sadly, millions of whales were slaughtered before a ban on whaling was agreed upon in 1982. Since then, whaling has been prohibited and successfully suppressed.

But almost all kinds of whales still suffer because of the extensive whaling in the past. Some whales, like the gray whale, have recovered quite nicely. Their numbers continue to grow. Others, like the northern right whale, continue to be in danger of extinction. At the present time, fewer than 400 northern right whales exist in the whole world. Only time will tell if whales can survive the effects of centuries of whaling.

1. What is the passage mostly about?

2. What finally stopped widespread whaling?

Oral Fluency Record Sheet

Name _____ Date _____

Oral Reading Accuracy: _____%   Circle: Fall Winter Spring

Oral Reading Fluency Score: _____ words correct per minute

Prosody Rubric: (Circle Score) 1 2 3 4

Comprehension Question Responses

#1 _____

#2 _____

Centuries of Whaling

	When Vikings roamed the Atlantic Ocean long ago, one
9	of the greatest prizes they sought was whales. Way back in
20	the 1100s, the struggle between whale and sailor was a fairly
31	even one, but over time, whaling methods grew more and
41	more advanced. By the mid-1800s, whaling had become a
51	big business.
53	Norwegian whalers, the modern relatives of the Vikings,
61	were among the leaders in whaling technology. In 1863, a
71	Norwegian sea captain created a new type of whaling ship. The
82	82-foot-long boat was sleek and swift, fast enough to catch up
95	with even the fastest swimming whale. It also had bomb harpoons.
106	These harpoons were tipped with bombs that would explode inside
116	the whale. They caused death much sooner than ordinary
125	harpoons. Suddenly, the seas were even more dangerous than
134	ever for whales.
137	By the late 1800s, many whale species were endangered.
146	The numbers of both the right whale and the bowhead whale
157	dropped sharply. Because these whales were slower than the new
167	boats, they were easy to kill. Sadly, millions of whales were
178	slaughtered before a ban on whaling was agreed upon in 1982.
189	Since then, whaling has been prohibited and successfully
197	suppressed.
198	But almost all kinds of whales still suffer because of the
209	extensive whaling in the past. Some whales, like the gray whale,
220	have recovered quite nicely. Their numbers continue to grow.
229	Others, like the northern right whale, continue to be in danger of
241	extinction. At the present time, fewer than 400 northern right
251	whales exist in the whole world. Only time will tell if whales can
264	survive the effects of centuries of whaling. **271**

Number of words read: _____ Number of errors made: _____

Nikki on Stage

Nikki was a very talented dancer, but she was also very shy. When Holly, Nikki's dance teacher, asked her to play the role of Tinkerbell in a show, Nikki said that she was afraid to perform in public.

"You know," Holly said, "I used to be very shy myself."

At first, Nikki didn't believe Holly. But then Holly explained how she had gotten over her stage fright. Once, several years ago, Holly said she was supposed to play a tiger in a dance production. The show's director told her that the only way to make it through the show was to turn into a tiger.

"So that is what I did," Holly said. "Everywhere I went, I thought of myself as a tiger. When I went on stage, I was the tiger. If I make a mistake, it was not me who got things wrong. It was the animal."

"Hmm," said Nikki. "That is not a bad technique." For the next six days, Nikki did everything as Tinkerbell. She ate, drank, walked, talked, and slept as Tinkerbell. When people called her, she answered only to the name Tinkerbell.

On the day of the show, Nikki was completely ready. With her costume on, she waited in the wings at the side of the stage. Suddenly, Holly told her she was on.

"Nikki," Holly whispered, "it's time." Nikki was so focused on being Tinkerbell that she did not even recognize her own name. It was only when Holly whispered Tinkerbell that Nikki went out. Tinkerbell's performance was excellent. Clearly, so was Nikki's. From that point on, Nikki never worried about being shy on stage again. She had learned to deal with her fears.

1. Why did Holly tell Nikki about her experience with stage fright?

2. How did Nikki get ready for her performance as Tinkerbell?

Oral Fluency Record Sheet

Name _____ Date _____

Nikki on Stage

	Nikki was a very talented dancer, but she was also very
11	shy. When Holly, Nikki's dance teacher, asked her to play the role
23	of Tinkerbell in a show, Nikki said that she was afraid to perform
36	in public.
38	"You know," Holly said, "I used to be very shy myself."
49	At first, Nikki didn't believe Holly. But then Holly explained
59	how she had gotten over her stage fright. Once, several years ago,
71	Holly said she was supposed to play a tiger in a dance production.
84	The show's director told her that the only way to make it through the
98	show was to turn into a tiger.
105	"So that is what I did," Holly said. "Everywhere I went, I
117	thought of myself as a tiger. When I went on stage, I was the tiger.
132	If I make a mistake, it was not me who got things wrong. It was
147	the animal."
149	"Hmm," said Nikki. "That is not a bad technique." For the next
161	six days, Nikki did everything as Tinkerbell. She ate, drank, walked,
172	talked, and slept as Tinkerbell. When people called her, she answered
183	only to the name Tinkerbell.
188	On the day of the show, Nikki was completely ready. With
199	her costume on, she waited in the wings at the side of the stage.
213	Suddenly, Holly told her she was on.
220	"Nikki," Holly whispered, "it's time." Nikki was so focused
229	on being Tinkerbell that she did not even recognize her own name.
241	It was only when Holly whispered Tinkerbell that Nikki went out.
252	Tinkerbell's performance was excellent. Clearly, so was Nikki's.
260	From that point on, Nikki never worried about being shy on stage
272	again. She had learned to deal with her fears. **281**

© Macmillan/McGraw-Hill

Number of words read: _____   Number of errors made: _____

Name _____ Date _____

The Frozen North

It was another red-hot summer day in the desert along
Highway 30. Cindy Tupper was dozing off in the back seat of the
car. Just before dozing off completely, she spotted an intriguing
sign: The Frozen North, Arctic Amusement for All.

"Can we stop, Dad?" she asked. Moments later, they pulled
into the parking lot and were hailed by a strange-looking man.

"Greetings from the Frozen North!" he boomed. "My name
is Andrew and I am your guide. You will need to put these parkas
on before you descend."

"Parkas?" Cindy asked. "Where are we going?" They rode
an escalator to a deep underground cavern. When they got off the
escalator, they found themselves in an entirely new universe. There
was ice and snow, and it was very cold.

"Look, Dad," Cindy said. "Penguins!" Sure enough, behind
a very large trough of water, penguins were playing, along with seals and a
walrus. A bit later, a huge white figure emerged from behind a
door and pushed itself into the water. "A polar bear!" cried Cindy.
"But how?"

"The Frozen North creates the illusion of an Arctic
ecosystem," Andrew explained. Andrew kept talking, but Cindy
soon dozed off on a very comfortable sofa. When she woke up
minutes later, she was perspiring.

"Wake up, Cindy," her mom said. "We're almost home."
They were back in the car, still driving through the desert. The ice
and snow were gone, along with the penguins, the walrus, and the
polar bear.

"I had the best dream," Cindy said.

1. Where does this story take place?
2. Why did Cindy dream about the Frozen North?

Oral Fluency Record Sheet

Name _____ Date _____

Oral Reading Accuracy: _____% Circle: Fall Winter Spring

Oral Reading Fluency Score: _____ words correct per minute

Prosody Rubric: (Circle Score) 1 2 3 4

Comprehension Question Responses

#1 _____

#2 _____

The Frozen North

	It was another red-hot summer day in the desert along
11	Highway 30. Cindy Tupper was dozing off in the back seat of the
24	car. Just before dozing off completely, she spotted an intriguing
34	sign: The Frozen North, Arctic Amusement for All.
42	"Can we stop, Dad?" she asked. Moments later, they pulled
52	into the parking lot and were hailed by a strange-looking man.
64	"Greetings from the Frozen North!" he boomed. "My name
73	is Andrew and I am your guide. You will need to put these parkas
87	on before you descend."
91	"Parkas?" Cindy asked. "Where are we going?" They rode
100	an escalator to a deep underground cavern. When they got off the
112	escalator, they found themselves in an entirely new universe. There
122	was ice and snow, and it was very cold.
131	"Look, Dad," Cindy said. "Penguins!" Sure enough, behind
139	a very large trough of water, penguins were playing, along with seals and a
153	walrus. A bit later, a huge white figure emerged from behind a
165	door and pushed itself into the water. "A polar bear!" cried Cindy.
177	"But how?"
179	"The Frozen North creates the illusion of an Arctic
188	ecosystem," Andrew explained. Andrew kept talking, but Cindy
196	soon dozed off on a very comfortable sofa. When she woke up
208	minutes later, she was perspiring.
213	"Wake up, Cindy," her mom said. "We're almost home."
222	They were back in the car, still driving through the desert. The ice
235	and snow were gone, along with the penguins, the walrus, and the
247	polar bear.
249	"I had the best dream," Cindy said. **256**

Number of words read: _____ Number of errors made: _____

Page 15:   1. Sam the dog.
2. Sam runs. Sam digs in the mud. Sam gets wet.

Page 17:   1. A dog and a cat.
2. Dogs and cats are not usually friends.

Page 19:   1. A bug.
2. Possible answer: The sun is hot.

Page 21:   1. Jan the vet.
2. She likes to help animals get well.

Page 23:   1. Meg.
2. In the morning.

Page 25:   1. It is too hot.
2. The fox gets the fan to cool off the frog. The fox wants the frog to jump and hop again.

Page 27:   1. Ducks.
2. The oil stops water from getting to the feathers.

Page 29:   1. Fruit trees grow from seeds in the ground.
2. They can help plant new trees.

Page 31:   1. Jake wants to be fast like a snake.
2. Fred tells Jake that his turtle shell is a home, and that is better than being fast.

Page 33:   1. He likes the lake.
2. They like to fish and skate on the lake together.

Page 35:   1. You can brush its fur. You can make sure your pet eats, drinks, and plays.
2. Any two of these: dogs, cats, fish, pigs, or ducks.

Page 37:   1. They make it safe for people to swim.
2. Possible responses: swimming fast in high waves, and rescuing people.

Page 39:   1. Making a cake for Ben's birthday.
2. Ben was just one year old.

Page 41:   1. Possible answers: She sees a girl in a long white dress; She sees herself as she would have looked long ago.
2. Possible answers: She is frightened. She is confused.

Page 43:   1. A baby turtle.
2. The sand is cool at night and will not hurt the baby turtle.

Page 45:   1. A mask.
2. Possible responses: deciding on what kind of mask to make; painting the mask.

Page 47:   1. Twigs and fur.
2. Possible responses: happy; satisfied with herself.

Page 49:   1. In a rocket.
2. It is made up. You can tell because people do not go to work in rockets.

Page 51:   1. Stars are big.
2. Earth, sun, other stars.

Page 53:   1. Any three of these: trees, old mines, old houses, or bridges.
2. They like to be in the dark.

Page 55:   1. Mike and a bug.
2. So he can have one plant and the bug can have the other.

Page 57:   1. Ride on a dog sled.
2. Winter, or when it is cold outside.

Page 59:   1. Light.
2. The shadow would be long.

Page 61:   1. Each star stands for a state in our country.
2. You can take the flag down at night; you can take the flag inside when it rains; you can never let the flag touch the ground.

Page 63:
1. Play soccer.
2. She was used to going to camp with Ted and was afraid she would be lonely.

Page 65
1. Jane spent all her time with her new dog Pepper.
2. Jane probably missed Dean, too.

Page 67:
1. You can use many things. Two of them are an old shirt or a paper plate.
2. You need at least two people to run between the bases so that there is more than one person to tag.

Page 69:
1. Forests with trees that lose their leaves, forests with trees that stay green all year, mixed forests.
2. People wanted to create farms and build cities.

Page 71:
1. He loves to read.
2. He could count the number of dimes.

Page 73:
1. Having a flower sale.
2. The posters would give information about the flower sale and get people interested in buying flowers.

Page 75:
1. They breathe through their open mouths.
2. There are many things that are killing sharks. They can get caught in nets, be sold for food or clothing, or be hunted for sport.

Page 77:
1. How plants and animals get food.
2. People move around to get their food while plants make their own food.

Page 79:
1. A chair that she painted.
2. Rachel found and painted the chair all by herself. There was no other chair like it.

Page 81:
1. They want to watch animals.
2. Pete makes noise with his hiccups.

Page 83:
1. Jobs that dogs have.
2. The dog could let the person know that a fire alarm had gone off or that a doorbell was ringing.

Page 85
1. Their claws have pads that flatten out. The pads give off a sticky liquid that acts like glue.
2. House flies carry germs.

Page 87:
1. She wanted to see what children did there.
2. They were chasing balls just like cats like to do.

Page 89:
1. Everything was made from trash.
2. Many things can be made from what we think of as trash.

Page 91:
1. The White House.
2. Any three of these: living space for the President, rooms for friends, offices, celebrations, balls, parties, dinners.

Page 93:
1. Fruit bats.
2. They have long noses, large eyes, pointy ears, and furry bodies like foxes.

Page 95:
1. She doesn't hear very well.
2. She felt uncomfortable with Grandma Nell.

Page 97:
1. Karla's interest in participating in the play.
2. It asked for someone to run the spotlight for the play.

Page 99:
1. Accept all reasonable responses.
2. In zoos.

Page 101:
1. Abraham Lincoln.
2. The pictures on the penny, and what the penny is made of.

Page 103:
1. Molly played games, and ate snacks and birthday cake.
2. Molly's mother was giving Molly a surprise party.

Page 105:
1. Chris didn't play a musical instrument.
2. Chris and Beth could both join the band now. Beth would sit on a wagon, and Chris would pull it.

Page 107:
1. Acting properly when you win or lose.
2. Accept all reasonable responses.

Page 109:
1. They dig for them.
2. Sun and wind can destroy dead plants and animals before they can turn into fossils.

Page 111:
1. She would hit Nick and then put her head back as if she were laughing.
2. She missed Nick and only did the trick with him.

Page 113:
1. There would not be room for everything in the new apartment.
2. It was one thing that Mom could take with her that included all of her treasures.

Page 115:
1. Forests.
2. Possible responses: It makes more wooden toothpicks than any other state. The Camp Fire Girls started there. Earmuffs were invented there.

Page 117:
1. It uses its curved tail to attach itself to plants and reefs.
2. Its head looks like a horse's head. It can change colors like a chameleon.

Page 119:
1. He wasn't thin enough.
2. Possible response: He learned to plan ahead. He learned not to eat too much at one time. He learned to save his food.

Page 121:
1. Lucy added flags.
2. Liz felt happy.

Page 123:
1. The class sold food.
2. All the foods were delicious and healthy.

Page 125:
1. Traveling in a covered wagon.
2. Possible responses: A covered wagon ride is bumpier. With cars, you don't have to feed the oxen.

Page 127:
1. Possible responses: strength, ability to bounce the ball as you move, ability to pass, ability to work as part of a team, and ability to shoot.
2. Wheelchair basketball is an excellent way for children in wheelchairs to be on a team.

Page 129:
1. They use bright colors to show or pretend they are poisonous or to blend in with their surroundings.
2. There are many animals that would like to eat them.

Page 131:
1. This passage is about a little girl who made her mother a birthday cake.
2. Proud.

Page 133:
1. She had told her best friend that she didn't like her.
2. To try to make up with Anna.

Page 135:
1. How thunderhead clouds are formed.
2. There is a lot of rising and falling motion going on.

Page 137:
1. Because of the cold and ice.
2. Flowers, vegetables, berries, and animals.

Page 139:
1. He made it himself.
2. It was wrapped inside several boxes that had different kinds of wrapping.

Page 141:
1. He wanted Kyle to work hard.
2. He learned to explain himself more clearly.

Page 143:
1. Its thick fur and a layer of fat.
2. A polar bear is very large.

Page 145:
1. It gives warmth and energy to everything on Earth.
2. Accept all reasonable responses.

Page 147:
1. Rosa's fear of playing in front of an audience.
2. Rosa's father's wink gave her the confidence to perform solo for the first time.

Page 149:
1. How good friends make sacrifices for each other.
2. She traded her lucky marble for the gift.

Page 151:
1. In bamboo forests in China.
2. Giant pandas don't inhabit the wild in the United States. People could not see giant pandas unless they went to the zoo or to China.

Page 153:
1. A few people start doing something different and then everybody starts doing it.
2. Big shirts, felt skirts, blue jeans with fancy stitching, baggy pants and baseball caps, playing hacky sack.

Page 155:
1. Having one big birthday celebration for her whole family once a year.
2. Possible response: There are too many people, and in the summer the children can sleep outside.

Page 157:
1. Fruit.
2. Possible responses: She knew she had tricked him. She knew the fruit wasn't real.

Page 159:
1. A school for boys.
2. A teacher at Babe's school.

Page 161:
1. Possible responses: to pump water, to grind grain, to drain water, and to produce electricity.
2. There will always be wind.

Page 163:
1. To see where her turtle prefers to live.
2. She took notes on how Marvin acted.

Page 165:
1. Ruiz thinks he has outgrown them.
2. Ruiz remembers the good times he had with the giraffe.

Page 167:
1. Possible responses: grapefruits, olives, chocolate, coconuts, walnuts, cherries, peaches, and apples.
2. Answers will vary.

Page 169:
1. Teaching chimpanzees to talk with people.
2. With their hands and fingers.

Page 171:
1. Watched timber wolves in their natural environment.
2. Run away.

Page 173:
1. This story is about a fire in school.
2. Jason let people know there was a fire and he helped put the fire out.

Page 175:
1. A writer and artist for children.
2. His books discuss serious problems and give life lessons. They also make children laugh.

Page 177:
1. It may die out in the next 20 years unless special efforts are made to protect it.
2. Possible responses: Forests are cut down for new homes, businesses, and farms. Sheep and other animals eat all the food in an area. Coastal areas are filled in.

Page 179:
1. It gave him a shady, cool place in the summer, a place to build forts in the winter, and a place to go when he wanted to be alone.
2. It let more people know about the problem. More people expressed their opposition and forced the government to change its plans.

Page 181:
1. Lightweight plastic.
2. The new one moved.

Page 183:
1. They formed letters.
2. Excited.

Page 185:
1. The camping trip Tony and his family took last summer.
2. Possible responses: made a fire, toasted marshmallows, told stories, sang songs.

Page 187:
1. To survive the cold weather.
2. They have not eaten for a long time and are very hungry.

Page 189:
1. Cooking oil, margarine, eating, feeding birds and butterflies.
2. They can grow in many climates and soils and don't need a lot of water.

Page 191:
1. David made a special beach wagon.
2. He decorated the wagon with glue, sand, rocks, and shells.

Page 193:
1. Skunk was all black, and they couldn't see him in the dark.
2. He decided to paint Skunk's tail with stripes instead of white spots.

Page 195:
1. Clothing, tents, and boats.
2. Whalers and fur traders hunted the animals that Eskimos needed in their life.

Page 197:
1. Honoring people with special stamps.
2. First you write a letter about the person and a group discusses your letter. Then the Postmaster General makes the final choice.

Page 199:
1. Under the pictures.
2. The children laughed at the words and the pictures. It made Rob feel very proud.

Page 201:
1. For protection.
2. It wasn't what she expected. It was cold and damp, not nice and cozy like her own home.

Page 203:
1. New products that people have come up with.
2. New products help make people's lives easier. They can help people do things in a new or better way.

Page 205:
1. How to stop.
2. The author thinks that it is fun and good exercise.

Page 207:
1. How the writer helped save sea otters after an oil spill.
2. It matted their fur so that they froze. The otters licked the oil on their fur and it poisoned them.

Page 209:
1. How Claire tried to make a special dessert for her mother for Mother's Day.
2. She thought the new dessert would be three times as good.

Page 211:
1. It has a cork ball at the center. This is wrapped with rubber and yarn and then covered with cowhide.
2. The special equipment protects them. It also has other purposes. For example, spikes on their shoes help them start and stop quickly.

Page 213:
1. Making plant sculptures.
2. Almost any shape: balls, cones, animals.

Page 215:
1. How Jill learned about rock climbing so she could go rock climbing with her father.
2. She probably felt safe because her father was holding on to her with ropes.

Page 217:
1. They squeeze them out, boil them out, or put them on trays and cover them with fat.
2. She loves all kinds of different smells.

Page 219:
1. First they saw it walking along a fire line. Then they saw it in a tree.
2. The bear is a good symbol because it survived a forest fire.

Page 221:
1. Answers will vary.
2. Their eyes are on the sides of their heads.

Page 223:
1. She was too young to stay home alone.
2. He got to her very quickly and grabbed her shirt.

Page 225:
1. She was in such a hurry that she didn't pay attention to what she was doing.
2. Possible response: She is too busy and does too many different things.

Page 227:
1. How water slides are made.
2. What is happening to you as you slide down keeps changing.

Page 229:
1. The first successful flights planned by people.
2. Hot or warm air is needed to make the balloons rise.

Page 231:
1. He wanted to get a better view of the bus.
2. Possible responses: He didn't hear Munch. Munch probably squeaks and doesn't use words.

Page 233:
1. Paco's first experience with whitewater rafting.
2. The raft hit a wave and took a big bounce.

Page 235:
1. By flapping their ears, spraying themselves with water, and rolling in mud.
2. They are very big and need a lot of food and water to maintain their bodies.

Page 237:
1. It is the longest structure in the world.
2. As protection against enemies.

Page 239:
1. He ate the kitchen stove.
2. They lowered one man into Babe's belly.

Page 241:
1. How Kara saved people during a flood.
2. She braved the river to save the people.

Page 243:
1. He was spending too much time watching television.
2. Excited.

Page 245:
1. Possible responses: He sat on her bed while she was on the telephone. He watched her do homework and watch TV.
2. She made her realize that her brother was her friend as well as her brother.

Page 247:
1. The passage is about floods, which are caused by too much water in one place.
2. Possible responses: snow runoff melted by spring rains; rainstorms filling rivers to overflowing; hurricanes blowing water inland; storms causing floods; volcanoes.

Page 249:
1. People gathering or collecting antlers.
2. Antlers provide calcium to some animals.

Page 251:
1. Alex learning to play the bass.
2. He practiced every day.

Page 253:
1. He thought he was a strong swimmer and could handle anything.
2. He learned how powerful and dangerous it could be.

Page 255:
1. Sources of inspiration.
2. Fairs, books, sports events, or films.

Page 257:
1. Native Americans tracked the phases of the moon to measure days and months.
2. By observing what was happening.

Page 259:
1. Happy, fun to spend time with.
2. Lauren thought she was going to be bored at Grandma's, but she had a great time.

Page 261:
1. It would be less crowded, close to a playground, and had a garden.
2. They read together each evening.

Page 263:
1. A lasting reminder of someone, or something important from the past; or anything that makes you stop and remember a person or event.
2. Memorials can be for anyone or anything you want to remember.

Page 265:
1. Ships and crews that disappear without leaving any evidence behind.
2. It was top-heavy and might have turned over in heavy seas.

Page 267:
1. Being an immigrant.
2. To find a better job or way of life.

Page 269:
1. To tell a myth about why winter comes each year.
2. Demeter's sadness when Persephone is in the underworld.

Page 271:
1. How to be a hero in everyday life.
2. Put others first and be kind and helpful to friends and family.

Page 273:
1. How things can be preserved in amber.
2. Fossilized resin or sap from ancient trees.

Page 275:
1. To cross waterways and wide spaces.
2. For people without vehicles.

Page 277:
1. Tim and his family raise Luke until he is ready for guide dog training.
2. Helping blind people in their daily lives.

Page 279:
1. The outer shell is hard so they are protected. A hermit crab can wear the shells of other creatures as armor as well.
2. They have sea anemones sticking to the outside of their shells. These anemones have stingers to keep predators away.

Page 281:
1. About every five minutes.
2. People hunt them and the female produces only one calf per year.

Page 283:
1. Go to the museum, games, and movies.
2. Jason figured out how to spend time with his uncle, work on his parents' program, and help the community at the same time.

Page 285:
1. She told her she had been a soldier.
2. She learned that people may not be boring if you take the time to talk to them. People may have interesting stories to tell.

Page 287:
1. How and why dolphins save humans from drowning.
2. They think humans are playthings.

Page 289:
1. A log.
2. When nations controlled the seas, they gained great power. When they lost control of the seas, they lost their power.

Page 291:
1. The marks that a screwdriver made on the door of a safe.
2. They left no fingerprints or other clues.

Page 293:
1. Air pollution.
2. They suggested a "Frequent Biker's Program." People earned points for biking into town and could use their points for discounts at stores.

Page 295:
1. Each sled dog must carry out its specific responsibility for the team to win the race.
2. It often has to make decisions on its own.

Page 297:
1. To warn about the harm of noise pollution.
2. Loud music.

Page 299:
1. Fly a kite for the longest time.
2. He flew two kites, his own and his brother's.

Page 301:
1. They were upset because he hadn't caught the ball.
2. He shows him a clipping about a time when he was blamed for losing a game.

Page 303:
1. How Nancy started a garden.
2. Clever, creative, and determined.

Page 305:
1. They were tired of waking Carlos up.
2. It's important to be responsible and get up in time for school.

Page 307:
1. A cycle is a pattern that keeps repeating.
2. Do a little each day to change the cycle.

Page 309:
1. A Wordwatch gives you the time and the definition of a new word.
2. It can teach them new vocabulary.

Page 311:
1. He loved money and Mrs. Tinsley offered him money to walk her dog.
2. Hard work pays off. It is not good to be lazy. You have to work hard to earn money.

Page 313:
1. Arizona had arid air, a dull landscape, and a hot sun. Florida was green with lots of flowers, humid air, and rain.
2. He thought the road was turning into a river.

Page 315:
1. El Greco painted the way he saw things.
2. If you are colorblind, you see one color as another but you know the true color. El Greco saw things as tall and chose to paint that way.

Page 317:
1. Cloud formation.
2. They contain warm air.

Page 319:
1. Warbler migrations in his hometown.
2. He used the Internet at school.

Page 321:
1. She made a list of ideas and she took a short walk to clear her mind.
2. Hannah wrote about how she tried to write the story, instead of making up a story.

Page 323:
1. For being critical of the governor.
2. They found Zenger not guilty because the law he broke was a bad law.

Page 325:
1. To show people how terrible slavery was in an interesting and readable way.
2. People were shocked and thought this book helped start the Civil War.

Page 327:
1. The doctor.
2. She has to give away her dog but she wants to keep spending time with the dog.

Page 329:
1. Making a new friend.
2. She realized that she missed spending time with her best friend.

Page 331:
1. They may be seeking better jobs; fleeing from their country; displaced by natural disasters; looking for a good education.
2. Immigrants need to decide where they should live.

Page 333:
1. You have to live where your job is. Migrant workers, circus performers, military people, and physicians may have to move around.
2. Because you are always packing up and saying good-bye to friends.

Page 335:
1. The discovery of a book and a computer by two people 100 years from now.
2. People no longer read books in the future, so Jada did not know what one looked like.

Page 337:
1. Henry played soccer like a one-person team. He would always hog the ball.
2. Give the other players time with the ball.

Page 339:
1. It was covered with cinders, ashes, and stone instead of being destroyed by lava.
2. We can see what life was like then because so much of the city is preserved.

Page 341:
1. The oceans.
2. It is difficult to travel to the bottom of the ocean and see through the darkness.

Page 343:
1. The Greeks could not figure out a way to get through the walls of the city.
2. A huge wooden horse for the warriors to hide in so they could enter the city.

Page 345:
1. The Sirens' song could cause the crew to forget to steer and make their boat crash.
2. To stop him from trying to go to the Sirens.

Page 347:
1. They drew pictures while we use letters.
2. Experts used the translations on the Rosetta Stone to decode hieroglyphics.

Page 349:
1. His children's books.
2. The sound of an engine on an ocean liner.

Page 351:
1. His dog had ruined his report.
2. Max chased a cat into the classroom, saving Walter from getting into trouble.

Page 353:
1. What Todd and Maria decided to do with the old Thelma Cross recording.
2. They thought Thelma should get money.

Page 355:
1. People put a particle into a mollusk to grow a cultured pearl. A natural pearl forms when a grain of sand sets inside a mollusk.
2. Cultured pearls are more available and cost less than natural pearls.

Page 357:
1. The history of whaling.
2. A ban on whaling agreed upon in 1982.

Page 359:
1. She wanted to help Nikki by showing how she overcame her own stage fright.
2. She did everything as Tinkerbell for days.

Page 361:
1. In Cindy's mind, while she was driving.
2. It was an extremely hot day, and the dream was a way for Cindy to cool off.

		Fall		Winter		Spring		
Grade	%ile	Num	LNC	Num	LNC	Num	LNC	ROI
K	90		37		55		65	0.8
	75		25		45		54	0.8
	50		11		33		42	0.9
	25	13377	3	12037	20	12653	31	0.8
	10		0		8		19	0.5
	Mean		15		33		42	0.8
	StdDev		15		17		18	
1	90		65		76		79	0.4
	75		55		66		69	0.4
	50		44		55		58	0.4
	25	10887	32	2518	44	1455	47	0.4
	10		22		32		36	0.4
	Mean		44		55		58	0.4
	StdDev		17		17		17	

Num = Number of Students   **LNC** = Letter Names Correct   **ROI** = Rate Of Improvement
ROI is Spring Score minus Fall Score (or Winter minus Fall) divided by 36 weeks (or 18 weeks)

AIMSweb® Growth Table
Phoneme Segmentation Fluency
Multi-year Aggregate

		Fall		Winter		Spring		
Grade	%ile	Num	PC	Num	PC	Num	PC	ROI
K	90		44		48		62	0.5
	75		32		34		51	0.5
	50		14		14		37	0.6
	25	1870	3	13234	5	14103	15	0.3
	10		0		0		5	0.1
	Mean		19		20		35	0.4
	StdDev		17		19		22	
1	90		56		62		67	0.3
	75		46		54		59	0.4
	50		33		43		50	0.5
	25	13615	15	10197	31	8269	39	0.7
	10		6		16		26	0.6
	Mean		31		42		48	0.5
	StdDev		19		18		16	

Num = Number of Students   **PC** = Phonemes Correct   **ROI** = Rate Of Improvement
ROI is Spring Score minus Fall Score (or Winter minus Fall) divided by 36 weeks (or 18 weeks)